BEHAVIOR THERAPY IN TERMINAL CARE

BEHAVIOR THERAPY IN TERMINAL CARE
A Humanistic Approach

HARRY J. SOBEL

Harvard Medical School
Massachusetts General Hospital

The Cushing Hospital Series on Aging and Terminal Care

Series Editors: Robert J. Kastenbaum
Theodore X. Barber

BALLINGER PUBLISHING COMPANY
Cambridge, Massachusetts
A Subsidiary of Harper & Row, Publishers, Inc.

International Standard Book Number: 0-88410-716-7

Library of Congress Catalog Card Number: 81-1995

Printed in the United States of America

Library of Congress Cataloging in Publication Data

Sobel, Harry J.
  Behavior therapy in terminal care.

  Bibliography: p.
  Includes index.
  1. Terminal care. 2. Death—Psychological aspects.
3. Behavior therapy. I. Title. [DNLM: 1. Behavior
therapy. 2. Terminal care—Psychology. WM 425 B677b]
R726.8.S6   616'.029   81-1995
ISBN 0-88410-716-7   AACR2

DEDICATION

In Memory of
Bernard Lerner and Chester Herzog

CONTENTS

FOREWORD

Robert J. Kastenbaum

". . . being is not enough."

What is this man saying? Perhaps, like myself, you would be tempted to reply, "Maybe so, but non-being is *too* much!"

This is but one of many points in this volume that might elicit the startle reaction from readers well-set in their orientations toward terminal care. All hackles worthy of the name will be on alert and ready to rise when the mere idea of behavior therapy is introduced in this context. Dr. Sobel and his colleagues know this full well. They have accepted the challenge of presenting an alternative approach associated in the minds of many with pigeons a-pecking rather than with humans confronting the ultimate of life and death. Now it is our turn: are we ready to accept the challenge of considering behavior therapy in terminal care?

May I share my personal reaction? As something of an ancient in thanatology and (forgive the word, but it does seem to follow) thaniatrics, I have seen the helping professions edge slowly toward the bedside of the terminally ill. What terrors that little journey has held for us! And with what sense of inner triumph and sprouting maturity do we finally come eye-to-eye with brother or sister mortal! Yes, fine, splendid! (But also: how ordinary and natural.) Here we are. What next?

Essentially the same answer to this question has been given by many voices. *Being-with* is seen as the fundamental approach. There is much to be said for this approach, which is perhaps more philosophy than technique. The dying person often experiences social isolation, loneliness, and a sense of abandonment. Being-with is not to be underestimated. A nonintrusive companionship, an availability, a caring attitude—these serve, I think, as general comforts in the presence of general stress. We feel better when we are with somebody who cares about us. This approach has another decided merit. If we recognize that being-with is valuable and legitimate, then we are less likely to engage in activity for activity's sake. This translates into fewer unnecessary medical manipulations, fewer anxiety-fueled interpersonal maneuvers. Not doing what does not need doing is a treatment principle that applies very well to this situation.

The distinction between being-with and doing-nothing has not always been appreciated. As a notoriously industrious and aggressive people, Americans are inclined more to action than meditation. Even a hint of passivity in the face of danger threatens our self-image. After years of trying to make being-with acceptable, I wonder if we have got just a little carried away with it. The answer is in the affirmative if, in our advocacy for a natural type of relationship with the terminally ill, we have neglected to explore what might be called "rightful doing."

The behavior therapy that inhabits this book has come a long way from its tough-new-kid-on-the-block introduction to psychology. I think its depth and maturity will quickly become apparent to you. And it is behavior therapy, after all, that has accumulated the most practical experience (and the richest data-base) in systematic interpersonal "doing." Sooner or later there would have to be a mutual reaching out between those most intimately concerned with terminal care and those who would make behavioral techniques available to people at moments of greatest stress. Sooner is better, and here it is.

Volunteers and professionals who are drawn to the hospice movement will find suggestions and points of view that can be put to practical use. Pain management, helping the bereaved, and gaining a better idea of the consequence's of one's own actions—these are among the many relevant topics addressed. Experienced clinicians are likely to recognize that they have been utilizing certain elements of the behavioral approach all along. This will make it easier to build new skills on top of those already existing. Even the most dedicated skeptic will benefit from this book, if only to sharpen his or her claws against a real adversary, not a strawperson.

My own problems with the behavioral approach are regarding the specific questions that must be raised with any attempt to influence human behavior and experience. Behavioral therapy with the terminally ill and their families can be as human as the people involved. How effective can it be? The answer to that question must properly await further experience and research. All of us who judge that our knowledge remains incomplete and our skills imperfect have the opportunity—and perhaps the responsibility—to examine this new approach.

Robert J. Kastenbaum

PREFACE

Harry J. Sobel

The field of thanatology has grown considerably over the past decade, perhaps even becoming faddish at times, as clinicians and theoreticians attempt to understand a vital aspect of our lives that remains ambiguous, uncontrolled, and often demoralizing. Twentieth century technology and medicine, however, consistently redirect us away from the naturalness of the dying process, often negating our right to participate actively in how we die. As the hospice movement gains wider acceptance and as increasing numbers of patients and families claim their "right of choice," there will be a significant demand for integrated humanistic approaches in clinical care. The care of the dying cannot be left solely to the physician. Patient and family needs are far too broad to be delegated only to biomedical services. As an alternative, holistic or biopsychosocial care of the dying patient will involve a multidisciplinary approach for helping people cope with terminal illness.

This book is about the application and integration of behavior therapy into terminal care. Until recently, the mere thought of a *behavioral thanatology* might have seemed a dehumanized and decadent notion, replete with implications for "controlling" the vulnerable dying patient. Certainly my own clinical training, and its roots in the psychoanalytic-existential tradition, made it difficult for me to consider using behavior therapy to help the dying. However, over the past four years at Project Omega I have become more and more aware of the benefits of constant examination and alteration of our existing clinical paradigms. Behavior therapy and its offspring, cognitive therapy, offer thanatologists many valuable insights for changing and developing intervention strategies, not the least of which is the value of a preventative orientation. It has been one of my personal goals to define an integrated model for terminal care, a preventative model that incorporates the humanistic and empirically grounded dimensions of behavior therapy. It is my hope that readers of this volume will avoid the pitfalls of theoretical preconceptions and stereotypes, and begin to analyze, critically, the future directions and problems inherent in this very complex, stress-producing, and demanding discipline. Dr. Jerrold Pollak and I have tried to clarify these issues in the first two chapters of the volume. The remainder of the book examines specific issues in terminal care and practical methods of behavioral intervention.

In preparing this book I have had the advice, support, and assistance of many people both directly and indirectly. I would like to take this opportunity to thank those friends, colleagues, and family members who have consistently encouraged me to pursue my professional work in the true spirit of behavioral humanism:

Avery D. Weisman, M.D., for his daily and dedicated supervision, friendship, loyalty, and scholarly guidance. The unique opportunity to learn, to question, and to laugh with a man of his talent and creativity will undoubtedly remain the highlight of my professional life. I am deeply appreciative of our experience together at Project Omega.

J. William Worden, Ph.D., Dorothy Wingquist, M.S.W., and the entire Project Omega team for their constant help in teaching me to become a flexible and "coping" clinician and researcher in the face of uncertainty, ambiguity, and much patient sadness.

Robert Kastenbaum, Ph.D., for his kind invitation and challenge to attempt this project. I look forward to many future professional collaborations.

Michael J. Follick, Ph.D., for his consistent ability to blend sincere friendship and personal understanding with professional support and intellectual critique. Our work together has indeed solidified a rare combination of mutual respect and sensitivity.

Bernard O'Brien, Ph.D., for his insight, advice, encouragement, guidance, and respect over the past seven years. There are few individuals whom I admire and care for as much as Bernie. In many ways, this book is a tribute to him, his openness to new ideas, and his capacity to expose the hazards of cognitive rigidity to all his students and friends.

My friends and colleagues at Massachusetts General Hospital and Harvard Medical School—Gerald Borofsky, Ph.D., Ward Cromer, Ph.D., James Muller, Ph.D., William Falk, M.D., Ginger Chappell, Ph.D., Charles Welch, M.D., and Jane Thorbeck, Ed.D.—for their compassionate understanding and cooperative spirit in all of our work together. I owe special appreciation to Jerry Borofsky and Ward Cromer for much more than what this book represents.

Thomas P. Hackett, M.D., for his direct support of our research at Project Omega and his continuing help in developing a nationally recognized psychology intern program at Massachusetts General Hospital.

My many patients for all they have taught me about the painful and life-enhancing realities of illness and dying.

Carol Franco, senior editor at Ballinger Publishing Company, for her ability to make the editing process an exciting and creative venture, and for allowing this project to become a foundation for beginning a friendship.

Larissa Taylor for her expert and sophisticated editorial assistance in preparing this manuscript. I cannot imagine how others complete their work without Larissa, her knowledge of medieval history and French food, and her appreciation of life's existential confusions.

To all of the contributors of this volume I wish to acknowledge my sincere gratitude for their scholarly efforts and willingness to participate in a controversial topic. As an editor, I could not have asked for more.

To my parents, who, as "contributors" for over three decades, have always been my two most loved teachers and friends. I thank them for their limitless support, love, and confidence.

To Elliot Sobel and Sharon Greenberg I extend a profound appreciation for helping me to realize and to enjoy the fact of how little I really know about anything. Their influence on my personal and professional life has been immeasurable; their friendship, essential; their humor, a life force.

Finally, to Dr. Wendy Sobel—wife, colleague, companion, contributor to this volume—I send my love and deep respect. My appreciation of our friendship and marriage, and my admiration of her talents, spirit, kindness, and tolerance, remains unmatched. She has made the last eleven years a joy to be alive.

Harry J. Sobel, Ph.D.
January, 1981
Boston, Massachusetts

THEORETICAL PERSPECTIVES IN BEHAVIORAL THANATOLOGY

1 TOWARD A BEHAVIORAL THANATOLOGY IN CLINICAL CARE

Harry J. Sobel

We live in an era of extraordinary changes. Questions thought to lie beyond comprehension are gradually answered comprehensively by a growing scientific technology. Answers, however, lead to further questions and complexity, and thus the process continues as we learn more about existence, our environment, and life systems in general. Death remains a question and an ambiguous yet firm answer despite technological advances. As such, the fears and fascinations about it seem to challenge and mock our computerized expertise. The fact of death, its purpose and presence—even its biological reality—is uncontrolled but inevitable. In an age of written guarantees for products, death's warranty lasts a lifetime, never faltering in its contract. No one escapes its inevitability or its finality. Even with all of the changes and stresses that we experience daily and survive, death remains the one we dread most. Our lust for control has brought us no closer to making the fact of death a choice or option rather than a certainty. It is with us throughout the lifespan, yet few of us ever integrate its ubiquity.

In all likelihood, death will continue to evade our attempts to control how, when, and where it occurs, but the process of dying will

This work has been supported by Public Health Service Research Grant No. CA–27020 from the National Cancer Institute to Project Omega, Department of Psychiatry, Massachusetts General Hospital, Boston.

3

be amenable to personal control, choice, and self-direction for many. As thanatologists have already noted, death and dying are different events leading to varying alternatives for the patient, the family, and the clinical caretaker.

Clinical thanatology is by no means a new discipline within the behavioral sciences and health care professions. Major works have appeared, clinical prescriptions discussed, and the significance of death awareness underscored (Feifel 1977; Garfield 1978; Kastenbaum and Aisenberg 1976; Kubler–Ross 1969; and Weisman 1972). Certainly there is no dearth of reports that delineate ways the clinician or counselor might approach dying patients and their families. Various stage and phase-specific models are manifest in much of the current literature and tend to represent a need to redefine the clinical process in precise developmental terms. Unfortunately, a great deal of the clinical literature clones itself, preferring to resuscitate *generally acceptable paradigms*. Impetus to formulate new models is the exception, not the rule. As professionals, many of us often stay within known theoretical boundaries and therefore avoid seeking new syntheses and integrations. This predilection does not foster the design of a scientific clinical thanatology.

In the field of clinical thanatology, the generally acceptable paradigm almost always leads to the various vicissitudes and descriptions of client-centered, existential, or analytic models of intervention. These models have held significant positions within the therapeutic armamentarium of terminal-care specialists. Part of this can be attributed to clinical tradition, the remainder, one hopes, to a proven efficacy with dying patients.

The accepted models of terminal patient care underscore a nondirective approach. Kubler–Ross (1969) and others emphasize such prescriptions, often giving patient care the spiritual overlay that we all have grown accustomed to in the past decade. Consider the following quote from Pattison (1978):

> Third, helping is not so much doing as being. In our anxiety to accomplish something, to do something about dying, to feel we are valuable, or whatever, I find a zealousness to do things. But this may be for our own benefit, not that of the dying. To comfort is to share. To share is the willingness to be without having to do (162).

I cannot argue with the fact that it is common to observe professionals in the act of helping a patient "do something" for the sole pur-

pose of fending off the vulnerabilities of being a health caretaker. However, being is often not enough, nor is it in harmony with the humanistic tradition which this volume supports. Similarly, active helping, educating, or instructing within a therapeutic relationship need not always be identified as a countertransference response. Simply being with the dying is often more appropriately done by those close to the patient—those family members and friends who have known the patient intimately and who have been chosen by the patient. The generally acceptable paradigm in clinical thanatology omits the potential for brief, structured, and directed "doing" as part of patient care. I believe that the desire to help a dying patient can be successfully implemented without always seeking or cultivating an existential, nondirective encounter.

The purpose of this chapter is to present a brief overview of a discipline I am calling "behavioral thanatology." I intend to describe the general field as an alternative to traditional paradigms, but more so, to present the concepts in a way that underscores the humanistic, practical, and preventative implications of behavior therapy in terminal care. It is my hope that behavioral thanatology can fill the scientific and empirical gap the profession often avoids.

Any psychotherapy or counseling method should be based on science, regardless of our attachment to particular analytic, existential, or behavioral theories. Theories help us understand human behavior and organize diverse information, while the science of clinical psychotherapy dictates the most promising and empirically supported approach to change. As most of us recognize, this has not always been the case in psychotherapy. Theories have gone untested. Clinical prescriptions have been blindly applied by tradition or by a priori assumptions. Integration of paradigms often lags far behind relevant information on treatment efficacy (Garfield and Bergin 1978). Clinical thanatology is not an exception to these trends. In fact, the nature of its topic contributes to an even stronger detachment from empirical perspectives.

Somehow we seem to believe that death and dying should be quarantined from the so-called evil, mechanistic, or depersonalized onslaughts of the behavioral scientist. This attitude is a common stereotype, and one that hinders the development of a significant thanatological method. An empirical clinical science or an experimentally based behavior therapy is not necessarily a polarity to humanism (Mahoney 1975).

WHAT IS BEHAVIORAL THANATOLOGY?

In light of the major emphasis given to behavioral and cognitive therapies over the past ten years, it is surprising to discover the almost total absence of these approaches in the clinical thanatology literature. Except for a few brief reports (Averill 1968; Preston 1973; Ramsay 1979; Ramsay and Happée 1977; and Whitman and Lukes 1975) and one initial review by Rebok and Hoyer (1979), thanatologists are not exposed to behavioral viewpoints. There are numerous reasons for this, perhaps foremost being the many misconceptions held by traditional therapists about behavior modification principles and techniques. I will attempt to note some of these myths later on.

How then can we define behavioral thanatology? Drawing upon recent descriptions of behavioral medicine from the Yale Conference on Behavioral Medicine (Schwartz and Weiss 1977), we can describe behavioral thanatology as a subfield of behavioral medicine concerned with the development of behavioral science knowledge and techniques relevant to the understanding of terminal illness, life-threatening behavior, and grief, and the application of this knowledge and these techniques to diagnosis, prevention, treatment and rehabilitation. It is a multidisciplinary field that aims to follow behavior therapy assumptions and to apply, in conjunction with medical care, behavioral and cognitive methods to the dying patient, the grieving patient or family, the professional caretaker within the health system, or the patient manifesting life-threatening behaviors and illnesses. One general aim, therefore, of this emerging discipline is to help a patient or family manage their own adaptive responses. The goal is not to control death or to dictate a one-dimensional strategy of coping. On the contrary, behavioral thanatology seeks to educate the patient to facilitate self-control leading to an awareness of one's own instrumentality, "coping potency" (Mechanic 1977), and capacity to maintain self-worth in the face of death. Understanding our self-concept and caring for that part of each of us that is unique is a behavioral as well as existential-humanistic goal. However, how the clinician assists in the process varies considerably in the behavioral model.

Despite the popularity and success of behavioral and cognitive-behavioral methods (Goldfried and Davison 1976; Mahoney 1974; and Meichenbaum 1977), many clinicians originally trained in traditional modalities continue to dismiss the salient findings and practical implications of these therapies. Either/or polarities promulgate dichotomous theorizing as opposed to tentative but necessary integrations (Goldfried 1980). Behavior therapy is typically conceived of as a dirty word, a profane label describing a set of techniques ostensibly practiced by a group of "pigeon-oriented" conditioners who usurp power and dignity from distressed patients. This stereotype is gradually dissolving as clinicians recognize that behavior therapies are much broader in scope than their ancestors of classical conditioning and systematic desensitization. Recent attempts at integration and contextualization are noteworthy (Wachtel 1977).

If behavior therapy lacked a hero's welcome into the general psychotherapy arena, then I am quite certain that it may not be warmly embraced by most thanatologists reading this volume. When I approached various colleagues prior to a decision to go ahead with the book, it was not uncommon to hear that the notion was dehumanized, absurd, potentially dangerous, disrespectful to the dying, or denial-enhancing. The myths, misconceptions, and stereotypes of behavior therapy made it seem paradoxical that behavioral methods could be useful in terminal care. Obviously there are many significant limitations to the science of clinical behavior therapy, limitations that tend to be no more or less profound than inadequacies manifest in traditional models of psychotherapy (Kazdin 1979). However, beyond these limitations, there are common misconceptions that interfere with a clear understanding of behavior therapy.

Misconceptions of Behavior Therapy

1. *Behaviorists are only concerned with overt behavioral events.* While this was true for early behavioral models, we now see a willingness to accept the importance of cognitions and mediational models. Observation of overt behaviors is a significant dimension of assessment and treatment, but not at the expense of ignoring covert events in the form of self-instructions, imagery, preferences and expectations, beliefs and cognitive styles, or private linguistic systems. Traditional operant models of reinforcement are now being significantly altered by cognitive-behavioral methods that take the "inferential leap" to mediation (Beck 1976; Beck et al. 1979; and Mahoney 1974) discounted by the classical behavioral tradition. As cognitive

models mature and are refined, we should see a very sophisticated paradigm develop.

2. *Behavior therapy and cognitive therapy are unilinear, one-dimensional techniques.* Any quick perusal of recent textbooks will discount this stereotype (Goldfried and Davison 1976). Behavior modification, and the cognitive therapies that are a distinct branch of behavior therapies, are a group of techniques implying many different strategies of intervention. Furthermore, most comprehensive treatment programs utilize a number of techniques and strive to avoid unitary perspectives on symptoms (Craighead 1980).

3. *Behavior therapy is manipulative and mechanistic.* There is little doubt that early behaviorists often transformed clinical intervention into a highly structured, rigid, and sometimes overly experimental procedure. Stimulus-response models from learning theory and experimental psychology were commonly and prematurely translated into symptom-oriented behavior modification procedures. The learning theory and animal laboratory foundations for these early attempts at clinical intervention gave behavioral psychotherapy a mechanistic image. It took very little time for clinicians to assume that an experimentally based therapy must inevitably manipulate patients, ignore relationship factors, and devalue the humanistic premises of individuality, uniqueness, and personal responsibility. The last ten years have proven the fallacy of these viewpoints. The therapeutic relationship within the context of precise assessment procedures is an important dimension of behavior therapy. Operational definitions are not in conflict with the recognition of a patient's individuality. In fact, what we do see is a collaboration model (Meichenbaum 1977; and Mischel 1968, 1977) far exceeding the humanism of many traditional methodologies. Patients are typically seen as students or apprentices in an educational sense: the assumption made is that self-control is a primary and necessary goal for change. Teaching specific coping skills should not be equated with unempathic manipulations of circumscribed behaviors. As will become more apparent, the self-control and psychoeducational notions have widespread implications for the behavioral thanatologist.

4. *Behavior therapy is too symptom-oriented and thus loses significant information.* The debate over unconscious mechanisms versus conscious awareness is always the scapegoated topic when nonbehaviorists review the state of the art and science. Theories of the unconscious are central to most psychotherapeutic models. As the

proverbial hidden nine-tenths of the personality iceberg, the unconscious has reigned supreme in keeping our understanding of behavior
afloat. For many of us, the iceberg melted when we observed that
what was assumed to be solid ice was merely very changeable and
haphazard water! The argument seems more appropriately redefined
when we admit that there are obvious factors of human consciousness that remain unexplained, but which may not be relevant for
behavioral, affective, or cognitive change. Ignoring the unexplained
dimensions of consciousness (e.g., memory structures and associa-
tions, dreams, spontaneous images) does not lead, as many have
claimed, to a superficial and short-lived modification of behavior.
Likewise, months or years of daily concentration on so-called unconscious processes does not guarantee an increased therapeutic success
rate (Garfield and Bergin 1978). Current behavior and cognitive therapies are not solely concerned with altering the snake-phobic patterns of college sophomores. This would be a serious misconception,
amply disproven by the sophistication of recent behavioral models
(Beck et al. 1979; and Wachtel 1977). With regard to terminal care,
I question any technique that emphasizes unconscious behaviors.
Patients are already vulnerable to fears about a process and event
they know little about. To introduce, purposely, an additional factor
lying beyond the patient's control is to ignore significant goals of a
humanistic, rational, and self-directed therapeutic encounter.

5. *Behavior therapy rejects the value of diagnosis and assessment.*
If diagnosis is portrayed as a mere labelling exercise, then I would
agree that behaviorists are not interested in diagnosis. Traditional
diagnosis in the service of consistently depicting pathological defenses, as opposed to coping strategies and skills, seems inappropriate
for designing relevant interventions. Weisman and I (1979) comment
on this distinction when consulting to the cancer patient, but it is no
less an important factor in terminal care. Labelling a dying patient as
an anxiety neurotic or an hysterical personality, for example, has
little clinical value if our intention is to facilitate an individual's
self-controlled, dignified, or "appropriate death" (Weisman 1972).
Behavior therapists, and most recently cognitive therapists, are making impressive strides in formulating realistic and reliable assessment
procedures. Behavior therapy cannot be separated from assessment,
for its theory of change specifically requires a direct correspondence
between that which is observed, recorded, and analyzed, and that
which is instituted therapeutically. If anything, behaviorists spend

even greater time assessing cognitions and behaviors prior to the beginning of treatment. The uniqueness of each patient's plight and coping repertoire is reiterated during the assessment phase. Diagnostic labels within traditional psychiatric systems rarely provide such a framework.

There are obviously additional misconceptions that the reader may harbor toward behavior therapy. Over time some of these may vanish; others will no doubt appear. My intention in this chapter, and in editing the entire volume, is to provide evidence that behavior therapy has changed, that it has a broader based perspective, and that it offers an extremely practical and humanistic channel for terminal-care specialists. My major request of the reader is that he or she remain receptive to ideas that may initially seem paradoxical, and not be thwarted by the experimental or technical tone of the behaviorist's language. Behavior therapy, like this volume, prefers to view clinical intervention as a scientific experiment. For the reader, we suggest that the experiment is to monitor and to self-observe personal conceptualizations while listening to alternative explanations and options.

BEHAVIORAL THANATOLOGY: BASIC PRINCIPLES

Recently I had the opportunity to visit with a dying patient after her physician requested a consultation from the Psychiatry Department of the Massachusetts General Hospital. What made this consultation different was a very brief statement by the patient. Within a few moments of my initial visit, the patient looked up and stated quite forcefully, "Dr. Sobel, I'm so tired and bored with everyone trying to help me die correctly!" Mrs. M.'s statement is a simple yet profound comment on what has occurred in certain sectors of the so-called death and dying movement. Clinicians and counselors have a propensity to accept preconceived notions about dying, about what is necessary for a "proper" death experience, and about stages that the patient must pass through on the way to a "good death."

The basic assumptions and principles of behavioral thanatology are an attempt to short-circuit the focus on helping patients die correctly or stage-appropriately, goals that are seen as the antithesis of humanism. Instead, the aim is to help patients live realistically, comfortably, and practically with their terminal condition. The behavioral consultant offers the death-bored patient an alternative strategy for living with dying, a strategy that teaches problem-solving in the service of comfort, flexible morale, self-control, and, to borrow Weisman's (1972) concept, an appropriate death. An appropriate death does not mean that a patient is maneuvered to die the way we as clinicians might choose to die, as is often the case in current clinical practice.

There are a number of key elements in the development and practice of behavioral thanatology with terminal patients. I will outline these in some depth so that the reader will have a general perspective from which to evaluate the remaining chapters in this volume.

The Biopsychosocial Perspective

If we accept the notion that dying is a biopsychosocial process, then any relevant strategy should acknowledge a multifaceted systems approach to intervention. Behavioral thanatology is not oriented solely toward the patient. Although patient coping and adjustment are primary therapeutic goals for the clinician, the behavioral thanatologist also seeks to include and integrate the contributing effects of family, the hospital environment, physicians, nurses, and other health-care professionals. The patient's behaviors, concerns, life tasks, and presenting complaints are not viewed in isolation. In effect, and oversimplified for our purposes here, a $3 \times 3 \times 3 \times 3$ interaction is apparent when one considers that each part of the system has its own biological (or biomedical), psychological, and social dimension interacting with each other dimension (see Figure 1). Thus, for example, the social reinforcement patterns maintained by the family affect both the dying patient's biological condition and the physical health of health care professionals. The possible combinations of interacting biopsychosocial dimensions of each member or relevant environment of the dying system increase even further when we recognize that the psychological component includes cognitions, affects, and overt behaviors. My point, however, is not to complicate matters, but to emphasize the interacting and multifaceted perspective that should become part of patient care. This is a critical component of behavioral assessment (Mash and Terdal 1976; and Turk et al. 1980) and seems quite distinct from the patient-centered,

Figure 1.   A Multifaceted Systems View of Intervention. (*B* = Biomedical Factors, *P* = Psychological Factors, *S* = Social Factors).

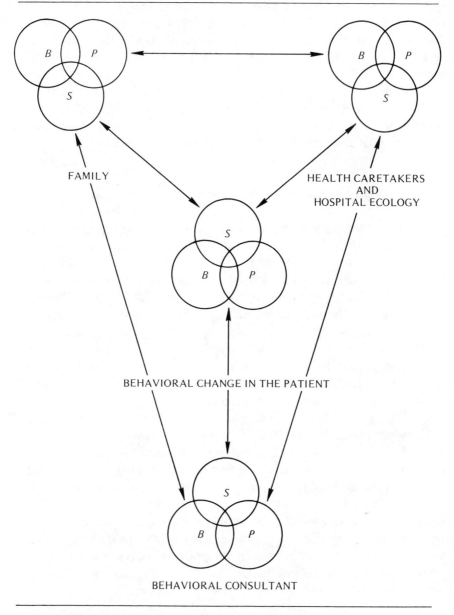

intrapsychic focus of many traditional paradigms. Unilinear assumptions detract from a humanistic model, often causing a loss of resources for fortifying patient coping.

A systems perspective guides the initial assessment, moving it toward a realization that direct intervention with the patient may not always be the appropriate treatment or strategy. Dying, like health care and health maintenance in general, is as much an interpersonal process as it is an intrapsychic event (Friedman and DiMatteo 1979). It is assumed that the behavioral consultant does not prefer and value one or the other. For example, a brief, problem-focused session with family members who maintain a depression-enhancing reinforcement pattern may successfully focus on what individual counseling may never have even uncovered. (See Chapter 7). Based on clinical and research experience, I believe that individual counseling without an interpersonal or systems context and assessment is greatly overvalued in terminal care. For the dying, time and meaningful personal encounters are not surplus commodities. This demands a careful overview of the multiple channels available for helping the patient.

Behavioral Assessment

It is impossible to pick up any book on contemporary behavior or cognitive-behavior therapy and not find the major emphasis given to assessment. As is apparent from my first point on basic principles, behavioral assessment is predicated on a multidimensional systems model. During the last ten years behaviorists have made significant contributions to the science of psychological assessment, consistently underlining the many deficits of traditional diagnostics from both tests and evaluation interviews (Goldfried and Kent 1972; Goldfried and Sprafkin 1974; Mash and Terdal 1966; Mischel 1968, 1977; and Sobel 1981). For our purposes, it is most important to acknowledge the following principles of a behavioral assessment: (1) behavior or symptoms are observed and recorded in relationship to antecedent events, consequences, and ongoing reinforcement patterns, and are not viewed as representations of underlying dynamics, unconscious processes, or unfulfilled wishes; (2) cognitions are behaviors, often amenable to the same functional analysis that can be performed on overt behaviors (Merluzzi, Glass, and Genest 1981); (3) direct assessment, with the patient's cooperation and collaboration, is seen as more practical and empirically valid than indirect attempts to tease out hidden material blocked by defense mechanisms; (4) coping strategies and skills, personal preferences, conscious requests, and problem-solving behaviors require observation by the clinician; (5) the assessment of broad personality characteristics or traits of patients is more likely to interfere with than to facilitate intervention; (6) diagnosis and assessment accepts the notion that individual variability is generally the rule, not the exception; (7) assessment data are psychosituational, a *sample*, not a fixed *sign*, of a patient's functioning within a given context (Bersoff 1973); and (8) the patient or family has the capacity and right to function as participating colleagues, "co-evaluators," or apprentices (Fischer 1970; Meichenbaum 1977; and Mischel 1977) to the behavioral consultant, and should not be placed in a role of passive patienthood if self-control, choice, and self-management are major therapeutic goals.

A functional health-oriented analysis of behavior has always been a prominent characteristic of behavioral assessment and therapy. Many clinical disciplines, however, including traditional models of terminal care, maintain static and undifferentiated approaches to assessment that seem to reinforce a pathological understanding of the patient. Once a diagnosis is made, a defense strategy proclaimed, or a character type highlighted, clinicians will often cease the assessment process. Furthermore, the labels—so often pathological in orientation—are seldom linked to the design and implementation of treatment programs. Nosological systems tend, simultaneously, to begin and end the process of understanding the patient. The terminal patient is not just a terminal patient, not a death and dying problem, not merely a denier. To reinforce the individuality of a dying patient, and therefore to design a relevant intervention strategy, it is necessary to observe the changing patterns and stimuli surrounding that patient's current experiences, environments, and responses. This is a key humanistic foundation of behavioral assessment. It is the basis for perceiving assessment as continuous, contextual, and health-directed (Mash and Terdal 1976).

The Patient as Student and Collaborator

A third basic principle of clinical behavior thanatology relates to the roles of the patient and the counselor. As traditional psychotherapists and counselors, we are accustomed to our role as experts. At times this role can preclude an acceptance of the patient's capacity to teach us more about himself or herself than we can ever hope to observe.

The behavioral thanatologist is a consultant, an educator, and a preceptor who is requested to facilitate some specific change, or to make a set of recommendations. A consultant-educator role includes therapeutic responsibilities when called for, but it also assumes that a collaboration with the patient-as-student or family-as-student may be more practical and effective. What does this imply? Basically, the behavioral thanatologist will approach each case with the assumption that many patients, families, or health professionals are capable of self-observation. The terminal phase is not synonymous with inexorable psychological regression. Certainly many patients are infantilized more as a result of the therapist's motivation than by personal wish. Seeking the patient's help and assistance as a colleague begins the process of reinstating self-control in the face of impending death. Furthermore, it de-emphasizes any magical expectations thrust upon the therapist while re-orienting the entire family and larger system to the therapy as an educational process. The behavioral consultant cannot cure death, and may not stimulate existential actualizations, but can indeed help the patient choose how final days are to be self-managed.

As much of the literature already shows, patients choose whom, when, and how to talk about existential issues during the terminal phase. Seldom is the psychological counselor chosen, and when a therapist is in fact chosen, this may be due to a choice by resignation, as family and close friends withdraw. The behavioral consultant does not assume that "here and now" practical concerns about finances, medical information, pain, anxiety, depression, personal hygiene, loss of control, food, work, or physical appeal are surface issues hiding the more profound thoughts on the acceptance or denial of death. Resolution of these biopsychosocial issues by active and direct behavioral techniques tends to elicit the *acceptance response* which traditional interventions strive so fervently to bring about through indirect discussions. The final result and benefit for the patient may be the same; the process is, again, quite different.

Consider the case of severe anxiety reactions in a cancer patient who was readmitted for yet another recurrence. The staff and the patient acknowledged the terminal condition, and the family sensed the looming event. The patient, however, continued to complain about the discomfort of anxiety and hyperventilation episodes. On interviewing the staff, I heard that the patient was denying, that the symptom must be a sign of her death fears. The staff and the family requested that I talk to the patient and see if I could help break through the denial, end the patient's "incessant bargaining," and facilitate acceptance.

My strategy as a behaviorist was quite different. After completing a behavioral assessment that included an analysis of current reinforcers for the patient, I asked the patient, (1) what she had observed; (2) what she would like to change; and (3) whether she would like me to help her learn some techniques that she could practice on her own. I had no doubt that the patient was frightened of dying. But more so, the patient felt that the anxiety prevented her from completing certain important life tasks, communicating with loved ones, and maintaining a satisfactory self-image. I described an anxiety-management program, using daily relaxation exercises, imagery of pleasant scenes, and staff reinforcement for anxiety-free periods. For approximately one week, the patient was both my student and a colleague. We recorded the frequency of anxiety episodes and together practiced the relaxation-meditation exercises. This brief intervention was very successful, despite the fact that we never spoke about death. I did not reinforce a naive denial of her terminal cancer plight, nor did I assume a controlling and mechanistic therapeutic posture. My goal was simply to facilitate self-instruction and primary symptom relief as part of encouraging choice and realistic self-control.

The role of the behavioral thanatologist incorporates Lazare's concept of the patient as a consumer (Lazare, Eisenthal, and Wasserman 1975). Too often psychotherapists do not consider the direct requests of the dying patient and family, the feasibility of negotiation, and the value of forming a contract. As I have reiterated above, the therapist is misdirected when he or she assumes some special knowledge of what is best for all dying patients. Patient requests are extremely diverse, perhaps as great as the symptoms that inhibit the attainment of these requests. Assessing patient preferences and requests, observing behavioral changes, negotiating all requests with those requests obtained from other components within the system, and avoiding uniform clinical prescriptions that may not match a particular request or problem are important factors in clinical behavior therapy. I view these dimensions of care as vital to a humanistic orientation.

Primary Prevention

Prevention is now receiving significant attention as a necessary component of health care. The rising popularity of holistic medicine and its emphasis on personal responsibility (Pelletier 1977) urges the medical and behavioral science professions to consider the necessity of preventative health care. This trend has major economic, social, and psychological implications as we enter the 1980s. The exorbitant increases in health care, for one, make it imperative that disease management and general mental health be confronted prior to the first sign of individual pathology.

Clinical thanatology should not be exempt from this push toward prevention and lifestyle modification. (See Chapter 10.) In one sense, it seems paradoxical to suggest that a principle of behavioral thanatology is prevention. However, in the spirit of the death education movement, I want to suggest that behavioral thanatologists assume responsibility for instituting preventative educational interventions with patients, families of the dying, and health-care professionals. Such an orientation belongs to a coping skills perspective in which the therapist-educator teaches principles of psychosocial inoculation (Meichenbaum 1977).

Dying is often a continuous chain of stressful stimuli. Death, when seen as a stressful life event, does not mean that all patients will react with traumatic symptoms. It does, however, imply that the potential for distress is always present as the patient and family navigate a new developmental phase, one very dissimilar to prior stages. Preparation for dying and the dying role is limited. Practice is even rarer. In order to strengthen or to alter coping, and thereby increase a patient's expectancy of self-efficacy (Bandura 1977) during stressful times, the behavioral thanatologist does not wait until problems or vulnerabilities become obtrusive. By assessing coping profiles early on, by holding psychoeducational seminars for staff, or by teaching a seemingly well-adjusted patient some methods for future use (e.g., use of imagery for pain reduction or ways of self-controlling possible depressions), the behaviorist attempts to *prevent* distress, *prepare* for change, and *foster* practice where reasonable. The prevention model also has major implications for staff adjustment and burn-out. (See Chapter 9.)

Over the past five years I have had the unique opportunity to participate in Project Omega at the Massachusetts General Hospital, where a prevention model was designed, tested, and exported to other health-care facilities (Sobel and Worden 1981; Weisman, Worden, and Sobel 1980; and Worden and Sobel 1978). The Omega model for psychosocial intervention with cancer patients is predicated on the assumption that not all patients require assistance but that certainly all should be screened and given a predictive score for possible future distress. This model then permits the health-care team to reach those who are identified "at risk" for emotional distress very early in the course of their illness. Project Omega has, therefore, been able to apply a behavioral and cognitive-behavioral treatment package on a preventative basis to a select group of cancer patients. This model does not wait for psychological symptoms to appear or intensify, nor does it assume that physicians and support staff will recognize distressed patients.

One further comment on Project Omega. A careful reading of relevant publications (Sobel and Worden 1979; Weisman and Sobel 1979; Weisman and Worden 1977; and Weisman, Worden, and Sobel 1980) underscores our commitment, as clinical thanatologists, to accept both the patient's capacity for self-observation and self-instruction, and the value of a therapist assuming the teacher role. Despite Weisman's psychoanalytic background, his recent writings demonstrate a shifting awareness and integration of behavioral and cognitive-behavioral principles (Weisman 1979; and Weisman and Sobel 1979). His original notion of an appropriate death serves as an early foundation for a self-controlled and preventative behavior modification approach to terminal care.

Cognitive Variables

A fifth principle of behavioral thanatology is the acceptance of cognitive or mediational variables. Ten years ago, as mentioned previously, a cognitive component to a behavioral model would not have been as readily accepted as it is today. Cognitive therapies are popular modalities, but more significantly, they have broadened the therapeutic channels for patient care. For terminal care, the contribution of cognitive perspectives is even greater, for in many instances the reality of a patient's situation precludes behavioral options that require overt procedures or the change of concrete reinforcers.

The terminal condition does not automatically subvert, destroy, or undermine a patient's private thoughts, images, daydreams, problem-solving behaviors, or perceptions. All of these cognitive variables have the potential to serve as rewards, reinforcers, stimuli of change, or focal points in the design of coping-skills programs that patients can use on their own. The dying process may demoralize the patient as it gradually inhibits normal activities, bodily functions, or environmental interactions. However, assuming that medications are handled humanely and appropriately, a patient's cognitive world will remain intact for much valuable time. Cognitions—such as daydreams, fantasies, and inner conversations—have distinct utility and practicality for the therapist concerned with maintaining a humanistic orientation. Cognitions are always present and available; they do not require staff or family participation when used therapeutically; they touch the heart of a person's individuality and creativity; and of utmost importance, they are amenable to self-control strategies. Cognitions, then, are often sufficient to guarantee an appropriate death, a self-controlled resolution of life's final role.

Nonbehaviorists are not accustomed to viewing cognitions as specific factors in behavior modification. Psychoanalytic and client-centered principles have always recognized cognitions as elements of psychological functioning, but typically this recognition has portrayed cognitions in a subservient role to affects. Thus traditional intervention strategies attempt, by and large, to employ cognitive factors as secondary links or structures in any change process, and not as primary agents having a direct effect on behavioral, affective, or further cognitive alterations. Terminal care paradigms almost always place a patient's affective world at the core of adjustment.

Cognitive therapies, and indeed there are now innumerable types of "thinking-oriented" psychotherapies (Beck 1976; Ellis 1973; Mahoney 1974; and Meichenbaum 1977), redirect the terminal-care specialist to a patient's cognitive style, and the personal power (Thoresen and Mahoney 1974) that can be found by becoming aware of the cognitive ecosystem. If we see dimensions of dying as cognitive processes, then the stress effects are controlled significantly by how the patient integrates and appraises what is happening. Emotional reactions and perceived behavioral options stem from the personal constructs and beliefs made by the dying patient. Dying is not synonymous with stress or distress. Between stressful stimuli and response possibilities lie the patient's cognitions, the family's cognitive patterns, and the system's preferences, attitudes, and expectations for dying. All three dimensions contribute to the success of coping and adaptation in the face of death.

The importance of cognitions in behavioral thanatology is emphasized throughout the present volume, and represents an exciting change in practical patient care. As Turk and Rennert note (see Chapter 4), even pain reduction through cognitive therapies is developing as a viable alternative and adjunct to biomedical possibilities. This type of approach, combined with imagery training and belief system modification as Achterberg, Lawlis, W. Sobel, and Ellis describe in their respective chapters, forms a central basis for a new cognitive paradigm in behavioral thanatology.

Depression and Behavioral Problem-solving Therapy. There is little doubt that behaviorists have made major contributions to the understanding and treatment of depression (Lewinsohn 1974). Those of us who have worked with the dying cannot deny the prevalence of dysphoria and depression during many terminal illnesses. Psychopharmacological treatments and traditional talk therapies often do little, unfortunately, to help patients regain a sense of control, learn how to manage depression on their own, or recognize more scientific and practical steps for preventing destructive mood changes. At times mood changes can be constructive, fortifying a patient with a necessary belief in his or her coping strengths, and stimulating creative alternatives. However, other depressions are incapacitating, precluding personal freedom and blocking social interaction during the final weeks or months. The use of problem-solving methods, attribution analysis, and self-instructional training are powerful antidepressant prescriptions for terminal care. The following description of a behavioral problem-solving program is one example of intervention.

Mr. S., a 48-year-old colon cancer patient, was admitted to the hospital after a regular follow-up exam revealed that the disease had spread to his liver. Three years had passed since his initial surgery and chemotherapy. Shortly after arriving at the hospital, Mr. S.'s wife, a social worker, and the mother of their three children ranging in age from 14 to 24, requested a psychiatric consultation for her husband. The hospital record showed a brief note from the family physician stating that "the patient's wife asked for a psychologist or psychiatrist to visit with her husband. Husband is aware of the metastasis and appears quite distressed."

Prior to visiting the patient, the therapist read the entire medical history and asked to meet with Mrs. S. During this brief session the consultant learned from Mrs. S. that her husband was frightened, "seemed to be withdrawing from the family," had lost his sense of humor, and talked a great deal about his fear of pain and fear of medication that might alleviate pain at the expense of personal control. The therapist asked that Mrs. S. inform Mr. S. of her consultation request, and of her initial meeting with a psychologist. Mrs. S. complied, reporting back that her husband seemed amenable to a first meeting.

After informing the family's physician of the patient's consent, the consulting psychologist met with Mr. S. Following brief introductions and conversation between the patient and the psychologist, the psychologist described his role.

Therapist: As you know, your wife asked that I meet with you to see if there were some things we might do together, now that your illness has recurred.

Patient: Right. I think she's pretty worried about me and what's going to happen.

Therapist: Yes, I got that impression, but I also sensed that you were worried about your current situation, and perhaps wanted to investigate what could be done to make things more comfortable.

Patient: Yes . . . I know how serious it is now . . . the pain, you know, I hope I can take it all because what I don't want is to be all drugged up and then not feel as if I'm really with my family and all.

Therapist: You would like to feel as much in control as is possible and that really feels frightening at times. Not knowing what to expect, and not having had to confront pain before, makes things seem overwhelming, like you're not sure whether you can really do it on your own.

Patient: Exactly . . . who the hell has died before? (Patient gets tearful and starts to cling to the bed rail. A couple of minutes pass.)

Therapist: Unfortunately, I can't cure your illness although I wish I could, but I would like to help you learn how to handle some of the things that are frightening you now. If we could work together for a while I believe that certain things might seem less overwhelming for you, and that you would feel more in control of your situation. For example, take your fear of pain. It's a normal and realistic fear, but certainly it is also something which we can work on, together, very specifically, so that you could have some method for confronting the pain, if and when it occurs. I would like to teach you a method for problem-solving, and also a way to relax your body so you and your family can spend some pleasant times together.

Patient: I would like that very much . . . I can't stand just doing nothing . . . it makes me depressed and then I don't want to think or do anything.

Therapist: I understand. The way I like to work with people is to work together. There are certain things which I have experience doing, but basically I need your help and cooperation. I can only be a kind of teacher. You're the student, but also you are the teacher as well. Together we can set up very specific goals and try to evaluate how we're doing as we go along. I'm going to give you some homework to do, and expect you to practice.

Patient: I like that. What about my wife, can she participate?

Therapist: She certainly can, but initially I would like us to work alone. It would be helpful for you to keep her informed of what we are doing, and why.

Patient: Yes . . . sure.

Therapist: There is one other thing I would like to say. If, at any time while we are focusing on specific issues, you would just like to talk about something, ask questions, or just let me know how you feel, please just do it. Most people in your situation have a great deal on their minds, but aren't quite sure where to direct it all. I will be happy to help you sort out whatever comes up.

Patient: Thank you, I really appreciate it. I get frightened that everyone else around here just wants me to be 'okay' and keep everything to myself . . . I can't always do that!

Therapist: Precisely. Most of the nurses and doctors are very busy. Sometimes they just don't realize when someone is upset or in need of comfort. On the other hand, I also feel you have the responsibility to ask questions, to make direct requests, and to let others know how things are affecting you. It is a tough responsibility but I believe it is the only way for you to preserve your self-respect and gradually adjust to the reality of what is happening.

Patient: I suppose so, but sometimes I get so damn angry at these smiling little nurses wanting me to cheer up. Dying ain't a happy experience.

Therapist: I know. It hurts a great deal. We don't know what to expect.

Patient: (Silence) . . . Well, I want to work on some of the things.

Therapist: Good. I would like to visit with you tomorrow morning. Between now and then it will be important for you to begin constructing a list of the various concerns you have, or some of the things you would like to accomplish. When I come back, I would like to begin by teaching you a form of body relaxation which you will be able to practice on your own. Okay?

Patient: Fine. I'll be here waiting for you.

At the next session, the psychologist went over Mr. S.'s list of concerns, helping him to define each task or problem clearly. Following this discussion, progressive muscle relaxation was introduced. The psychologist presented a clear rationale for its use (e.g., calming the body, time-out from concerns, reducing anxiety, focusing on some pleasant scenes, and anti-pain applications). The patient was taken through a 30-minute relaxation procedure using progressive tensing and relaxing of each muscle, deep breathing, and repetitive focusing on the numbers '1' and '2' while inhaling and exhaling. This exercise was taped on a cassette so that the patient could practice on his own. At the conclusion of the relaxation, the psychologist introduced the notion of careful problem-solving as a way to regain a sense of control over what appear to be overwhelming issues. The patient again brought up his fears of depression and pain, and anticipatory anxiety over not being able to obtain clear information from the medical staff. The psychologist stated that their next session would focus on methods of problem-solving.

After another relaxation session at the next meeting, the psychologist restated the purposes of learning how to solve problems in a step-by-step manner while becoming conscious of how we talk to ourselves. The notion of self-talk (Beck and Meichenbaum) was presented. Recognizing that the patient was very much concerned with depression, the psychologist used a card from the Cancer Problem-Solving Instrument (Weisman, Worden, and Sobel 1980; and Sobel and Worden 1981) to initiate a problem-solving intervention. The card chosen portrayed a woman who is concerned and worried about her uncontrollable crying episodes. This card asks the patient to generate alternative solutions to the vignette, and thus, in effect, aims to help the patient cope by resolving the woman's concerns. A second card showing the problem solved is presented to the patient to facilitate the cognitive pathway.

Therapist: As you have correctly perceived, the lady in the card is having difficulty controlling her emotions as a result of her cancer recurrence. What I would like us to do together is to go through a precise series of problem-solving steps and not try, immediately, to solve her dilemma.

Patient: Okay . . . you know, this lady reminds me of myself a bit.

Therapist: Well, then that should help us quite directly. I have given you a list of problem-solving steps which we find are practical. I'm sure there are many other ways of approaching a problem or concern, but let's start with the list I have given you.

Patient: Fine.

Therapist: As you can see, the first step suggested is that a person clearly define the problem. So many people want to jump to solutions that they often forget to narrow the problem down to its realistic dimensions. After defining a problem, it is often best to get away from it, to do nothing, to try not to think about what it is, or how to solve it. This is why I have taught you relaxation. In a way, it can be used as time-out, a brief period to clear the mind.

Patient: You know, I had a lot of trouble last night trying to relax. My mind kept racing and thinking.

Therapist: Right. It takes a time of practice before the exercises will work. Try not to fight the thoughts. Just watch them flow by, and pass right from your mind. We can work on that together in a little while.

Patient: Good.

Therapist: Back to our cards. Step three is the step of trying to imagine what this woman says to herself, the kind of self-talk she has. Given what we know about her, what do you think she says, inside?

Patient: I suppose she says things like, "I'm no good anymore," or "Why me, why should I have cancer?" . . . or even "I feel guilty for messing up my family by being sick and all."

Therapist: Okay. I'm going to write these down so later we can study how these thoughts might affect how she feels, and even what she does.

Patient: I guess I say some of these things to myself also.

Therapist: Well, that can really help us. Why don't you try to keep a log, between now and our next session, of the types of private thoughts you have. Could you do that?

Patient: Sure.

Therapist: Now that we have some sense of her possible thoughts, the next step in problem-solving is to generate as many possible solutions as we can, solutions which will get this lady from Card 1 (her dilemma) to Card 2 (the resolution). One other thing. I find that people always want to find the best solution, and because of this tendency they often can't solve a problem at all. What I would like you to do is to think of any solution, think of many alternatives, even try to create a poor solution so that we can compare and contrast each option.

At this point in the session the patient began to give a number of alternative solutions to the card. In effect, Mr. S. described ways of coping with depression that included changes in thinking, acting, and feeling. Solutions were recorded on a separate index card, then rank-ordered after each one was evaluated. The final steps in the problem-solving session were: (1) making a choice, and (2) redefining the original problem to see if any positive dimensions could be uncovered. In analyzing the patient's solution and general cognitive style, the psychologist was able to assess the patient's disease attributions, for example, "This lady feels guilty for bringing on this disease." Furthermore, the nature of the patient's self-instructional style was clarified as was the degree of flexibility in recognizing solutions, and decentering from initial responses. One interesting observation was the quantity of 'should' statements which became part of the patient's projected problem solutions. Such statements would be dealt with later, via techniques described by Ellis in his rational-emotive therapy (See Chapter 6.)

After completing the problem-solving exercise, the psychologist requested that the patient study the various steps, in addition to continuing the relaxation. The need for self-observation was underlined, especially in the context of monitoring 'how we talk to ourselves and control our behaviors.' Intervention with Mr. S. continued for two weeks, during which time additional cards were used as well as applications to his list of personal concerns. The patient learned both a 'cognitive-behavioral approach to pain control before any substantial pain was manifest, and began to anticipate how thoughts influence feelings and behavior. A significant amount of time was spent on preventing depression through personal problem-solving and interpersonal assertiveness. By the end of three weeks the nursing staff reported that Mr. and Mrs. S. were utilizing the relaxation tapes together during their early evening visits. The psychologist made periodic follow-ups in the hope of reinforcing the continued use of techniques.

This case report demonstrates the feasibility of designing a fairly structured interview which respects the patient's individuality and capacity to learn while dying. Furthermore, it clearly portrays the active, preventative orientation of the behavioral thanatologist. In this brief case study, both cognitive and behavioral techniques were used in the hope of teaching the patient a methodology for coping. One goal was to educate the patient in cognitive coping skills that are applicable within a self-control paradigm. The therapist wanted to reinforce the notion that depression was indeed controllable, that a sense of self-worth could be preserved directly, and that mediational structures are always available for self-help, despite the dying process. As Bandura (1977) clearly states, the change and coping process seem quite dependent on the expectancy of self-efficacy as an individual confronts stressful situations.

Self-Control

I want to draw attention to one final principle that is implied throughout this chapter, namely, the practice of behavioral self-control (Thoresen and Mahoney 1974). The acceptance of self-control techniques into clinical behavior therapy is indeed a significant step for contemporary psychotherapy, despite the fact that self-control is not a new principle. For centuries philosophers emphasized the importance of personal freedom, choice, self-control, and responsibility. On the other hand, behavior therapists translate these constructs into very practical programs of intervention and behavioral change. Self-control research—and its components of self-observation, self-reward, and covert self-regulation—demonstrates the many benefits of viewing a patient as an agent of his or her own change process.

Self-control should not be confused with will power or common ideas of restraint. For the behavior or cognitive therapist, self-control strategies represent a precise model of humanistic psychotherapy whereby patients are taught to be "personal scientists" (Kelly 1955; and Mahoney 1978) of their overt and covert behaviors. The patient exercises self-control when: (1) observations are made on the internal and external environment; (2) data and recordings are collected; (3) interdependent relationships are perceived between individual behaviors and environmental conditions; (4) positive and negative reinforcers are understood; (5) self-administered consequences (e.g., rewards) to specific behaviors are instituted (6) environmental planning and stimulus modification are made by the patient; and (7) new behaviors or cognitions are maintained, recorded, and assessed through time. Self-control behavior modification is, therefore, a specific technology of change that the professional teaches to a patient in the hope that the process will continue as the patient becomes his or her own therapist. All models of therapy strive for this result, but few structure the encounter in such concrete and pragmatic terms. (For the reader interested in learning exact prescriptions for a self-control program I suggest a careful reading of Thoresen and Mahoney 1974.)

Self-control principles and strategies have significant implications for the behavioral thanatology paradigm. The issue of control is central to an understanding of the dying patient, the family, and the health care system. Most of us do not have a learned coping response to a life-threatening illness. Our responses are generally more defensive, biological, and automatic while stressful emotions are rapidly fended off. Typically, we do not immediately confront or redefine the stress of dying through problem-solving (which I interpret as the essence of coping). The dying patient or the grieving family fears the loss of psychological, biological, and social control. It is due to the primacy and salience of these control concerns that I underline the benefits of a self-control behavioral orientation in terminal care and behavioral medicine. (See Chapter 10.)

To reinstate a sense of personal control, and thus to prevent future distress during the dying process, a behavior therapist can guide a patient to an awareness of how many things can be altered, modified, or preserved despite the reality of death and life-threatening illness. Even the simple act of teaching a patient how to reduce bodily anxiety through progressive muscle relaxation seems to be a first step in helping to fortify personal control and morale (Sobel and Worden 1981). Learning to recognize how one can control and choose very specific responses, both in the internal and external environments, may be more helpful than confronting the existential pain of saying goodbye. In fact, I believe that the latter is more possible and rewarding when elicited from a patient who has first coped with specific vulnerabilities through a self-managed process.

As Weisman (1972) and others have stated, dying brings on an inevitable confrontation with choice, sometimes even a total demolition of our capacity to choose. The hospital environment may reinforce a patient to relinquish the right of personal choice; physicians often negate the right; nurses can indirectly dismiss it; the well-intentioned family may even take it away. Allowing a patient to perceive the potential for self-control and the option for choices (Perlmutter and Monty 1977), however limited, may in and of itself prevent destructive dysphoria, learned helplessness (Seligman 1975), or alienation. Self-control strategies, whether behavioral, cognitive, or decisional as Averill (1973) describes, can serve the practical clinical demands for assuring "safe conduct, an appropriate death, and dignified dying:"

> Dignified dying is not an exotic concept; it simply means that one continues to regard a dying patient as a responsible person, capable of clear perceptions, honest relationships, and purposeful behavior, consistent with the inroads of physical decline and disability (Weisman 1980: 756).

While working toward a self-control program for the dying, the clinician must also take heed of Averill's (1973) finding that "no simple relationship exists between personal control and stress." At times a perception of possible control and multiple choices will inoculate an individual against distress. Having control and managing available options, however, do not guarantee stress reduction and adaptation, any more than empathic discussion with a dying patient automatically facilitates acceptance of death. It is the *meaning and type* of control that is the blueprint for the eventual effectiveness of a particular intervention.

The *control response* varies considerably with each patient or staff person, making it essential for the clinician to assess attitudes, expectations, and general cognitions of control and death. This assessment of personal philosophies is central to a rational, humanistic approach to thanatology, as Ellis discusses in Chapter 6. The critics of behavior therapists certainly cannot accuse us of manipulating patients and inhibiting personal control when in fact our aim is to help patients perceive and choose their own type of control in a rational, self-determined, and self-maintaining manner (See Chapter 2.) Simple behavioral self-control techniques, such as practicing imagery or mentally rehearsing assertive behavior with an overbearing nurse or relative, are promising components for terminal care when reality shows that professional time is limited, psychotherapy expensive, and inpatient learned helplessness an infectious psychosocial pattern. I believe that the behavioral self-control option is significantly more humanistic and helpful to a patient than hearing that "the complex mechanisms of defense must be analyzed carefully" (Feigenberg 1975, 1980).

Problem-solving, as described in the prior section, is a salient part of the self-control paradigm. In the final analysis, and in a very general sense, a dying patient will succeed in maintaining adaptive and creative control to the extent that decisionmaking is resourceful, flexible, optimistic, and practical (Weisman and Sobel 1979). The aim, then, of the short-term intervention is to assess deficits in decisionmaking, teach self-observation, and finally, to reinforce a vigilant (Janis and Mann 1977) style of problem-solving. A step-by-step decision process can include the following components:

1. Identifying primary affects.
2. Defining uppermost problems and subsidiary concerns.

3. Generating alternatives and observing covert structures (e.g., imagery, self-instructions).
4. Imagining how others might respond if asked to solve similar problems.
5. Considering pros and cons of each proposed solution.
6. Rank ordering all possible solutions.
7. Selecting the most acceptable or feasible solution.
8. Re-examining and redefining the original problem in light of the assessment.

We live in a world where control is so earnestly sought after that often we misattribute events to preserve a semblance of some control. This is especially true when highly stressful events, like dying, are encountered. The final redefinition phase of problem-solving underlines the value of a self-control orientation for it is here that the behavioral consultant helps the patient recognize personal attributions.

It is not uncommon for a clinician to discover that a patient's attributions are unbalanced, and therefore interfere with realistic self-control (Janis and Rodin 1979). For example, one cancer patient may attribute the onset of disease solely to psychological factors, and thus feel quite guilty and rejected. Another patient might attribute the disease's etiology to environmental or ecological factors, resulting in angry projections on everyone providing care. Such attributions are very much a part of a patient's cognitive coping profile, despite the obvious limitations that they place on adaptation. At times these attributions are similar to the use of positive denial (Lazarus 1979), for they temporarily reinstate self-control at a time of heightened fears, low morale, and alienation. The goal for the behavioral consultant is to facilitate realistic appraisal and choices that are not just tied to pseudo or defensive control. In short, through a careful process of teaching decisionmaking, the behaviorally oriented clinician hopes to stimulate a patient's information-seeking behavior, leading to new attributions, practical expectations, and eventual self-control (Sobel and Worden 1981; and Weisman and Sobel 1979).

My overview of the basic behavioral thanatology principles is by no means an exhaustive or comprehensive discussion. There are additional components that will develop as the field gains wider attention. My intention here is to generate a tentative outline, suggesting for the reader some factors that are necessary for a paradigm shift in the behavioral and cognitive-behavioral direction.

MYTHS OF CANCER AND TERMINAL CARE

In the process of applying behavioral thanatology principles to clinical practice, I have become aware of a number of myths that can inhibit the adoption of the structured, humanistic approaches discussed in this volume. As I noted earlier, general misconceptions about behavior therapy are typically first-order blockades for the traditional therapist. Following these initial preconceptions on the nature of behavior therapy, many terminal care and cancer counselors—regardless of their professional background—will accept one or more of the common myths.

Here is a brief description of the typical myths that I observe directly:

1. Psychosocial care, including grief counseling, necessitates helping the patient or family reach deep or profound insights into character.
2. A good death is a totally resolved death. All life concerns are worked through, integrated, or at least discussed openly.
3. A therapist can teach a patient how to die correctly and appropriately.
4. When working with dying or grieving patients, we must always be cautious because they are psychologically fragile. Vulnerability to stress means that regressive trends will occur as therapeutic confrontations are made.
5. A here-and-now focus during a session is inevitably superficial, leads to symptom substitution, and avoids the more significant unconscious dynamics. Existential concerns are at the core of observable stress among dying patients.
6. Catharsis, or aiming the patient toward intense emotional release, is synonymous with successful intervention.
7. Denial and defensive avoidance are always countertherapeutic. A denying patient can never be a coping patient.
8. All people cope poorly with cancer and other life-threatening illnesses, and thus require professional counseling. Serious depression is always present if you search hard enough.

9. Rational problem-solving, as a therapeutic strategy, is the same as encouraging defensive rationalization. Step-by-step instructions for learning a particular coping skill fortifies a patient's avoidance of feelings.
10. Coping is a uniform, unilinear, and constant process: once a poor coper always a poor coper.
11. Coping and adaptation during a terminal illness are orderly processes that inevitably follow precise psychological stages. In order to experience a healthy resolution of grief, a patient must progress through specified stages.
12. Depression, anxiety, or the overall plight of patienthood cannot possibly lead to personal growth and development. Resolution of life issues, which had been occurring prior to the illness, is always a higher priority for the patient than continuing to learn during a living-with-dying phase. Heightened personal awareness and integration are extremely rare for patients.
13. Dying, and the thoughts or images of death iteslf, are the most frightening, tragic, and catastrophic dimensions of the patient's life. Fear of death reigns supreme over fears of other biopsychosocial events, such as pain, bodily disfigurement, and isolation.
14. A therapist should and must like each patient he or she works with since the patient is nearing death. Empathy and unconditional positive regard for a patient guarantee intervention efficacy. Genuine warmth, on the part of the consultant or counselor, combined with "just being there" for the patient, will insure a highly successful encounter.
15. There are only fourteen myths of terminal care, and once we understand how and when they appear, we will then be perfectly competent counselors.

Space does not permit me to expand on these common myths by describing case examples where the negative effects of each misconception were manifest. I urge the reader to consider them as an exercise for self-evaluation, a personal review of how easily we can preclude the discovery of creative paradigms and intervention strategies. Myths and unvalidated assumptions are cognitive ferris wheels for the clinician, often leading the well-intentioned helper into an inescapable circle that never alters its views or boundaries. To question our long-held clinical precepts at least increases the chance that we might recognize inconsistencies and subsequently experiment with flexible alternatives.

Myths of terminal care are inextricably tied to standards of care. Unquestioned standards can indeed become myths. Likewise, myths disguised as valid assumptions cannot but dissolve thanatology's design of family or patient-centered standards of humanistic care. I suspect that many traditional thanatologists may read the present volume only to proclaim that standards of care would be destroyed by such a behavioral model. Most of us are so conditioned to equating behavioral empiricism with a controlling, dehumanizing authoritarianism that it is difficult to conceive how standards might be preserved.

Recently, Kastenbaum (1977) reviewed patient-centered standards of terminal care that emerged from a task force. In no instance are the seven highly humanistic standards of care negated by the principles or practice of behavioral thanatology. In all cases, they both reiterate the value of an "empirical humanism" (Mahoney 1975) and underline, indirectly, the clinical benefits of the techniques discussed in this volume. I believe that behavioral thanatology principles and techniques follow from these important standards of terminal care and outline where the future of hospice and holistic medicine might go. It is a clinical methodology that can match, in a practical way, our humanistic-existential theories and standards. Rather than becoming a polarity, or forcing us to bifurcate paradigms, the behavioral or cognitive-behavioral option emphasizes the benefits of synthesis and integration in terminal care. Humanism is preserved, not hindered, by examining feasible alternatives.

CONCLUSIONS AND SUMMARY

It has been my intention in this chapter to lay the groundwork for a new interdisciplinary dimension within thanatology and behavioral medicine. An overriding issue for the present volume is whether or not behavioral thanatologists can integrate emerging concepts and still preserve both the humanistic and empirical standards which, independently, have taken so long to develop and to cultivate. I have underscored this point a number of times because it suggests the most likely pitfall. The history of clinical psychotherapy, as well as the current state of the profession, are replete with examples of how polarities are constructed and synthesis is avoided. Empirically oriented clinicians, such as those trained in the behavioral tradition, tend to ignore valuable theoretical contributions on human development offered by other disciplines. Similarly, representatives from traditional psychoanalytic and existential schools often are phobic to data-based interventions and the methodologies of empirical investigation. The two do not seem antithetical to each other, nor should they continue the paradigmatic sparring we constantly witness.

Behavioral thanatology offers a practical opportunity for clinicians to pursue a scientific study of death and dying, while emphasizing the importance of personal and familial responsibility, goal-setting, self-control, choice, and pro-active interaction with one's internal (e.g., cognitions) and external environments (Bugental 1967; and Buhler 1971). The principles and practice of behavioral thanatology seem to provide realistic methods to facilitate the appropriate deaths that Weisman conceptualizes.

As humanism and applied holistic medicine continue to overlap, we will observe an increasing emphasis on personal responsibilities for health. The study of chronic illness and even dying itself are part of a health psychology that accepts the necessity for teaching individuals that patienthood is not the sole responsibility of medical practitioners or health-care systems (Matarazzo 1980). Medical specialization, high technology, and professional expertise can coexist with patients who choose to control many aspects of their care, whether it be during a healthy life phase or a dying process. The behavioral thanatologist, like the behavioral medicine consultant, will reinforce personal options, attempting to guide patients away from a reliance upon physicians and other health care professionals (Pelletier 1979). The sickness role and the dying transition do not have to be invitations to passivity.

Creative dying is not necessarily a cliché, but it can be taken seriously only if we recognize the limits of individuals and our interventions. Grandiose plans for total consciousness raising, personality integration, or a final death acceptance, seem to define the field at its most unsophisticated and one-dimensional level. Creative dying, in the behavioral-humanistic tradition, means helping a patient visualize options, engage in active problem-solving, review and renegotiate contracts, and participate — where medically feasible — with his or her own biopsychosocial care. It does not imply infantilizing the patient, insisting on the paradox of healthy dying (Kastenbaum 1979), or viewing the individual as a temporary intruder into a well-functioning hospital or hospice. The patient is a participant and a collaborator, as are physicians, nurses, family members, and psychosocial consultants. Creative dying, then, is the result of efforts from a dynamic, interacting system that supports the value of self-control.

Any new or emerging clinical paradigm runs the risk of being prematurely generalized to all situations and to all patients. Behavioral thanatology is no exception. I have attempted to prevent this occurrence by noting a very simple fact: *behavior therapy in terminal care is a tentative hypothesis.* My intention has not been to pronounce an absolute model bound to a rigid set of clinical prescriptions. As a hypothesis, behavioral thanatology requires intensive experimental investigation with divergent populations in specific settings. A dying patient is not just a dying patient and therefore behavioral interventions will not be appropriate for all individuals, health professionals, or systems. The need for a critical perspective is paramount. As empirical humanists in terminal care, we should not forget our commitment to scientific inquiry nor relinquish our dedication to human individuality. Ongoing clinical research can reasonably maintain these requirements and still continue to scrutinize the efficacy of behavioral thanatology (Epstein 1980; and Lazarus 1978).

Psychosocial researchers and clinicians will undoubtedly continue to study behavioral thanatology. However, I also urge my colleagues not to assume inadvertently that behavior therapy can become a technological answer for overcoming the inevitability of death, and the many emotional realities inherent in the dying process: "Expecting the ancient human concern with death to disappear miraculously because of breakthroughs in science or technology may be an exercise in naivete" (Kastenbaum 1977: 319).

No psychotherapeutic technique can afford to ignore the physical and psychological pains that so often accompany terminal diseases. Behavioral thanatology can, on the other hand, become one dimension of health-care planning, hospice programming, and behavioral medicine; a methodology for assisting patients, families, and staff to preserve self-efficacy, to define realistic self-management, and to reclaim dying as a personal responsibility. Behavior therapists in terminal care will not cure death, but they may indeed ease difficulties dramatically while directly uncovering options for patient coping and problem-solving.

In a philosophical and practical way, behavioral thanatology opens up the possibility for a final life experiment. Similar to Mahoney's (1978) personal scientist model, I believe that behavior therapists in terminal care settings have an opportunity to guide patients and families into a creative experiment with their remaining days. Goals and contracts can be generated, old ones rejected or redefined, and new data sought as the patient attempts to die with a relaxed, but self-controlled uncertainty. As a joint venture, the patient–therapist encounter aims for both a respite from normal anxieties and a realization of new capabilities in response to a very significant stress.

Dying is a developmental task. Similar to adolescence, it also poses a major challenge to our struggle to be independent and unique, yet receptive to social supports and our common connection to biological sameness. Behavioral thanatology suggests a new approach for resolving the *developmental task of living* with an approaching death.

REFERENCES

Averill, J.R. Grief: Its nature and significance. *Psychological Bulletin*, 1968, *70*, 721–748.

Averill, J.R. Personal control over aversive stimuli and its relationship to stress. *Psychological Bulletin*, 1973, *80*, 286–303.

Bandura, A. Self-efficacy: Toward a unifying theory of behavior change. *Psychological Review*, 1977, *84*, 191–215.

Beck, A. *Cognitive therapy and the emotional disorders*. New York: International Universities Press, 1976.

Beck, A., Rush, A., Shaw, B., and Emery, G. *Cognitive therapy of depression*. New York: Guilford Press, 1979.

Bersoff, D. Silk purses into sow's ears: The decline of psychological testing and a suggestion for its redemption. *American Psychologist*, 1973, *28*, 892–899.

Bugental, J. *The challenge of humanistic psychology*. New York: McGraw-Hill, 1967.

Buhler, C. Basic concepts of humanistic psychology. *American Psychologist*, 1971, *26*, 378–386.

Craighead, W. Away from a unitary model of depression. *Behavior Therapy*, 1980, *11*, 122–128.

Ellis, A. *Humanistic psychotherapy*. New York: McGraw-Hill, 1973.

Epstein, S. The stability of behavior: II. Implications for psychological research. *American Psychologist*, 1980, *35*, 790-806.

Feifel, H. *New meanings of death*. New York: McGraw-Hill, 1977.

Feigenberg, L. Care and understanding of the dying: A patient centered approach. *Omega*, 1975, *6*, 81-95.

Feigenberg, L. *Terminal care: Friendship contracts with dying cancer patients*. New York: Brunner/Mazel, 1980.

Fischer, C.T. The testee as co-evaluator. *Journal of Counseling Psychology*, 1970, *17*, 30-36.

Friedman, H.S and DiMatteo, M.R. Health care as an interpersonal process. *Journal of Social Issues*, 1979, *35*, 1-11.

Garfield, C. (Ed.). *Psychosocial care of the dying patient*. New York: McGraw-Hill, 1978.

Garfield, S., and Bergin, A. *Handbook of psychotherapy and behavior change*. New York: John Wiley and Company, 1978.

Goldfried, M.R. Toward the delineation of therapeutic change principles. *American Psychologist*, 1980, *35*, 991-999.

Goldfried, M.R. and Davison, G.C. *Clinical behavior therapy*. New York: Holt, Rinehart and Winston, 1976.

Goldfried, M.R. and Kent, R. Traditional versus behavioral personality assessment: A comparison of methodological and theoretical assumptions. *Psychological Bulletin*, 1972, *77*, 409-420.

Goldfried, M.R. and Sprafkin, J.N. *Behavioral personality assessment*. Morristown, N.J.: General Learning Press, 1974.

Janis, I.C. and Mann, L. *Decision making: A psychological analysis of conflict, choice, and commitment*. New York: MacMillan, 1977.

Janis, I.C. and Rodin, J. Attribution, control, and decision making: Social psychology and health care. In G. Stone, F. Cohen, and N. Adler (Eds.), *Health psychology*. San Francisco: Jossey-Bass, 1979.

Kastenbaum, R. *Death, society, and human experience*. St. Louis: C.V. Mosby, 1977.

Kastenbaum, R. Healthy dying: A paradoxical quest continues. *Journal of Social Issues*, 1979, *35*, 185-206.

Kastenbaum, R. and Aisenberg, R. *The psychology of death*. New York: Springer, 1976.

Kazdin, A. Fictions, factions, and functions of behavior therapy. *Behavior Therapy*, 1979, *10*, 629-654.

Kelly, G. *The psychology of personal constructs*, Vol. 2. New York: Norton, 1955.

Kubler-Ross, E. *On death and dying*. New York: MacMillan, 1969.

Lazare, A., Eisenthal, S., and Wasserman, L. The customer approach to patienthood. *Archives of General Psychiatry*, 1975, *32*, 553-558.

Lazarus, R. Strategy for research in hypertension. *Journal of Human Stress*, 1978, *4*, 34-39.

Lazarus, R. Positive denial: The case for not facing reality. *Psychology Today*, 1979, November, 44-60.

Lewinsohn, P. A behavioral approach to depression. In R.J. Friedman and M.M. Katz (Eds.), *The psychology of depression: Contemporary theory and research*. New York: Winston-Wiley, 1974.

Mahoney, M.J. *Cognition and behavior modification*. Cambridge, Mass: Ballinger, 1974,

Mahoney, M.J. The sensitive scientist in empirical humanism. *American Psychologist*, 1975, *30*, 864-867.

Mahoney, M.J. Personal science: A cognitive learning therapy. In A. Ellis and R. Grieger (Eds.), *Handbook of rational-emotive therapy*. New York: Springer, 1978.

Mash, E., and Terdal, L. *Behavior therapy assessment: Diagnosis, design and evaluation*. New York: Springer, 1976.

Matarazzo, J.D. Behavioral health and behavioral medicine: Frontiers for a new health psychology. *American Psychologist*, 1980, *35*, 807-817.

Mechanic, D. Illness behavior, social adaptation, and the management of illness. *Journal of Nervous and Mental Diseases*, 1977, *165*, 79-87.

Meichenbaum, D. *Cognitive behavior modification: An integrative approach*. New York: Plenum, 1977.

Merluzzi, T., Glass, C., and Genest, M. (Eds.). *Handbook of cognitive assessment*. New York: Guilford Press, 1981 (in press).

Mischel, W. *Personality and assessment*. New York: Wiley, 1968.

Mischel, W. On the future of personality assessment. *American Psychologist*, 1977, *4*, 246-254.

Pattison, E.M. The living-dying process. In C. Garfield (Ed.), *Psychosocial care of the dying patient*. New York: McGraw-Hill, 1978.

Pelletier, K.R. *Mind as healer, mind as slayer*. New York: Delta, 1977.

Pelletier, K.R. *Holistic medicine*. New York: Delacorte Press, 1979.

Perlmutter, L., and Monty, R. The importance of perceived control: Fact or fantasy? *American Scientist*, 1977, *65*, 759-765.

Preston, C. Behavior modification: A therapeutic approach to aging and dying. *Postgraduate Medicine*, 1973, *54*, 64-68.

Ramsay, R.W. Bereavement: A behavioral treatment of pathological grief. In P.O. Sjoden, S. Bates, and W.S. Dockins (Eds.), *Trends in behavior therapy*. New York: Academic Press, 1979.

Ramsay, R.W. and Happee, J.A. The stress of bereavement: Components and treatment. In C.D. Spielberger and I.G. Sarason (Eds.), *Stress and anxiety*, Vol. 4. New York: Wiley, 1977.

Rebok, G.W. and Hoyer, W.J. Clients nearing death: Behavioral treatment perspectives. *Omega*, 1979, *10*, 191-201.

Schwartz, G. and Weiss, S. What is behavioral medicine? *Psychosomatic Medicine*, 1977, *39*, 377–381.

Seligman, M.E.P. *Helplessness: On depression, development, and death*. San Francisco: W.H. Freeman, 1975.

Sobel, H.J. Projective methods of cognitive analysis. In T. Merluzzi, C. Glass, and M. Genest (Eds.), *Handbook of cognitive assessment*. New York: Guilford Press, 1981.

Sobel, H.J. and Worden, J.W. The MMPI as a predictor of psychosocial adaptation to cancer. *Journal of Consulting and Clinical Psychology*, 1979, *47*, 716–724.

Sobel, H.J. and Worden, J.W. *Helping cancer patients cope: A problem-solving intervention program*. New York: BMA and Guilford Press, 1981.

Thoresen, C. and Mahoney, M. *Behavioral self-control*. New York: Holt, Rinehart and Winston, 1974.

Turk, D., Sobel, H., Follick, M., and Youkilis, H. A sequential criterion analysis for assessing coping with chronic illness. *Journal of Human Stress*, 1980, *6*, 35–40.

Wachtel, P.C. *Psychoanalysis and behavior therapy*. New York: Basic Books, 1977.

Weisman, A.D. *On dying and denying*. New York: Behavioral Publications, 1972.

Weisman, A.D. *Coping with cancer*. New York: McGraw-Hill, 1979.

Weisman, A.D. Thanatology. In H. Kaplan, A. Freedman, and B. Sadock (Eds.), *Comprehensive Textbook of Psychiatry*. Baltimore: Williams and Wilkins, 1980.

Weisman, A.D. and Sobel, H.J. Coping with cancer through self-instruction: A hypothesis. *Journal of Human Stress*, 1979, *5*, 3–8.

Weisman, A.D. and Worden, J.W. *Coping and vulnerability in cancer patients*. Cambridge, Mass.: A Project Omega–MGH Research Monograph, 1977.

Weisman, A.D., Worden, J.W., and Sobel, H.J. *Psychosocial screening and intervention with cancer patients*. Cambridge, Mass.: A Project Omega–MGH Research Monograph, 1980.

Whitman, H. and Lukes, S. Behavior modification for the terminally ill. *American Journal of Nursing*, 1975, *75*, 93–101.

Worden, J.W. and Sobel, H.J. Ego strength and psychosocial adaptation to cancer. *Psychosomatic Medicine*, 1978, *40*, 585–592.

2 HUMANISTIC PERSPECTIVES ON BEHAVIOR THERAPY IN TERMINAL CARE

Jerrold M. Pollak

By virtue of the power to reason and to project into the future, we are the only animals aware of our basic biological limitation—that we are going to die (Becker 1974). However, that to which one gives intellectual assent, one rejects as an emotional being because of the intense anxiety engendered. In an often-quoted statement, Freud (1915, 1963) maintains that it is impossible to imagine one's own death and that in the unconscious we are all convinced of our immortality.

On a completely conscious level people may not be particularly bothered by or fearful of death. On less conscious levels of experience, attitudes become increasingly ambivalent while intense feelings of aversion and dread come to the fore (Feifel 1959, 1968; Feifel and Branscomb 1973). The thanatology literature is replete with findings indicating that some degree of denial is an omnipresent strategy used in dealing with the reality of death, particularly among individuals with life-threatening illnesses (Schneidman 1973; Weisman 1972, 1974).

Like their predecessors, twentieth century individuals must confront the inevitability of death. But they must do this at a time when there is a breakdown of traditional societal structures and belief sys-

The author wishes to thank Ms. Diane Taraskiewicz for her editorial assistance on this chapter.

tems that historically conferred meaning on existence by serving as repositories of abiding transcendent truths. This enabled the individual to maintain at least a psychological sense of immortality, even after a belief in life after death had begun to lose its credibility. With the advent of doomsday weaponry, however, contemporary people cannot console themselves with the certainty that they will live on though their children or personal works. Perhaps at no other time in our brief history has death come to represent such total isolation and complete severance of one's vital connection to all that is familiar.

In the face of a universe seemingly devoid of meaning and value, in a world where individual desires and efforts appear to count for little or nothing, and where all that lives will all too quickly pass away into oblivion, humanism affirms each person's uniqueness, value, dignity, and significance. It maintains that people are free to make choices and to create personal meanings; to care and show concern for the struggles of fellow human beings.

Is behavior therapy humanistic in the means and ends it tries to achieve, particularly when applied to terminal care? Historically, the question of the compatibility of behavior therapy with humanistic values and practices has stirred considerable controversy. This was particularly true a generation ago when behavior therapy was in its infancy. Behavior therapy practice then consisted largely of the application of classical and operant conditioning techniques, based on nonmediational paradigms inspired by research on stimulus-response learning. These techniques were typically employed within various institutional settings, often with captive populations exhibiting an array of behaviors deemed undesirable by caretaking staff. Humanists argued that behavior therapy was an essentially coercive, even reactionary enterprise forcing people to behave in accord with the dictates of institutional power relationships. The exception to this accusation was the use of procedures such as systematic desensitization which were usually employed within outpatient settings among patients ostensibly coming for help on their own volition. Even this procedure, however, was criticized for fostering a conception of the human being as an essentially passive and reaction organism, at the mercy of the same conditioning principles as dominate the lives of animals.

From within the humanistic framework, it is said that behavior therapy derives from a set of beliefs that are overly deterministic, reductionistic, and mechanistic about the nature of people. Critics also note that behavior therapy is tied to a narrow definition of what constitutes scientifically legitimate clinical phenomena and methodology. More specifically, behavior therapy is accused of ignoring the individual's subjective world of personal meanings and existential concerns, and of paying insufficient attention to the impact of future time on behavior and personality change. In the last analysis, behavior therapy is seen as violating time-honored humanistic values of individuality, creativity, freedom of choice, and personal responsibility (Matson 1973; Rogers and Skinner 1956; Wandersman, Popper, and Ricks 1976; and Wann 1964).

Despite these criticisms, the practice of behavior therapy continues to find acceptance in many quarters of the psychiatric and health-care community. In recent years there has been an expansion in the application of behavior therapy to the developing field of behavioral medicine and to the treatment of medical conditions where stress and anxiety play a major role in the etiology or maintenance of the disorder (Wolpe 1980). Given these developments, it is not at all surprising to observe the application of behavior therapy to the care of those with life-threatening illnesses. This latter trend is reflected in several papers (Brown 1977; Preston 1973; Rebok and Hoyer 1979; and Whitman and Lukes 1975) and in this volume. With the expansion of behavior therapy into the domain of clinical thanatology, however, there will most likely be a resurgence of the above concerns and criticisms about the place of these practices in such a traditionally humanitarian enterprise as caring for the dying.

Psychotherapy Process and Outcome

In re-examining the issue of the compatibility of behavior therapy with humanism, and specifically in assessing the place of behavior therapy within a humanistic psychosocial orientation to terminal care, I would like to consider the current state of affairs on psychotherapy process and outcome.

Over the past two decades the often acrimonious debate between proponents of behavioral approaches to psychotherapy and adherents of more traditional neoanalytic-psychodynamic and existential-humanistic orientations has diminished in intensity (Strupp 1978). There are many reasons for this in a field where polemics and ideology were once popular. Among these is the recognition that behavioral methods, such as systematic desensitization and assertiveness training, have demonstrated utility in the amelioration of specific maladaptive habits, fear disorders, and other avoidance patterns. A more flexible behavioral practice has also developed, characterized by a growing appreciation for the role that private events (e.g., thoughts, beliefs, feelings, images, and a patient's own self-control strategies) may play in the maintenance and modification of an array of fairly complex behavior patterns (Ledwidge 1978; Mahoney 1974; Mahoney and Arnkoff 1978; and Meichenbaum 1977). There is also a growing awareness and acceptance, by adherents of different orientations, of the common elements and dimensions in psychotherapeutic practice, including relationship and other "nonspecific" factors influencing desired personality and behavior change (Kazdin 1979; Murray and Jacobson 1978; Shapiro 1980; Shapiro and Morris 1978; Strupp 1978; and Wilkins 1979).

In recent years attempts have been made, with varying degrees of success, to integrate behavioral and nonbehavioral approaches from the standpoint of both theory and practice (Sloane 1969; Wachtel 1977; and Woody 1971). Murray and Jacobson (1978) tried to integrate behavioral and nonbehavioral practices by examining the role of cognitive processes in both orientations (e.g., arousal of expectation for therapeutic gain and correction of nonadaptive beliefs about the self and the world). The reader is also referred to Sobel's discussion on behavioral thanatology (see Chapter 1) which focuses on the possible integration of diverse psychotherapeutic practices in caring for the terminally ill patient.

Currently there is a relatively peaceful coexistence between adherents of different schools as well as a greater willingness on the part of at least some practitioners to move toward the adoption of a broader and more eclectic clinical stance. This is occurring even though clinicians may continue to identify themselves with a particular orientation (Dimond, Havens, and Jones 1978; Garfield and Kurtz 1977; and Lazarus 1973, 1976). The trend coincides with a research emphasis on individualizing methods and goals of psychological treatment, with the aim of determining which specific interventions result in what kind of changes for particular patients in specific circumstances (Bergin 1971; Bergin and Lambert 1978; Beutler 1979; and Strupp 1978).

If one views behavior therapy in the context of these contemporary trends in psychotherapy, and considers some of the changes occurring specifically within behavior therapy itself, then it would appear that a monolithic behavior therapy practice no longer exists. What we can currently include under the rubric of behavior therapy are really a multiplicity of often diverse clinical procedures. This development reflects a loosening of conceptual boundaries between behavioral and nonbehavioral orientations, characterized by a shift from an exclusive focus on mechanistic conditioning models to a concern with cognitive processes and strategies and self-control paradigms (Kanfer 1975; Mahoney and Arnkoff 1978; Mahoney, Kazdin, and Lesswing 1974; and Meichenbaum 1975, 1977).

Thus in recent behavior therapy literature one observes an emphasis on "developing and refining the methodology of self-directed behavioral analysis and change" (Rebok and Hoyer 1979). This is reflected in the development of an array of self-instructional, self-management, and self-monitoring techniques that are ostensibly designed to provide people with better ways to regulate their behavior in line with their own expectations, desires, and motivation for change. The individual is helped to become a "personal scientist replete with skills in self-observation and experimentation" (Mahoney 1975) with the ultimate goal of restoring or enhancing a sense of self-efficacy or mastery (Bandura 1977). Given these conceptual shifts, and the diversity in technique that now characterizes the field, it is not easy to dismiss behavior therapy, by definition, as incompatible with humanistic values and practices, or to negate its potential helpfulness as a humanistic practice in terminal care. One must first consider the particular kinds of behavioral techniques that are contemplated for use, and then assess them in terms of patient needs and desires and the understanding that a patient has of what these procedures are intended to achieve. Techniques must also be evaluated in light of the goals, intentions, and values of the practitioner and the health-care institution. Behavioral thanatology cannot only be patient-centered.

To the extent that behavior therapy can help particular patients and approximate or achieve what Weisman and others label an appropriate death (Pattison 1978; Weisman 1972, 1977), it may be considered a set of interventions that fall within the domain of humanistic caregiving. Weisman (1977) defines an appropriate death as:

> . . . one we might choose, had we a choice. It is not necessarily an ideal death, whatever that might mean. . . . It means an absence of suffering, preservation of important relationships, an interval for anticipatory grief, relief of remain-

ing conflicts, belief in timeliness, exercise of feasible options and activities and consistency with physical limitations all within the scope of one's ego ideal (119).

For Pattison (1978), an appropriate death refers to a manner of dying that preserves identity and integrity, is adaptive for the individual patient, and is consistent with prior coping styles and the personal meanings (i.e., cognitions) attached to living and dying. Ultimately, what constitutes an appropriate death is an individual matter, reflecting the diversity of human experience, personality, and lifestyle.

BEHAVIOR THERAPY AND THE HISTORICAL CONTEXT

In the following discussion I will place the practice of behavior therapy within a larger historical and cultural context and elucidate some of the reasons why this broad group of procedures may begin to play an important role in terminal care.

The evolution of personality theories and methods of psychological treatment are significantly influenced by the historical and cultural context out of which they emerge. In turn, theory and technique mirror and shape both the prevailing climate of opinion and the ideological belief structure of the culture of which they are a part.

It has frequently been said that belief in the mastery and control of the environment is a key tenet of the value system held by advanced Westernized industrial societies. Parsons and Lidz (1967) refer to the concept of "instrumental activism," defined as a "dedication to activity that can be expected on rational grounds to maximize human control over the conditional elements of the life situation," as characteric of Western beliefs about the nature of truth and reality.

In advanced industrial societies the pre-eminent goals of mastery and control are achieved primarily through attempts to adopt as strict an attitude of scientific detachment and objectivity as possible. This orientation is in turn employed in the service of ensuring continued technological advances. In a highly technological society, social, political, and even existential dilemmas tend to become problems solved largely through the application of empirically based, scientifically tested techniques (Ellul 1964). Certainly in the field of medicine one can readily observe that specific technological advances have led to increased longevity and enhancement in the quality of life for many individuals who, only a generation ago, suffered from debilitating and often fatal illnesses. However, the awareness and acceptance of death's inevitability belies our more extreme and naive cultural beliefs in the idea of progress (Nisbet 1979) and in the limitless power of science or technology to ameliorate life's travails and to resolve its paradoxes.

Howard and Scott (1965) argue that at the core of the American value system is a set of beliefs that actually serve to enhance the fear of death. One belief is that individuals can and should master nature and thereby gain total control over the environment through continued scientific and technological advance. Another pertains to the equation of activity, hard work, and self-control with productivity, ambition, and in the last analysis, with rectitude. One consequence of the belief that nature can and must be made subservient to our wishes is a view of death as a defeat by nature; death as a thwarter, if you will, of our struggle for supremacy. Therefore, because death is experienced as a direct threat to our strivings for omnipotence, it becomes a source of anxiety, fear, and revulsion. Death also represents a state of total inactivity. Since inactivity is viewed in negative terms—accompanied by intense feelings of guilt and anxiety—death, understood as a state of immobilization or stasis, is also a state to be feared and denied.

In cultures reflecting Western values, an "overcoming response" to death predominates, defined by Kastenbaum and Aisenberg (1972) as an "eternal menace eager to bring us down and strip us of our achievements." Death is seen as an external contingency; cultural values require an assertion of power against external, malicious forces such as death, which carry overtones of defeat, humiliation, and failure. In cultures where a participatory relationship with death prevails, the culture is in a natural and intimate relationship with the environment. Death has an internal locus; it connotes honor, reunion, and fulfillment, and is experienced as an integral part of the inherent rhythm of nature and life.

Of all social character structures, the obsessive-compulsive personality, or anal character, embodies the predominant values of modern, urban, industrialized cultures with the latter's emphasis on pragmatism, rationalism, efficiency, and, most importantly, self-control

(Pollak 1979). Central to the psychodynamics of obsessional individuals is the issue of control (Salzman 1968, 1979). More specifically, the goal of the obsessional lifestyle is to gain as much control over one's self and one's environment as is possible in order to achieve some measure of security in an uncertain world. In so doing, the individual defends against painful and frightening feelings of vulnerability and helplessness. In the last analysis, the obsessive style is an attempt to ensure what cannot be ensured, to make certain and predictable what will always be unknown: one's future. To achieve control the obsessive individual strives to impose rationalistic understandings and solutions, and thus manipulates the environment in keeping with needs for order and predictability. Ultimately the individual sacrifices the full experience of the moment for the sake of shoring up an imagined safe tomorrow.

The existential psychologist Erwin Strauss (1966), in an essay on the phenomenology of obsessive lifestyle or what existentialist thinkers call the obsessive-compulsive's way of "being in the world" (May, Angel, and Ellenberger 1958), argues that obsessive style represents a failure to accept the passage of time and eventual death as inherent in life. The obsessive-compulsive is viewed as preoccupied with the uncontrollable elements of human existence, such as decay, disintegration, and eventual death, despite a great need to deny that this is in fact the case. Thus one could say the obsessional lifestyle reflects an "overcoming response" to death. Miller and Chotlos (1960) similarly view obsessive style as an elaborate defensive system or "armoring of the personality" (Becker 1969, 1974). The purpose of such armor is to allow the individual to live effectively and to act in the world with some measure of security and personal control, thus circumventing panic and immobilization in the face of threats to physical or psychological survival. The obsessive-compulsive style can be considered an often effective and resilient normative defense and life adaptation.

Of all psychological approaches aimed at understanding and effecting changes in human behavior, behavior therapies appear to reflect the prevailing ethos of advanced industrialized societies with their emphasis on operationalism, empirically based methodologies, and prediction and control through the application of technique. Furthermore, we may understand the introduction of behavioral approaches into terminal care as a natural outgrowth of our culture's particular preoccupation with empirical verifiability and validation, personal control, and fears of helplessness and dependency, and its proclivity for fostering an overcoming response as opposed to a participatory relationship with death.

Thus, the application of behavior therapies to terminal care can be understood, at least in part, as reflecting culturally normative obsessional defenses against the feelings of rage, frustration, and helplessness that the fact of terminal illness can engender. Culturally syntonic obsessional solutions, in the form of specific reinforcement schedules, desensitization programs, or coping-skills training, can be interpreted as an attempt to preserve or restore an acceptable measure of control. One might speculate that a culture that encouraged a truly participatory relationship with death would have little if any need to develop behavior therapy approaches in caring for its dying members.

Nonetheless, at least in our culture, retaining a sense of control is a primary if not predominant need of all participants in the dying process (Kastenbaum 1978). This need must be addressed by all involved in caring for dying persons. It is not surprising then to find behavioral approaches emerging within terminal care.

What follows is an attempt to highlight, within a broad humanistic framework, some of the potential blind spots and limitations of behavioral formulations and methods within terminal care. I also intend to explore some alternatives to formalized behavioral interventions when trying to foster feelings of self-control and attempting to preserve a patient's personal identity and integrity.

PROBLEMS AND PITFALLS OF
BEHAVIORAL THANATOLOGY

Clearly, future clinical practice and research with behavioral methods will permit a more objective assessment of the relevance of the points discussed below. However, in discussing the place of any psychological therapy in terminal care, it should be pointed out that many dying persons may require little or nothing in the way of formalized psychotherapeutic assistance because of their natural ability to cope effectively with the stress of their illness (Weisman and Sobel 1979; and Worden and Weisman 1980).

Historically, behavioral practice has been faulted for ignoring the patient's inner life, for minimizing the importance of individual differences, and for generally focusing diagnosis and intervention at the level of overt behavior. This kind of orientation fails to consider that the individual's personality is often an integral part of the therapeutic problem. In many instances, therefore, it is important to assess the totality of a patient's functioning. This includes both the dimensions of overt behavior and inner experience and all variables, such as temperament and early life history, that may be influential (Strupp 1978).

Meaningful and effective therapeutic involvement with the dying patient requires that the therapist view the individual as a unique person. This means that the therapist adopts a phenomenological perspective, attempting to enter as much as is possible into the patient's subjective experience of his or her situation, trying to perceive the world as the patient does (Havens 1974). This implies a moving away from death and dying as medical, biological abstractions or external, technical problems, and confronting the reality of the imminent ceasing of a unique, living person. It also implies a sensitivity to the personal meanings that this particular person attaches to his or her own dying. In this regard, Feifel and Branscomb (1973) remind us of the multiplicity of meanings death may have for different people. Death may, for example, connote "the gentle night" or "great destroyer." It may reflect cessation from suffering, reunion with loved ones, loss of control, separation, and loneliness, or, as Greenberger (1964) notes, punishment and seduction. Sensitivity is focused on actual concerns and fears, what was and is of personal significance in the life of the patient, and what, if anything, this particular person continues to live for. What is a trivial occurrence or insight to the outsider may be enormously meaningful to the patient, and can be the occasion, depending on how it is construed, for a major disruption in coping ability (Weisman 1974) or for a renewed sense of hope and will to live.

An understanding of the inner subjective reality of any one person's struggle with the imminent dissolution of the self will enable the therapist to gain valuable insights into how an individual copes and adapts. It will also shed light on which changes in self-perception or life events may prematurely precipitate disequilibrium and irreversible decline, and thus prevent the achievement of an appropriate death. Our attempts to grasp the subjective reality of the patient's experience will be made easier to the degree that we come to grips with our own finitude and realize the shared existential situation, that is, a recognition that "sooner or later we shall be they" (Feifel 1977).

In contrast to the importance of maintaining a phenomenological framework, at least some behavior therapy is still geared to assessment and intervention at the level of overt behavior. By failing to incorporate the phenomenological dimension, a behavioral treatment program runs the risk of making the patient feel managed rather than understood, and of encouraging behaviors that are important and desirable to the staff or family but not necessarily to the patient. However, some of the newer developments in behavior therapy which stress evaluation of the particular ways people interpret events and talk to themselves about their experiences (Mahoney and Arnkoff 1978) suggest the possibility of clinically wedding phenomenology to behavioral practice. While the evolution of behavior therapy has been characterized by the development of several models of change and a multiplicity of techniques, clinical practice retains an emphasis on the therapist as a highly directive and powerful influence for change in the patient. Hollander (1975) characterizes the relationship in behavior therapy as an essentially "educative teacher–pupil relationship." Mahoney and Arnkoff (1978) refer to the role of the cognitive-behavioral therapist as that of a diagnostician–educator who isolates and helps correct faulty beliefs and self-statements in the patient.

Less generous descriptions are offered by Ehrenwald (1966), who argues that behavior therapies have abandoned the "methods of the couch" for "the methods of the classroom and pulpit," as well as by those who view the behavior therapist as an "implacable manipulator" (Devoge and Beck 1978). In contrast, psychodynamic and existential-humanistic approaches attempt to be considerably less directive by limiting involvement to such things as reflection, clarification, empathic responding, and, on occasion, interpretation of latent meanings and underlying dynamics.

Within a nondirective orientation, therapists may feel a strong pull to become more directive in response to the patient's insistent demand for something specific and tangible to ameliorate emotional pain. This kind of situation may develop at times of crisis, when the patient is experiencing a profound threat to self-esteem and basic life adaptation. Coming to grips with life-threatening illness constitutes just such a crisis situation for all concerned—patient, family, and caregivers. In response to the sense of helplessness that can pervade the dying situation, ther therapist may feel an intense need to assume more control. This can be reflected in the impulse to instruct the patient, family, or staff in specific ways to modify undesirable coping behavior.

What may be overlooked is that the therapist may respond to his or her own fears of loss of control and concerns about dying, and thus seek ways to assuage personal anxieties as much as to ease the anxieties of others. Second, one can fail to appreciate that within the "holding environment" (Winnicott 1958) maintained by the empathic and compassionate, albeit essentially nondirective therapist, the requisite conditions can be established to shore up adaptive coping in many dying persons. This therapeutic framework provides the patient with the opportunity to develop the trust that will allow for the ventilation and at least partial working-through of painful feelings and fears in the absence of assuming a directive stance where structured task-oriented strategies are provided to the patient, family, or staff. Pattison (1978) reminds us that caring for the dying is "not so much doing as being" or as Nouwen (1959) eloquently states:

> When we honestly ask ourselves which persons in our lives mean the most to us we often find that it is those who, instead of giving much advice, solutions, or cures, have chosen rather to share our pain and touch our wounds with a gentle and tender hand. The friend who can be silent with us in a moment of despair or confusion, who can stay with us in an hour of grief and bereavement, who can tolerate not knowing, not curing, not healing, and face us with the reality of our powerlessness, that is the friend who cares (1959: 34).

In an age when the process of dying in urban industrial societies has evolved from the "moral to the technical sphere of control" (Benoliel 1977), there is the danger that for both caretakers and patients the experience of dying can easily become a depersonalized and fragmented experience. The dying person may have the unrelenting experience of being "done to," or instructed by an array of technical experts involved in the caretaking process. In this situation the individual feels little if any sense of participation in important decisions, and hence may feel that the freedom to achieve personally significant life goals in the time that remains has not been retained.

Garfield (1977) points out that a significant obstacle to providing effective emotional support to the dying person is the rigid distinction between "we and them," between health care providers with their presumed expertise and the patients, presumed without knowledge or personal resources to help themselves in any meaningful way. Despite the practitioner's intention, behavioral approaches, by virtue of their directiveness, may easily be construed by some patients as yet another set of dehumanizing, technocratic procedures imposed from without. Such procedures may thus intensify the experience of being done to and controlled, when the primary need is really to be with understanding figures with whom the individual can feel an emotional connection.

Are there other ways to preserve or to restore a patient's sense of control in the absence of formalized, behaviorally geared interventions and techniques? Kastenbaum (1978) urges that we permit patients the widest latitude possible, in keeping with realistic constraints imposed by illness, with regard to choices concerning work, travel, diet, medication, and visits by relatives and friends. With the acceleration of physical decline and increased dependency, these options will likely have to be reduced in scope but nonetheless should be retained if at all possible. Kastenbaum (1978) further points out the value of making available to the patient accurate and intelligible information about the nature, course, and management of the illness.

A third point has to do with the role of human relationships in terminal care. From a humanistic perspective, meaningful psychotherapy with the dying person involves primarily the quality of the relationship established between therapist and patient. The treatment relationship is seen as egalitarian, and is conceptualized not as parent to child, clinician to patient, or teacher to student, but as human being to human being. Each is a participant and may potentially be wholly present to and affected by the other (Feigenberg 1975; Karasu 1977). The importance of the relationship between therapist and patient has been the subject of considerable debate in the psychotherapy process and outcome literature (Parloff, Waskow, and Wolfe 1978). Typically cited as a critical factor in effective treatment is the therapist's capacity to offer at least minimal levels of accurate empathy, nonpossessive warmth, unconditional positive regard, and genuineness over a sustained but unspecified length of time (Truax and Carkhuff 1967; Truax and Mitchell 1971).

In the early years of behavior therapy practice the role of the therapeutic relationship was deemphasized, and primary if not exclusive importance was placed on the techniques themselves for bringing about desired changes. Recently there has been a greater acknowledgment and acceptance of the role that relationship factors play in behavioral treatment, even though at times it is cast essentially as a vehicle by which to reinforce the therapist's technical influence over the patient (Devoge and Beck 1978). At the other end of the continuum, existential-humanistic approaches have viewed the therapeutic relationship as a necessary and, in some cases, sufficient condition for bringing about desired personality and behavioral changes. Psychodynamic-neoanalytic practitioners have usually occupied a middle ground on this issue, but more current developments have placed renewed stress on alliance-building and similar relationship-oriented concepts, particularly in the treatment of more disturbed crisis-ridden patients (Adler 1980).

Several studies attest to the operation of relationship factors in behavior therapy (Klein et al. 1969; Patterson 1968; Sloane 1969; and Wolowitz 1975) and to the perceived importance of the therapeutic relationship to the behavior therapy patient (Ryan and Gizynski 1971; and Sloane et al. 1975). There have also been suggestions to complement behavioral techniques with traditional relationship factors (Devoge and Beck 1978; and Sloane 1969).

As the practice of behavior therapy proliferates, it is not uncommon to hear about patients who, even after a successful behavioral treatment for a well-defined problem, have returned to the same or another therapist. This is apparently done to develop or retain a relationship with the therapist or to work on problems in more traditional ways. Occasionally individuals will enter into behavioral treatment, ostensibly because of a disturbing concern or symptom, when the primary and often unacknowledged motivation is to establish an emotional connection with another person who is seen as trusting, warm, supportive, and nonjudgmental. While behavioral practitioners have generally become more attuned to the importance of relationship factors, behavior therapy still reflects an orientation to treatment that elevates technique considerably above other important factors.

The behaviorally oriented terminal-care practitioner needs to remain cognizant of the insights and findings derived from clinical thanatology that reveal the critical importance of establishing and maintaining significant relationships with the dying. The dying situation can easily induce retreat from meaningful personal involvement with the patient and family on the part of the caregiver (Weisman 1972, 1974), even without the presence of techniques that may foster social distance. Changes in relationships with significant others, in the direction of real or perceived abandonment, may constitute a psychosocial stress of such magnitude as to precipitate disequilibrium, decline, and death, as clinical case studies suggest (Weisman 1974). A significant relationship involves mutuality and intimacy, but need not be unambivalently supportive or necessarily involve formal kinship relationships (Weisman 1974). For the dying patient, one or more professionals rather than family members may become the "significant key others" with whom a sustaining emotional connection is sought and maintained throughout the terminal phase.

The critical importance of valued human relationships in terminal care can also be seen in the role played by denial. Denial is a ubiquitous and often necessary defense used to a greater or lesser degree by all patients at different points in the dying process (Schneidman 1973; Weisman 1972, 1974). If we reconceptualize denial as a social strategy rather than an intrapsychic defense mechanism, then its purpose is not only to avoid a potential threat but to ensure against loss of sustaining and mutual relationships (Weisman 1972). Thus denial is apt to be evoked if and when the patient perceives that a significant relationship is in jeopardy. Behavioral intervention may stimulate an increase in denial by its direct limitations of the human relationship.

Another consideration germane to the possible pitfalls and limitations of behavior therapy in terminal care has to do with the fact that the dying process stirs up intense feeling and anxiety in all concerned. Schneidman (1978) has commented on the intensity of transference and countertransference reactions encoutered in psychotherapy with the dying person. Obviously, the greater the investment made by the therapist and the more a personal relationship is established with the patient, the more intensely distressing and immobilizing the feelings of anger, depression, guilt, and helplessness will be in the therapist. Weisman (1977) reminds us that when dealing with the painful realities of life-threatening illness, clinicians often resort to defenses of detachment, isolation, and intellectualization, mirroring to a greater or lesser degree tendencies toward emotional withdrawal on the part of the patient's loved ones. It is certainly tempting to gravitate toward involvement in the minutiae of biomedical

assessment and technical dimensions of care as a defense against dealing directly with the psychological reactions engendered within ourselves (Garfield 1978). These countertransference reactions, while
understandable, can be detrimental to the degree that they arouse
or intensify feelings of isolation and abandonment in the patient.
They often have concurrent negative repercussions for the clinician,
in that they foreclose opportunities to experience solidarity with
another human being that through identification with his or her suffering and struggle. This, in turn, depends on the ability to remain
emotionally open and available to the other person. In so doing, one
becomes more fully aware of one's own frailty and finitude, but also
of one's courage and capacity for concern.

It is debatable that, in the terminal care situation, behavior therapy interventions may lend themselves to rigid detachment and professional objectification. Behavior therapy approaches can be seduc-
tive for the practitioner because they offer a persuasive rationale for
making death an impersonal, objective, external problem rather than
a very real subjective experience of individuals. In the name of being
a behavioral scientist proffering objective, empirically grounded,
functional analyses of maladaptive behaviors, the practitioner can
conclude that an attitude of detachment (and a focus on the details
of design and implementation of specific techniques and objective
measurable outcomes) is necessary for effective intervention. This
would be an unfortunate development for both patient and caregiver.
Although I do not believe behavior therapists need fall into the pro-
crustean bed of a narrow dogmatic scientism, the potential for this
occurring in clinical work exists, particularly if the approaches become a routine part of patient care and are applied institutionally
with large numbers of hospice patients.

When it was first introduced, behavior therapy was often viewed
with skepticism. This was especially so when its more zealous proponents claimed it would soon supplant well-established psychodynamic and existential-humanistic approaches and be effective with a
wide range of mental health problems. In subsequent years, behavior
therapy was criticized for its focus on specific and circumscribed
behavioral problems and for its presumed failure to conceptualize
and treat more complex and diffuse psychiatric conditions which
constitute a large proportion of problems encountered in clinical
practice. Occasional research reports notwithstanding (Kohlenberg
1973; and Nawas 1971), there are still a wide range of patient con-

cerns, difficulties, and dilemmas which, at best, can be only partially conceptualized using existing behavioral paradigms or treated using the present armamentarium of behavioral techniques (Ledwidge 1978).

The terminally ill person is forced to cope with an array of anxiety-producing problems, many of which are existential concerns and dilemmas replete with ambiguity, ambivalence, and paradox. These do not lend themselves easily, if at all, to the delineation of relevant overt or covert target behaviors, operational definitions, a functional analysis, or easy and quick diminution or resolution.

The dying situation will often stimulate reactions of anticipatory grief and mourning, a sometimes painful review and appraisal of one's life, and a seeking of personally relevant meaning to living and dying. In some cases this will include a reappraisal of one's relationship to the spiritual domain. The reality of dying may also stir up the need to work toward completion of unfinished business (Cassem and Stewart 1975; Kubler–Ross 1969; and Kutscher 1973). This may include working toward a better understanding and at least a partial working-through of problematic self-perceptions, feelings, and experiences, as well as emotionally laden aspects of significant relationships. The dying patient will also have to decide how and in what manner to say goodbye to loved ones (Woodson 1979).

For some people the terminal phase can be an impetus for the attainment of meaningful insights, important changes in attitudes, and creative achievement. This is exemplified in Leo Tolstoy's short story, "The Death of Ivan Ilyich" (Tolstoy 1960), which depicts the struggle of a man who, confronted with the certainty of his imminent demise, recognizes fully for the first time the wasted opportunities and essential pointlessness of his existence. However, in the last days of his life he succeeds in achieving an authentic and meaningful existence with the recognition of his genuinely felt love for his family and his courage to face death honestly in the midst of those who attempt to deny the truth of his situation. Tolstoy's character may be said to be experiencing what in the existential literature is referred to as "ontological" or "existential guilt" (Lifton 1973; and May, Angel, and Ellenberger 1958), a painful state of awareness of having failed to act on one's deepest and most genuine impulses and desires. This sense of having freely forfeited the opportunities for becoming the person one wanted to be can easily be stimulated at the end of one's life. Although existential guilt often leads to profound feelings of regret and depression it can also be an opportunity for constructive insight and personal growth.

The concerns described above are a critically important dimension of psychosocial care and fall most appropriately within the purview of relationship-based, existential-humanistic approaches to counseling and psychotherapy (Feigenberg 1975; Feigenberg and Schneidman 1979; Frankl 1966; and Garfield 1978). I question whether the behavioral thanatologist can integrate these factors into ongoing care.

A last point concerns the problem that all psychological therapies, especially in their more orthodox applications, fail to appreciate and address certain aspects of the complexity of human personality and behavior. Behavior therapies are often rebuked for their insensitivity to the intrapsychic and interpersonal dynamics at work in the treatment situation.

Schneidman (1978) points out that psychotherapy with dying people needs to be flexible. The therapist must be able to shift easily in accord with changes in the patient's physical condition, needs, moods, and efforts at maintaining control. Psychotherapy also requires a sensitivity and capacity to respond to both the manifest and latent meanings of the patient's communications and to the various ways that concerns and anxieties about dying can be masked (Feifel and Branscomb 1973). Perhaps most importantly, the therapist must appreciate the dynamics of the denial process, specifically the role denial plays in coping and adapting to life-threatening illness.

Weisman (1972) distinguishes three levels of denial among patients who are terminally ill. These are: denial of the fact of illness (first-order denial), denial of the implications of the illness (second-order denial), and denial of extinction (third-order denial). Weisman (1972) introduced the concept of "middle knowledge," referring to a state of "uncertain certainty" in dying persons when they have a dim awareness of their situation while they deny the reality of their condition. Thus, denial and acceptance will often fluctuate throughout the terminal phase. While denial is not to be encouraged, it may be psychologically necessary and adaptive for the patient at various times. Forceful attempts to encourage the patient to relinquish denial and face the reality of the situation more directly may be detrimental (Garfield 1978; Lazarus 1979; Schneidman 1978; and Weisman 1972).

Although awareness of the delicate interplay of denial and acceptance, and their importance in psychosocial care, tends to fit comfortably within traditional psychodynamic and existential-humanistic approaches, this significant clinical phenomenon is typically overlooked or treated with less significance than it deserves by behavioral clinicians. One can imagine, for example, a behavior therapist attempting to reduce a particular patient's anxiety about dying through some form of imagery or systematic desensitization, or applying a specific cognitive decisionmaking technique to enable a patient to work toward the completion of an important unfinished task. However, after an apparently fruitful beginning, the therapist may find that the patient, who seemed able to acknowledge the reality of his or her condition and was cooperating fully with the behavioral treatment regimen, now reverts rather abruptly and unpredictably to denial. The patient begins to talk unrealistically about leaving the hospital, embarking on a new business career, and so forth. Continuation of a specific, goal-oriented, behavioral approach would be incongruent with the patient's experience and situation, and might be deleterious if it significantly interrupts an essential adaptive strategy.

CONCLUSIONS AND SUMMARY

Despite the increased attention paid to the terminal phase of life over the past twenty years, empirically based, unified, systematic findings relevant to clinical practice are fairly modest in scope (Feifel 1977; and Kalish 1978). Much remains to be known about how individuals respond to and cope with a fatal illness. A literature on the comparative utility of different therapeutic approaches in facilitating coping with life-threatening illness is only in its infancy (Weisman, Worden, and Sobel 1980).

Although there have appeared a number of substantial reviews of the voluminous literature on psychotherapy outcome in general (Bergin 1971; Bergin and Lambert 1978; and Luborsky, Singer and Luborsky 1975), the amount of clinically germane, empirically based knowledge about intervention remains quite modest (Frank 1979). When examining this research one finds that, perhaps with the exception of the short-term superiority of behavior therapy in modifying specific habits and fear-avoidance behaviors, behavioral methods have not been shown to be more effective than nonbehavioral methods across a range of psychiatric difficulties (Beutler 1979; Frank 1979;

Shapiro 1980; Sloane et al. 1975; and Strupp 1978). In addition, a recent review comparing traditional behavior therapy approaches with cognitive-behavior therapy methods could find no differences in the effectiveness of these two behavioral strategies (Ledwidge 1978).

Behavioral therapists generally have insisted on the need for controlled empirical tests of the relative effectiveness of diverse psychotherapeutic approaches, repeatedly trying to adduce hard evidence for the effectiveness of their own methods and techniques. In this regard, proponents of behavior therapy have shown a strong commitment to the idea that all psychotherapists must be made accountable for their activity by having their methods subjected to scientific experimentation and validation. However, one of the continuing issues in psychotherapy process and outcome research, and one that will likely pose particular difficulties for the behavioral thanatologist, is how to demonstrate that effects from behavioral techniques are significantly in excess of what might be attributable to one or more nonspecific influences, referred to in the literature as hope, faith, suggestion, expectancy, demand, and placebo (Bernstein and Neitzel 1973; and Shapiro 1980).

After years of dismantling research on behavioral procedures such as systematic desensitization, it appears that nonspecific effects do in fact play a significantly greater role in behavioral treatment success than was originally thought (Kazdin and Wilcoxon 1976; and Murray and Jacobson 1978). For a sizable number of people, coping with a life-threatening illness engenders intense feelings of vulnerability and dependency which can be associated with heightened compliance. Thus the potential for the operation of nonspecific factors is significantly enhanced. The more the procedure(s) carries with it a persuasive, seemingly scientific rationale, is inherently credible, and is accompanied by relaxation exercises (as is true of many behavioral programs), the more likely it is that a strong expectancy of therapeutic gain will be aroused, resulting in some or all of the intended changes in behavior or attitudes (Murray and Jacobson 1978). Nonspecific effects may also be stimulated in certain patients as a result of the directive-didactic stance of the behavioral practitioner. An orientation of this kind will significantly augment patient attributions of therapeutic potency to the practitioner.

Given the apparent power of nonspecific effects in psychotherapy, it may be that the therapeutic relationship, understood as a multidimensional variable capable of powerful, nonspecific therapeutic effects, will be shown to account largely, if not completely, for the benefits that accrue from various psychotherapeutic interventions with dying persons. This is suggested by the reported positive response of patients receiving traditional, relationship-oriented care in hospice settings (Kalish 1978; Saunders 1977; and Woodson 1979).

Given current trends, behavior therapies will be increasingly used as one of many broad groups of approaches aimed at providing more adequate psychosocial care for dying persons and their families. In some cases they may constitute the primary mode of intervention, while in other cases they may serve as a supplementary set of procedures. As ancillary techniques they will likely be drawn upon to reduce immobilizing anxiety, depression, or physical pain, and to enhance deficient coping in certain individuals who may, as a result, be able to respond more favorably to traditional psychotherapeutic approaches.

In the terminal care situation, behavior therapies will have particular relevance and value for patients who *a priori* define, or can be persuaded to believe, that at least some of their difficulties are the result of detrimental habitual ways of thinking and behaving. Behavior therapy may also be favorably responded to by patients who comply easily with authority, and who desire concrete expert instruction as to what they or others can do differently to decrease distress and anxiety. If these conditions exist, then the patient's theory of what is helpful would be consistent with the beliefs of the practitioner, ideally setting the groundwork for a reasonable working alliance (Wile 1978).

On the other hand, for those who hold varying theories of what would be helpful for themselves, are struggling primarily with diffuse existential problems, possess high reactance (e.g., seek internal direction) or have specific kinds of characterological styles (e.g., obsessional or passive-aggressive), behavioral methods may be received with considerably less confidence and may even be actively resisted.

Despite indications and contraindications for behavior therapy, in the last analysis psychosocial care must be a flexible undertaking that is geared to the needs, desires, lifestyle, and physical condition of the dying person. It should not be rigidly dictated by the prevailing ideology about the meaning of human existence, or the theory and practice of psychotherapy. Following the lead of others who have recommended an eclectic stance in the general practice of psychotherapy (Dimond, Havens, and Jones 1978), I would like to suggest the adoption of an eclectic framework for therapists attempting to make themselves helpful in the terminal care situation. This would allow for the integration of ideas, concepts, and methods from various conceptual bases, with the aim of developing a truly patient-specific approach to psychotherapy that fully appreciates each dying patient as a unique individual who is coping with particular difficulties within a special environment.

In our search for greater knowledge and certainty about the terminal phase of life and what we as therapists can do to make the experience of dying more tolerable, dignified, and acceptable, we may easily lose sight that human existence—and dying as an inherent part of what it means *to be*—will elude our attempts at a comprehensive definition and understanding, thus frustrating our wishes for developing technologically correct caregiving programs. As Weisman (1974: 139) so eloquently states: "At the heart of human existence is ambiguity about what we know, ambivalence about what we feel, and anxiety about what we are. . . ." It behooves us to remain emotionally in tune with the personal struggle of each patient and to maintain a critical, yet receptive attitude toward new therapeutic applications in terminal care.

REFERENCES

Adler, G. A treatment framework for adult patients with borderline and narcissistic personality disorders. *Bulletin of the Menninger Clinic*, 1980, *44*, 171–180.

Bandura, A. Self-efficacy: Toward a unifying theory of behavioral change. *Psychological Review*, 1977, *84*, 127–190.

Becker, E. *Angel in armor.* New York: George Braziller, 1969.

Becker, E. *Denial of death.* New York: Free Press, 1974.

Benoliel, J. Q. Nurses and the human experience of dying. In H. Feifel (Ed.), *New meanings of death.* New York: McGraw–Hill, 1977.

Bergin, A. E. The evaluation of therapeutic outcomes. In A. E. Bergin and S. L. Garfield (Eds.), *Handbook of psychotherapy and behavior change.* New York: Wiley, 1971.

Bergin, A. E., and Lambert, M. J. The evaluation of therapeutic outcomes. In S. L. Garfield and A. E. Bergin (Eds.), *Handbook of psychotherapy and behavior change* (2nd ed.) New York: Wiley, 1978.

Bernstein, D.A., and Nietzel, M.T. Demand characteristics in behavior modification: The natural history of a "nuisance." In M. Hersen, R.M. Eisler, and D.M. Miller (Eds.), *Progress in behavior modification* (Vol. 4). New York: Academic Press, 1977.

Beutler, L.E. Toward specific psychological therapies for specific conditions. *Journal of Consulting and Clinical Psychology,* 1979, *47,* 882–897.

Brown, M.A. A behavioral approach to post-catastrophic illness work phobias. *International Journal of Psychiatry in Medicine,* 1977, *8,* 235–241.

Cassem, N.H., and Stewart, R.S. Management and care of the dying patient. *International Journal of Psychiatry in Medicine,* 1975, *6,* 293–304.

DeVoge, J.T., and Beck, S. The therapist-client relationship in behavior therapy. In M. Hersen, R.M. Eisler, and P.M. Miller (Eds.), *Progress in behavior modification* (Vol. 6). New York: Academic Press, 1978.

Dimond, R.E., Havens, R.A., and Jones, A.C. A conceptual framework for the practice of prescriptive eclecticism in psychotherapy. *American Psychologist,* 1978, *33,* 239–248.

Ehrenwald, J. *Psychotherapy: Myth and method, an integrative approach.* New York: Grune & Stratton, 1966.

Ellul, J. *The technological society.* New York: Vintage Books, 1964.

Feifel, H. Attitudes toward death in some normal and mentally ill populations. In H. Feifel (Ed.), *The meaning of death.* New York: McGraw–Hill, 1959.

Feifel, H. Attitudes toward death: A psychological perspective. *Journal of Consulting and Clinical Psychology,* 1968, *33,* 292–295.

Feifel, H. Death in contemporary America. In H. Feifel (Ed.), *New meanings of death.* New York: McGraw–Hill, 1977.

Feifel, H., and Branscomb, A.B. Who's afraid of death? *Journal of Abnormal Psychology,* 1973, *81,* 282–288.

Feigenberg, L. Care and understanding of the dying: A patient-centered approach. *Omega,* 1975, *6,* 81–93.

Feigenberg, L., and Schneidman, E.S. Clinical thanatology and psychotherapy: Some reflections on carying for the dying person. *Omega,* 1979, *10,* 1–9.

Frank, J.D. The present status of outcome studies. *Journal of Consulting and Clinical Psychology,* 1979, *47,* 310–316.

Frankl, V.E. Logotherapy and existential analysis—a review. *American Journal of Psychotherapy,* 1966, *20,* 252–261.

Freud, S. Reflections upon war and death. In P. Rieff (Ed.), *Character and culture.* New York: Collier, 1963. [Originally published, 1915.]

Garfield, C.A. Impact of death on the health-care professional. In H. Feifel (Ed.), *New meanings of death.* New York: McGraw–Hill, 1977.

Garfield, C.A. Elements of psychosocial oncology: Doctor–patient relationships in terminal illness. In C.A. Garfield (Ed.), *Psychosocial care of the dying patient.* New York: McGraw–Hill, 1978.

Garfield, S.L., and Kurtz, R. A study of eclectic views. *Journal of Consulting and Clinical Psychology*, 1977, *45*, 78-83.

Greenberger, E. Fantasies of women confronting death. *Journal of Consulting Psychology*, 1965, *29*, 252-260.

Havens, L.L. The existential use of the self. *American Journal of Psychiatry*, 1974, *131*, 1-10.

Hollander, M. Behavior therapy approach. In C. Loew, H. Grayson, and G. Loew (Eds.), *Three psychotherapies: A clinical comparison*. New York: Brunner/ Mazel, 1975.

Howard, A., and Scott, R.A. Cultural values and attitudes toward death. *Journal of Existentialism*, 1965, *6*, 161-174.

Kalish, R.A. A little myth is a dangerous thing: Research in the service of the dying. In C.A. Garfield (Ed.), *Psychosocial care of the dying patient*. New York: McGraw-Hill, 1978.

Kanfer, F.H. Self-management methods. In F.H. Kanfer and A.P. Goldstein (Eds.), *Helping people change*. New York: Pergamon Press, 1975.

Kastenbaum, R. In control. In C.A. Garfield (Ed.), *Psychosocial care of the dying patient*. New York: McGraw-Hill, 1978.

Kastenbaum, R. and Aisenberg, R. *The psychology of death*. New York: Springer, 1972.

Karasu, T.B. Psychotherapies: An overview. *American Journal of Psychiatry*, 1977, *134*, 851-863.

Kazdin, A.E. Nonspecific treatment factors in psychotherapy outcome research. *Journal of Consulting and Clinical Psychology*, 1979, *47*, 846-851.

Kazdin, A.E., and Wilcoxon, L.A. Systematic desensitization and nonspecific treatment effects: A methodological evaluation. *Psychological Bulletin*, 1976, *83*, 729-758.

Klein, M.H., Dittman, A.T., Parloff, M.B., and Gill, M.M. Behavior therapy: Observations and reflections. *Journal of Consulting and Clinical Psychology*, 1969, *33*, 259-266.

Kohlenberg, R.J. Behavioristic approach to multiple personality: A case study. *Behavior Therapy*, 1973, *4*, 137-140.

Kubler-Ross, E. *On death and dying*. New York: MacMillan, 1969.

Kutscher, A.H. Anticipatory grief, death and bereavement: A continuum. In E. Wyschogrod (Ed.), *The phenomenon of death*. New York: Harper & Row, 1973.

Lazarus, A.A. Avoid the paradigm clash. *International Journal of Psychiatry*, 1973, *11*, 157-159.

Lazarus, A.A. *Multimodal behavior therapy*. New York: Springer, 1976.

Lazarus, R.S. Positive denial: The case for not facing reality. *Psychology Today*, 1979, *13*, 44-60.

Ledwidge, B. Cognitive behavior modification: A step in the wrong direction? *Psychological Bulletin*, 1978, *85*, 353-375.

Lifton, R.J. On death and death symbolism: The Hiroshima disaster. In E. Wyschogrod (Ed.), *The phenomenon of death.* New York: Harper & Row, 1973.

Luborsky, L., Singer, B., and Luborsky, L. Comparative studies of psychotherapies: Is it true that "everyone has won and all must have prizes?" *Archives of General Psychiatry,* 1975, *32,* 995–1008.

Mahoney, M.J. *Cognition and behavior modification.* Cambridge, Mass.: Ballinger, 1974.

Mahoney, M.J. Sensitive scientist in empirical humanism. *American Psychologist,* 1975, *30,* 864–867.

Mahoney, M.J., and Arnkoff, D. Cognitive and self-control therapies. In S.L. Garfield and A.E. Bergin (Eds.), *Handbook of psychotherapy and behavior change* (2nd ed). New York: Wiley, 1978.

Mahoney, M.J., Kazdin, A.E., and Lesswing, N.J. Behavior modification: Delusion or deliverance? In C.M. Franks and G.T. Wilson (Eds.), *Annual review of behavior therapy theory and practice* (Vol. 2). New York: Brunner/Mazel, 1974.

Matson, F.W. (Ed.). *Without/within: Behaviorism and humanism.* Belmont: Wadsworth, 1973.

May, R., Angel, E., and Ellenberger, H. *Existence: A new dimension in psychiatry and psychology.* New York: Basic Books, 1958.

Meichenbaum, D. Self-instruction methods. In F.H. Kanfer and A.P. Goldstein (Eds.), *Helping people change.* New York: Pergamon Press, 1975.

Meichenbaum, D. *Cognitive behavior modification.* New York: Plenum, 1977.

Miller, M.H., and Chotlos, J.W. Obsessive and hysterical syndromes in the light of existential consideration. *Journal of Existential Psychiatry,* 1960, *1,* 315–329.

Murray, E.J., and Jacobson, L.I. Cognition and learning in traditional and behavioral psychotherapy. In S.L. Garfield and A.E. Bergin (Eds.), *Handbook of psychotherapy and behavior change* (2nd ed.). New York: Wiley, 1978.

Nawas, M.M. "Existential" anxiety treated by systematic desensitization: A case study. *Journal of Behavior Therapy and Experimental Psychiatry,* 1971, *2,* 291–295.

Nisbet, R. *History of the idea of progress.* New York: Basic Books, 1979.

Nouwen, H. *Out of solitude.* Notre Dame: Ave Maria Press, 1959.

Parloff, M.B., Waskow, I.E., and Wolfe, B.E. Research on therapist variables in process and outcome. In S.L. Garfield and A.E. Bergin (Eds.), *Handbook of psychotherapy and behavior change* (2nd ed.). New York: Wiley, 1978.

Parsons, T., and Lidz, V. Death in American society. In E. Schneidman (Ed.), *Essays in self-destruction.* New York: Science House, 1967.

Patterson, C.H. Relationship theory and/or behavior therapy. *Psychotherapy: Theory, Research and Practice,* 1968, *5,* 226–233.

Pattison, E.M. The living-dying process. In C.A. Garfield (Ed.), *Psychosocial care of the dying patient.* New York: McGraw–Hill, 1978.

Pollak, J.M. Obsessive-compulsive personality: A review. *Psychological Bulletin*, 1979, *86*, 225–241.

Preston, C.E. Behavior modification: A therapeutic approach to aging and dying. *Postgraduate Medicine*, 1975, *54*, 64–68.

Rebok, G.W., and Hoyer, W.J. Clients nearing death: Behavioral treatment perspectives. *Omega*, 1979, *10*, 191–200.

Rogers, C.R., and Skinner, B.F. Some issues concerning the control of human behavior: A symposium. *Science*, 1956, *124*, 1057–1066.

Ryan, V.L., and Gizynski, M.N. Behavior therapy in retrospect: Patients' feelings about their behavior therapists. *Journal of Consulting and Clinical Psychology*, 1971, *37*, 1–9.

Salzman, L. *The obsessive personality*. New York: Jason Aronson, 1968.

Salzman, L. Psychotherapy of the obsessional. *American Journal of Psychotherapy*, 1979, *33*, 32–40.

Saunders, C. Dying they live: St. Christopher's Hospice. In H. Feifel (Ed.), *New meanings of death*. New York: McGraw–Hill, 1977.

Schneidman, E.S. *Deaths of man*. New York: Quadrangle, 1973.

Schneidman, E.S. Some aspects of psychotherapy with dying persons. In C.A. Garfield (Ed.), *Psychosocial care of the dying patient*. New York: McGraw–Hill, 1978.

Shapiro, A.K., and Morris, L.A. Placebo effects in medical and psychological therapies. In S.L. Garfield and A.E. Bergin (Eds.), *Handbook of psychotherapy and behavior change* (2nd ed.). New York: Wiley, 1978.

Shapiro, D.A. Science and psychotherapy: The state of the art. *British Journal of Medical Psychology*, 1980, *53*, 1–10.

Sloane, R.B. The converging paths of behavior therapy and psychotherapy. *International Journal of Psychiatry*, 1969, *7*, 493–503.

Sloane, R.B., Staples, F.R., Cristol, A.H., Yorkston, N.J., and Whipple, K. *Psychotherapy versus behavior therapy*. Cambridge, Mass.: Harvard University Press, 1975.

Strauss, E. *Phenomenological psychology*. New York: Basic Books, 1966.

Strupp, H. Psychotherapy research and practice: An overview. In S.L. Garfield and A.E. Bergin (Eds.), *Handbook of psychotherapy and behavior change: An empirical analysis* (2nd ed.). New York: Wiley, 1978.

Tolstoy, L. *The death of Ivan Ilyich and other stories*. New York: Signet, 1960.

Truax, C.B., and Carkhuff, R.R. *Toward effective counseling and psychotherapy: Training and practice*. Chicago: Aldine, 1967.

Truax, C.B., and Mitchell, K.M. Research on certain therapist interpersonal skills in relation to process and outcome. In A.E. Bergin and S.L. Garfield (Eds.), *Handbook of psychotherapy and behavior change*. New York: Wiley, 1971.

Wachtel, P.L. *Psychoanalysis and behavior therapy: Toward an integration.* New York: Basic Books, 1977.

Wandersman, A., Popper, D., and Ricks, D. (Eds.). *Humanism and behaviorism: Dialogue and growth.* Oxford, England: Pergamon Press, 1976.

Wann, T.W. (Ed.). *Behaviorism and phenomenology.* Chicago: University of Chicago Press, 1964.

Weisman, A.D. *On dying and denying: A psychiatric study of terminality.* New York: Behavioral Publications, 1972.

Weisman, A.D. *The realization of death.* New York: Jason Aronson, 1974.

Weisman, A.D. The psychiatrist and the inexorable. In H. Feifel (Ed.), *New meanings of death.* New York: McGraw-Hill, 1977.

Weisman, A.D., and Sobel, H.J. Coping with cancer through self-instruction: A hypothesis. *Journal of Human Stress*, 1979, *5*, 3-8.

Weisman, A.D., Worden, J.W., and Sobel, H.J. Psychosocial screening and intervention with cancer patients: A research report. Cambridge, Mass.: Shea Bros. and Massachusetts General Hospital, 1980.

Whitman, H.H., and Lukes, S.J. Behavior modification for terminally-ill patients. *American Journal of Nursing*, 1975, *75*, 98-101.

Wile, D.B. Ideological conflicts between clients and psychotherapists. *American Journal of Psychotherapy*, 1977, *31*, 437-449.

Wilkins, W. Expectancies in therapy research: Discriminating among heterogeneous nonspecifics. *Journal of Consulting and Clinical Psychology*, 1979, *47*, 837-845.

Winnicott, D.W. *Collected papers.* New York: Basic Books, 1958.

Wolowitz, H.M. Therapist warmth: Necessary or sufficient condition in behavioral desensitization? *Journal of Consulting and Clinical Psychology*, 1975, *43*, 584-585.

Wolpe, J. Behavior therapy for psychosomatic disorders. *Psychosomatics*, 1980, *21*, 379-385.

Woodson, R. Hospice care in terminal illness. In C.A. Garfield (Ed.), *Stress and survival: Emotional realities of life-threatening illness.* St. Louis: C.V. Mosby, 1979.

Woody, R.H. *Psychobehavioral counseling and therapy: Integrating behavioral and insight therapies.* New York: Appleton-Century-Crofts, 1971.

Worden, J.W., and Weisman, A.D. Do cancer patients really want counseling? *General Hospital Psychiatry*, 1980, *2*, 100-103.

CLINICAL ISSUES AND METHODS

3 BEHAVIORAL TREATMENT OF DEPRESSION IN THE DYING PATIENT

Wendy K. Sobel

In the East, particularly in such countries as India and Tibet, death is viewed as a natural and completely acceptable component of the life cycle. For centuries the Tibetan Buddhists have conceptualized death in a manner that deviates radically from our Western philosophical code. Unlike the Western world, where death is feared and consequently devalued and denied, Tibetans are given significant preparation for the experience of death. Ram Dass, formerly a Harvard University psychologist who became extensively involved with Eastern philosophy, has written: "Every moment is our moment of birth and our moment of death, and here we are, . . . It's just a transformation of energy. Nothing more or less than that" (Ram Dass 1970: 165). To our Western sensibilities, these are strange constructs. We bristle at the nonjudgmental attitude toward death. We are perplexed by the notion that dying is merely a new form of energy, the next step in an ongoing and continually fluid vital process.

Just as we are perplexed by Eastern concepts, we may imagine the consternation of the Buddhist community at our respirators and other life-prolonging devices. The Karen Quinlan case painfully brought to consciousness the irony of our advanced medical technology. In numerous situations we are successful in prolonging physical survival, but not necessarily life in the sense of a meaningful existence. In less dramatic form this concept is evident in the millions of

69

people, young and old, whose lives are extended but who often must suffer with indignity and an almost constant awareness of impending death. Perhaps because of the tremendous increase in the number of people who must face the threat of death every day, we witness the fascination both in the media and in contemporary psychology with the process of dying. In the West it is fair to say that people have traditionally been obsessed with extending life without much consideration for the quality of existence. Immortality is the ideal, and seems to be encompassed in the continued functioning of the physical body. What about the emotional concomitants?

In this chapter I will be concerned with treating depression in the patient who is diagnosed with a disease that ultimately will result in death. Due to the technologies that extend the life span, particularly here in the United States, people are living longer with more debilitating diseases, and constitute a group highly susceptible to depression. One of the essential points I wish to communicate is that many terminally ill individuals have to learn how to cope with *life* in the context of a life-threatening disease. It is not only death that is the problem. Living with illness, living with treatments, living with the omnipresent knowledge of death: these are the adversities with which the terminally ill must cope.

In the following pages, I will examine the various concepts of depressive illness and the need for accurate evaluation and precise diagnosis. Second, special issues will be considered that may arise in conjunction with depression in the terminally ill, as well as variables that play an influential role in the course of the disorder. A rationale will then be outlined for the application of behavioral approaches for treating depression in the patient with a terminal illness. Finally, I will introduce three specific behavioral techniques: (1) the cognitive method, (2) an approach based on the self-control method, and (3) relaxation training. Due to the brevity of this chapter the focus must be limited to these few approaches. Other behavioral perspectives are presented in various chapters within this volume. It seemed appropriate to review in depth specific behavioral techniques since many readers may come from traditional schools of thanatology and be unfamiliar with behavior therapy. I have decided to describe these three approaches and encourage practitioners to integrate into their specific settings those techniques that may be applicable.

DIAGNOSIS OF DEPRESSION

The first recorded observations on melancholia were made in the fourth century B.C. by Hippocrates (Beck 1967). Descriptions of the disorder have changed little in the intervening years, although theories and treatments have proliferated. In terms of incidence, a recent National Institute of Mental Health report estimated that in any calendar year approximately 15 percent of the population, ages 18 to 74, experience depressive symptoms (Secunda et al. 1973). Depression has been with civilization through the ages and yet continues to mystify us as to causation and appropriate treatment modalities.

In this section I will explore various categorizations of depression to provide a framework in which to understand the type of depressed state we may encounter in the terminal patient. The accurate distinction between depressive disorders is essential, and inevitably leads to more precise treatment modes. According to Klerman, who has conducted extensive research in the area, there is a vagueness in diagnostic acuity, with many people receiving the undifferentiated diagnosis of depression (1971). Klerman additionally points to a "neo-Kraeplinian revival" (1971: 310) in which the roots of an affective illness are found in the biology and heredity of an individual.

Endogenous and Exogenous Classifications

The major differentiating categories with respect to etiology are the endogenous versus the exogenous or reactive classifications. Endogenous depressions originate from within the person and are commonly associated with psychosis. A biological disorder exists that may be genetic, metabolic, or constitutional, with no apparent connection to external factors. Manic-depressive illness and involutional melancholia are prime examples. The endogenous depression is time-limited, has no clear precipitant, and retains autonomy: that is, it is fairly independent of environmental configurations. It is interesting to note, as Klerman (1971) points out, that the premorbid personality bears little resemblance to the endogenously depressed state. Thus we often observe a stable, non-neurotic character structure prior to the actual depressive symptomatology.

The exogenous or reactive depressions are considered psychogenic and constitute the neurotic disorders that are so prevalent today. External stresses, often related to a significant loss, can be identified as reasonable precipitants of the depressed state. Reactivity to the psychosocial environment is evident, and vacillations of affect even within a 24-hour period can be observed in the exogenously depressed individual.

Although it appears that we have a neat and reliable way of distinguishing the two major categories of depressive illness, in actual practice the differentiation or diagnostic process is not so simple. For example, a person suffering from mania may initially be seen as schizophrenic and consequently be treated with a major anti-anxiety agent rather than Lithium, the appropriate treatment. Another complicating factor is that with certain endogenous depressions, an external precipitant can be delineated. We then enter the chicken and egg dilemma: Does the biological disturbance precipitate the depression as well as negative changes in the environment? Or does the environmental alteration influence the biological substrate and cause an imbalance and subsequent depression? These questions remain to be answered. With the neo-Kraeplinian revival, however, it appears that progress will be forthcoming.

Depression Among Medical Patients

Given the difficulties outlined above, it is clear that the medical patient with depressive symptoms presents a challenge to health-care professionals. Determining a precise diagnosis and formulating a corresponding treatment plan is not a simple task. As I stated previously, all too often the sad, dejected, complaining patient is labelled rather hastily as depressed. Little attention is given to the *specific* nature of the depression. Implications for appropriate care are extensive, and are illustrated cogently by Sachar (1975). Essentially, Sachar distinguishes five depressed states that manifest themselves in conjunction with disease: (1) depressive illness, which is equivalent to the endogenous depression described above, (2) grief reactions, (3) neurotic characterological depressions, (4) medical depressions, and (5) drug-induced depressions. Depressive illness, or endogenous depression, often presents as a medical problem and thus necessitates precise diagnosis. Sachar advocates somatic treatment as the only ethically sound approach. Grief reactions are denoted as the most typical depressive experiences among medically ill patients. They are deemed appropriate, which differentiates them from depressive illness, and consequently are amenable to short-term psychotherapy. It is to this common depressive reaction that the treatment section of the current chapter will be primarily oriented.

Sachar's third category, neurotic characterological depressions, refers to the patient with long-term chronic problems that have been exacerbated by a current physical stress. The hypothesis is that placebo medication may be as effective as an antidepressant. Medical depressions constitute a significant dimension and remind nonmedical professionals how important it is to have consultation channels with physicians. There are many biological syndromes that may initially manifest themselves as depression. The symptomatology in these secondary depressions does not differ from a primary depression; however, antidepressants will not alleviate the symptoms. Among the most common of these illnesses are acute and chronic brain syndromes, endocrine disorders, viral illnesses, psychosomatic diseases, and malignancies—particularly cancer of the pancreas, stomach, and other abdominal organs. Finally, there are depressions related to the ingestion of certain drugs. The most striking of these drug reactions is often found as a result of Reserpine, one medication for hypertension. Alphamethyldopa, Valium, and withdrawal from amphetamines can all induce a mild depressive reaction. In sum, Sachar has classified five distinct categories, and has facilitated an understanding of the implications for varying treatment modalities given a specific and carefully made diagnosis.

In the terminally ill patient, the health care provider may actually encounter an overlap of the depressed states, described by Sachar. There may initially be a grief reaction, or what I would call a normal depressive reaction to the potential loss of life. The person may be observed to experience fluctuating moods, crying spells, increased dependency, but nothing resembling a clinical depression. At some point in the illness, we might witness a drug-related depression with an organic basis. This phenomenon can be observed during the often painful, aversive treatments for various forms of cancer. Although the cancer is being attacked, the postsurgery and posttreatment individual most often feels much more ill, weakened and debilitated, and potentially depressed. One sometimes sees a psychotic depression, often temporary, which is precipitated by environmental circumstances in conjunction with the illness, and which is then alleviated by environmental manipulation. A familiar example is the elderly person who lives alone, develops a fatal illness, and after several weeks of hospitalization is informed that he or she must enter a nursing home. The patient may experience a psychotic depression and develop delusions and hallucinations to ward off the pain of the ultimate abandonment and hopelessness that is felt. If this same patient were told that a move to relatives could be an alternative, then a very different perspective might be entertained. A psychotic depression could be prevented. Obviously, many kinds of depressive reactions are possible among medical patients. It is the responsibility of healthcare practitioners to be constantly aware of the potential diagnostic configurations and the precise treatments that are available.

An aid in determining the exact nature of depressive symptomatology in the seriously ill patient is utilizing family members and friends to gain a more complete assessment of the situation. In the hospital setting with its constant flow of visitors and specialists, the skillful physician, nurse, psychologist, social worker, or priest can informally interview those people who have known the patient well and attain a much better understanding of the present depression.

Another important device is the team approach, in which communication channels between professional disciplines are maximized. For example, a behavioral psychologist is called in for a consultation on a hospitalized patient who has begun to manifest depressed affect. The psychologist makes it a point to speak with nursing personnel on the ward—if possible, from different shifts—reads the patient's chart, observes the system, and then arranges a meeting with the attending physician. In this way, there is maximum input into the diagnostic pool and the most accurate treatment plan can be formulated. Diagnosis is not merely a labeling process. It is a careful assessment and observation of multiple factors in a complex system.

Special Issues in Terminal Illness

How can we conceptualize the issues that arise in conjunction with a terminal illness and that may contribute to a depression? I would propose that we consider five major dimensions.

Perhaps the most significant and traumatic issue the newly diagnosed patient must confront is the acknowledgment of death, the profound loss of life. Avery Weisman has studied the dying patient at all stages of the process, formulating in-depth analyses of the psychological adaptations that are required. In reading his work we realize that one cannot discuss facing death as a unitary psychological entity. Weisman (1972) classifies the reaction to personal death awareness into stages and draws some parallels between the adjustment to a life-threatening illness and the denial process. He postulates the following sequence: (1) recognition of a reality, (2) repudiation of a threatening portion, (3) replacement with a more congenial, tolerable meaning, and (4) reorientation to the changes. In a psychosocial sense, Weisman observes three stages experienced by dying patients. Initially he encounters denial and postponement, then mitigation and displacement seem to occur; in the preterminal stage he sees the phenomena of countercontrol—the giving up of control to others—and cessation (i.e., psychological death). Weisman warns: "The overwhelming risk in caring for a dying patient is that the doctor may impose cessation and countercontrol long before it becomes necessary" (1972: 121). Clearly, depression may be a component at any one of the various stages described above. However, there are ways the health-care professional can alleviate symptoms, hasten the process toward a healthy and genuine acceptance of death, and promote a "reorientation to the changes."

A second issue that may constitute an even greater source of depression for the terminally ill patient involves the predicament of coping with life during a chronic illness. The medical and surgical procedures, the unpleasant and often painful tests, and the aversive treatments are not only uncomfortable and physically draining but also contribute to the identity of patienthood and loss of control over one's own body. Particularly in the case of cancer, there is often a sense of a foreign and yet unseen enemy spreading and taking over the system, as well as a profound helplessness and total reliance on external sources of help in the form of medical technology and personnel. The loss of meaningful control and the resulting pervasive helplessness can readily implicate a significant depression (Seligman, 1975).

Third, it is important to consider the issue of self-esteem in the context of the patient encountering a fatal illness. Weisman (1972) notes that some patients, in a magical way, conceptualize their death as a punishment, perhaps for an act committed years before. Typically, this is related to guilt, often a significant aspect of a depressive illness. Another component of self-esteem which can be extremely relevant to the dying patient is body-image. Again, to cite the obvious case of cancer, one thinks immediately of the severe damage to body self-concept that can accrue from loss of body parts and loss of functions.

A fourth area of concern is the reduction or cessation of normal pursuits. One can easily imagine the sense of dejection that may arise in light of the apathy, irritability, and low-grade depression that commonly follow a simple virus or a broken limb. In behavioral terms, the source of reinforcers has been dramatically reduced. For example, visualize a 42-year-old active woman who has been teaching for fifteen years at a university. She contracts a disease that forces her not only to terminate her work but also to give up her avid hobby of tennis as well as most of her other activities. The losses are immense and devastating. She no longer has the professional reinforcer, nor the positive feedback that she is athletic and, in a more general sense, a functional person engaged in many pursuits. Reinforcement is essential for healthy functioning and a sense of self-control. Among dying patients, direct reinforcements are scarce resources.

Finally, I wish to draw attention to the interpersonal alterations that can accompany a diagnosis of terminal illness. A phenomenon that is rarely discussed or admitted is the withdrawal that occurs on the part of other people when they become aware of the diagnosis. It is not clear what initiates the withdrawal. Is it the fear and denial of others, or is it the dying patient's subtly conveyed wish to be alone? It may of course be a combination. This is not universal, and naturally differs according to the individual, but I would maintain that some qualitative change appears in the interpersonal sphere. If this change precipitates an emotional loss, then depression is once again a possibility.

Before proceeding to treatment modalities, it is instructive to note some of the variables that influence the severity of a depressive reaction. Briefly, there are six such important variables: (1) age; generalizing, we can expect the younger, terminally ill patient to experience a more severe depression, (2) type of disease, (3) support system, inclusive of family, friends, and the primary physician involved, (4) premorbid personality, (5) premorbid coping style, and (6) societal reaction to the illness. (For example, some diseases—most notably cancer—retain an aura of secrecy. Despite its widespread prevalence, there remains a taboo about its acknowledgment, often precluding cathartic release and subsequent relief.)

TREATMENT MODALITIES

In presenting a rationale for the use of behavioral approaches for treating depression in the terminally ill patient, I would like to point out several factors. Behavior therapy tends to be short-term and goal-directed. We witness not only a more accelerated reduction of symptoms but also lowered expense to the patient who doubtless has overwhelming financial debts. Second, the focus in behavior therapy is generally on the present and on coping with the environment at hand. The approach is not geared toward unravelling dynamics, neurotic styles, or chronic long-term issues. This would seem then to be appropriate for treating the depressed patient with terminal illness. A third and crucial element of the behavioral approach is its basic philosophy that the patient assume ultimate control for treatment. This may sound odd to the reader unfamiliar with behavior therapy, but it should become apparent in the following pages that this transference of control is an integral dimension of the behavioral approach. Since the loss of control is such an underlying theme for the terminally ill patient, this aspect assumes great relevance. Finally, there is a high degree of humanistic value in the behavioral approaches; this can only be understood once we begin to examine the different modalities.

Typically, a review of the literature reveals a plethora of research studies that either support or refute a particular therapeutic modality. In the area of behavioral treatment for the dying patient, this is not the case. Recently Rebok and Hoyer (1979) reviewed the scarce literature on behavioral interventions with the terminally ill. Their major thrust is related to the achievement of self-control or behavioral self-management. Rebok and Hoyer (1979) cite research that has demonstrated both the importance of self-control for a dying patient, in terms of awareness and involvement in the medical treatment process, and of basic decisionmaking in daily affairs. Additionally, they present a self-management treatment program that places the patient in ultimate control while also encouraging involvement of family and friends.

Cognitive Therapy

It was not until the late sixties and early seventies that mediational processes, or cognitions, were recognized in the theoretical framework of behavior modification (Mahoney 1974). Prior to this time, the so-called pure behaviorists paid no heed to such unmeasurable, vague, and indefinable internal constructs; they focused rather on events, behavioral repertoires, and environmental contingencies. Similar to the over-Freudianization that occurred after Freud's death, one might contend that Skinner has been rigidly interpreted in a one-dimensional and limiting way. Mahoney (1974: 4) cites Skinner's comments: "It is particularly important that a science of behavior face the problem of privacy. . . . An adequate science of behavior must consider events taking place within the skin of the organism . . . as part of behavior itself."

The added dimension of cognitions led to the development of numerous cognitive therapies. These approaches differ significantly from traditional behavior therapies and yet behavioral principles are maintained and utilized. Although space does not permit an exploration of all the cognitive modes, the reader is encouraged to research the following areas: self-instruction (Meichenbaum 1977), coping skills training, problem-solving, and attribution (Mahoney 1974). All of these cognitively oriented techniques have direct relevance for helping the terminally ill patient cope with depression.

Perhaps the best known of the cognitive therapies is cognitive restructuring. Albert Ellis (1962), Aaron Beck (1972), and Arnold Lazarus (1971) are among the major theoreticians in this area, having written extensively on their particular paradigms. The underlying philosophy common to all the methods, as Ellis notes (1962), was stated long ago in 60 A.D. by the Roman philosopher Epictetus: "Men are disturbed not by things, but by the views they take of them." In other words, we are not upset by an event, but rather by the intervening, mediational system of beliefs and attitudes that we formulate about that event. The cognitive therapists hypothesize then that an event, by itself, is not capable of causing an emotional reaction; witness the myriad of different reactions in different people responding to the same event. It is the way in which one constructs the event, the particular cognitive style, which then produces the idiosyncratic emotion. Cognitive therapy is "based on an under-lying theoretical rationale that an individual's affect and behavior are largely determined by the way in which he structures the world" (Beck et al. 1979: 3).

Although Ellis and Beck essentially agree theoretically, they have differed in their description and understanding of cognitive styles. Ellis, (see Chapter 6) elaborates on the concept that specific be-liefs, which ultimately cause emotional upset, are basically irrational. Within this therapeutic system one first identifies, explores, and then challenges these irrational thoughts, finally substituting a more rea-sonable, rational thought process.

A discussion of Beck's approach to treating depression may prove more relevant to the topic of treating the terminally ill. It is a broader based theory, encompassing most of the concepts and prin-ciples outlined in other cognitive modes. Through a variety of cog-nitive and behavioral techniques, the patient is encouraged and taught first to recognize dysfunctional and distorted cognitions and subsequently to examine the inaccurate belief system that has pro-duced the distortions.

It is important to understand Beck's theoretical model and ration-ale of depression before delineating some of the techniques. Briefly, Beck et al. (1979) propose that there are three major components that contribute to depression: (1) the cognitive triad, (2) schemas, and (3) cognitive errors. The cognitive triad involves the individual's negative attitude toward self, the current experiential situation, and the future. The attitude toward these three crucial areas is negatively and unrealistically distorted in the depressed patient. Beck sees the symptomatology of depression as emanating directly from these dis-torted beliefs.

Schema refers to the "stable cognitive patterns [which] form the basis for the regularity of interpretations of a particular set of situa-tions" (Beck et al. 1979: 12). A schema thus represents the process of molding data into thoughts. Dysfunctional and inappropriate schemas may become active in a depressed state. The more depressed an individual becomes, the more prevalent are the inappropriate and negative schemas.

Beck, formerly a psychoanalyst, proposes that the negative atti-tudes evident in the cognitive triad and one's idiosyncratic schemas are learned in childhood. Later in life these schemas may materialize in response to environmental stressors. Beck et al. (1979) write:

> Alternatively, depression may be triggered by a physical abnormality or disease that activates a person's latent belief that he is destined for a life of suffering. Unpleasant—even extremely adverse—life situations do not necessarily produce a depression unless the person is particularly sensitive to the specific type of situation because of the nature of his cognitive organization (16).

The cognitive organization evident in the negative triad and schemas is supported by a patient's cognitive errors. These errors in thinking perpetuate the entire negative system and maintain the depressive outlook even when actual environmental data exist to counter the person's distorted evaluations. Beck et al. (1979) delineate six such cognitive errors: (1) arbitrary inference—drawing a conclusion without valid support or based on contradictory data, (2) selective abstraction—looking at a detail, not considering other more important aspects in a given circumstance, and interpreting the gestalt based on the one detail, (3) overgeneralization—making a broad conclusion based on narrow pieces of data, (4) magnification and minimization—attributing inaccurate significance to an event, and thus distorting the meaning, (5) personalization—relating environmental events to oneself inappropriately, and (6) absolutistic, dichotomous thinking—placing occurrences in either of two opposing descriptive categories (e.g., depressed individual tend to choose the negative category when evaluating themselves). For a complete review of Beck's theory and therapeutic approach, I refer the reader to the book, *Cognitive Therapy of Depression* (Beck et al. 1979).

A precautionary note from Beck and his colleagues reiterates the need for a thorough diagnosis of depression prior to the design of a specific treatment plan. One cannot jump into cognitive therapy without investigating medical components as well as other potential complicating factors. In the following section, I will describe some specific techniques that may be applicable to the patient who has been diagnosed with a terminal illness and who manifests depression.

Behavioral Techniques in Cognitive Therapy. Even within the framework of cognitive therapy, the use of behavioral techniques may be indicated. With the markedly depressed patient, for example, behavior therapy can be useful in generating some form of initial activity, in propelling the individual out of lethargy, and in so doing, enabling self-observation of action. Although behavioral change does not lead necessarily to cognitive change, it can often stimulate the challenging process by which the cognitive therapist helps the patient alter a particular belief system. Behavioral changes can provide a more conducive atmosphere in which increased motivation will develop. "Actually, the behavioral methods can be regarded as a series of small experiments designed to test the validity of the patient's hypotheses or ideas about himself" (Beck et al. 1979: 118).

In the behavioral phase of treatment, the therapist assumes a fairly active role in the initial prescription of therapeutic goals. In actuality, however, the patient assumes the responsibility for carrying out the therapy. For example, an important technique consists of scheduling activities and recording thoughts and feelings associated with each activity. The patient is given specific instructions regarding the scheduling procedure and is taught principles that serve to reduce the possibility of failure. This behavioral technique counters the tendency toward passive immobility, depressive ruminations, and simply negative thoughts such as, "I don't do anything" or "I'm worthless." As is true in all behavioral approaches, the therapist presents a rationale to the patient for the assignment; he or she explains how it will help alleviate the depressive symptomatology. The behavioral approach bears a resemblance to the medical model, and as such may be particularly appropriate for the terminally ill patient. Two crucial differences exist. The therapy is viewed as the joint task of both therapist and patient, and the patient understands the reasoning behind the particular treatment package.

In the case of the medically ill patient, the relevance of this technique is apparent. Medically ill people have often lost the ability to perform certain activities and experience a need to redirect their energy and to discover new channels. For example, consider the man who has undergone kidney surgery and subsequently must be connected to a dialysis machine for several hours, three to four days per week. Many activities have necessarily been curtailed, the individual has become reactively depressed, and has stopped performing many tasks within his capability. In this case, an active problem-solving style may be useful to help generate activities that are quite possible for the patient.

A second technique involves rediscovering activities that are reinforcing for the patient either in the sense of mastery or pleasure. Many depressed people report that they derive no feelings of well-being from their current behavioral repertoire. This in part results from their depression, but also from not taking an active role and engaging in activities that previously had been reinforcing. There are specially designed inventories such as the Reinforcement Survey Schedule (Cautela and Kastenbaum 1967) that can quickly elicit pleasurable activities. Once detected, these activities are assigned, and the patient is asked to record associated thoughts and feelings. In addition, the patient is instructed to note the degree of pleasure and feelings of accomplishment or competency that the activities generate. An essential principle here is the emphasis on noting *degrees* of pleasure and mastery, as opposed to a more rigid or dichotomous cognitive evaluation. Such statements as "I'm no good at this," "I'm a terrible racquet-ball player," or "I'm a lousy father" can be examined and re-evaluated more realistically. The important goal of this exercise is to discover activities pleasurable at least to some extent, and in so doing begin to lift some of the depressive affect. In the therapy session the clinician reviews the activity schedule along with the ratings and potentially uncovers cognitive distortions.

A common sense approach, labelled Graded Task Assignment, has been widely applied in many areas of behavioral treatment (Beck et al. 1979). Essentially, the method entails the prescription of more difficult and complex activities once simpler tasks have been accomplished with relative ease. Thus a woman who has isolated herself socially after a first diagnosis of lymphatic cancer may be assigned an initial task of calling one friend each day. Once comfortable with this, the patient is asked to invite a friend or relative over for coffee, and so on. The observing and evaluating processes continue and the therapist helps to correct and challenge the patient's erroneous or distorted negative evaluations.

An imagery technique, known as cognitive rehearsal is designed to visualize the various steps involved in a task. The concentration on detail aids in the actual completion of the task, deters daydreaming or ruminating, and helps to note potential obstacles. This is really a form of problem-solving in fantasy prior to attempting the behavior. Sometimes it is quite possible to assess what has blocked a particular response; for example, it may become clear why a patient has stopped engaging in an activity which has previously been quite pleasurable and reinforcing.

Beck and his colleagues (1979) include two more techniques within the category of behavioral approaches: assertive training and role-playing. My own view of assertive training is that there are indeed behavioral aspects, but primarily it is a cognitively oriented treatment approach. There is a vast literature on this subject (Alberti and Emmons 1974; Lange and Jakubowski 1976; McFall and Marston 1970; Rimm and Masters 1974; and Wolpe and Lazarus 1966) and its application has been useful in many different clinical areas. Again, with this technique, the therapist examines and challenges negative cognitions. Role-playing, as a method for practicing new behaviors, is utilized in conjunction with assertive training.

In concluding this section, it should be noted that initially we are interested in testing negative ideas about the self, increasing the overall activity level, stimulating motivation to examine negative cognitions, and elevating mood. The patient is taught the concept of gradualism, of movement toward goals as opposed to an all or none, success or failure paradigm.

Cognitive Techniques. As depression lifts, patients are more easily inducted into the cognitive mode of treatment. Clearly, there is overlap between the behavioral and cognitive techniques, and often a combination approach is indicated. As noted, the behavior therapy techniques are more closely aligned with the medical model and thus may be more appropriate during the initial treatment of depression in the terminally ill patient. Cognitive therapy becomes more readily applicable once the inertia has lifted, and the patient has greater motivation to deal constructively with emotions and thoughts. It represents a joint enterprise, with the patient taking on increased therapeutic responsibility.

The rationale behind the cognitive theory of depression must be presented first in order for the patient to engage fully in the therapy. The clinician illustrates the mutual interaction between a person's thoughts and existing feelings and behaviors. The patient is taught that some thoughts may in fact be inaccurate (as opposed to irrational, which may promote guilt in the highly vulnerable depressed individual). Therapist and patient become scientific collaborators with the intention of examining the patient's thinking and its connection to depression.

Specifically, and most importantly, the patient is instructed to become aware of and to record ongoing cognitions. With regard to the medical patient, this can provide an immediate source of a heightened sense of control. The patient is doing something, he or she is an active collaborator rather than a passive recipient of external help.

Beck and his colleagues (1979) outline the following steps as a method used to teach the process of gathering thoughts. The first lesson involves defining a cognition or what Beck terms an "automatic thought." It is important to explain that a cognition is one's image of reality, that it is automatic or habitual, and can be prematurely taken as fact when actually it should be subjected to analysis. Second, the therapist communicates the important connection among cognitions, behaviors, and feelings. This is accomplished most easily by the use of examples. A technique useful in eliciting cognitions and furthering the patient's comprehension of the process is noting experiences that have just occurred and the associated cognitions. For example, the patient might be asked: "What were you thinking when you called up to make this appointment with me?" In this way, the patient gains some consciousness of the existence of cognitions. A fourth step involves the recording of automatic thoughts, preferably as they arise. This is related to the concept of thematic cognitions whereby the patient examines cognitions to observe if there are any underlying similarities. For example, one might discover many thoughts expressing a theme of inadequacy in social situations. This can be quite helpful in providing material to be discussed with the therapist. Finally, the collected thoughts are reality-tested with the assistance of the clinician, which constitutes the essence of the therapy session. Herein lies the collaborative effort in which patient and therapist examine cognitions with an eye toward a more realistic appraisal of the individual, the present circumstances, and the future.

Beck et al. (1979) discuss two techniques designed to increase objectivity and to create a healthy distance between individuals and their cognitions. We are not inseparable from our thought processes; rather, we have the power or control to generate and to alter a cognition. This sense of control, however, is often lost or simply not recognized, particularly in an individual suffering from depression. The process of reattribution or "de-responsibilitizing is useful in modifying inappropriate self-blame. Many depressed patients assume an erroneously high degree of responsibility for negative situations. At the psychotic level, this process can manifest itself in such cognitions as, "It's my fault that the Southwest has had a drought," or

"It's because of me that the sanitation workers went on strike." As Weisman (1972) notes, patients facing death often experience strong guilt feelings. The cognitions preceding these feelings take the form of: "I deserve to die," "I haven't been a good husband, so this was coming to me," and so on. If the therapist is successful at lifting some of the inappropriate self-attribution then the patient's energy can be freed up to assume appropriate responsibility for present life circumstances.

Take the example of Mrs. B.:

Mrs. B., a 54-year-old married woman, was admitted to the hospital for a breast biopsy. The tissue was determined to be malignant and a mastectomy was then performed. The patient was informed that, given proper treatments, the prognosis was optimistic in terms of life expectancy, despite the fact that she had contracted cancer. Mrs. B. accepted this information with very little outward response. Hospital staff then began to notice a marked passivity, a lack of interest in her surroundings, a loss of appetite, and a general withdrawal from the people around her. A behavioral consultant was called in at this point to evaluate Mrs. B. and to help alleviate her apparent depression. In questioning the patient, it became evident that her father had died unexpectedly about a year ago and that she had been quite close to him. The grieving process had not been completed and Mrs. B. still maintained intense emotions about this death. Further assessment revealed Mrs. B. to be a rather passive and quiet woman, devoted to her husband and three children. She described herself as an easy-going person who rarely expressed anger. In addition, Mrs. B. had read a magazine article recently that attempted to correlate various forms of cancer with certain personality configurations which emphasized the inhibition of anger, and thus had begun to experience guilt for bringing the disease on herself.

The consultant realized that several issues were involved. The first task was to help Mrs. B. de-responsibilize, and show her that there was no substantial data to support theories linking personality to disease. It was important to remove the guilt and allow Mrs. B. to express her other strong feelings, notably resentment and anger toward being so ill. The therapist also explored the patient's attitude toward her father's death and was able to help resolve the grieving process. During the brief cognitive therapy, Mrs. B. was helped to examine her belief system and to become aware of her cognitive errors. Through the processes of arbitrary inference, selective abstraction, and overgeneralization, she had concluded that she would soon die of cancer despite the fact that her prognosis was quite good. Based on the one piece of data that she had cancer of the breast, she wrongly assumed that her life was coming to an abrupt end. When Mrs. B. was able to see how her thinking had actually distorted the facts, the depression began to lift.

A second technique—the search for alternative solutions—actually falls within the rubric of problem-solving. This should be utilized when the depressed patient becomes less dysphoric, more objective, and has the ability to evaluate cognitions in a more realistic manner. Solutions may surface which previously were either not acknowledged or rejected prematurely. Basically, once the depression is somewhat alleviated, the cognitive style becomes more flexible, and creative solutions can be generated. A positive and reinforcing cycle emerges: a solution is found and the patient feels better about himself or herself, feels competent and less depressed, expects further competency, and is better able to generate the next solution.

Finally, it is important to remember that a very large portion of cognitive therapy is the patient's responsibility. Specifically, a great deal of time is spent between therapy appointments in recording situations, responses, thoughts, and feelings. Beck and his colleagues (1979) have devised various recording forms for this purpose; these forms can be found in the appendices of their latest book.

The cognitive approach outlined by Beck has been criticized for being superficial, dealing for the most part with manifest versus latent content or cognitions (Mendelson 1974). In *Psychoanalytic Concepts of Depression*, Mendelson notes limitations of Beck's theoretical conceptualization, but essentially is in agreement with Beck (1979) as to the applicability of cognitive therapy to reactive depressions:

> Beck acknowledges that the major usefulness of cognitive therapy *during* a depression is with those reactively depressed neurotic patients who are not severely ill, whose depressions are precipitated by identifiable events and who do not have the characteristics of endogenous depressions (286).

The Self-Control Model

I would like to stress once more the importance of facilitating control for the terminally ill person. In this section I will briefly illustrate a model and treatment approach which has been developed by Rehm (1977) based on the dimension of self-control.

In Rehm's review of other theorists who closely approximate his view, he mentions Lewinsohn, Seligman, Beck, and Kanfer. Lewinsohn, in a very general sense, conceptualizes depression as "an extinction phenomenon," "a loss or lack of response contingent positive reinforcement" (Rehm 1977: 788). Therapy is aimed at re-locating sources of reinforcement. Seligman derives his theory of depression from a laboratory model of "learned helplessness" where-by "depressive retardation is caused by a belief in response-reinforce-ment independence" (1975). Seligman has observed many of the key depressive symptoms—for example, negative beliefs, lowered activ-ity, loss of libido, loss of appetite—with people in a learned helpless position. Rehm goes on to describe Beck's model, noting the primary negative triad and cognitive distortions discussed above.

Rehm's model, although sharing much in common with the above theorists, is most closely aligned to that of Kanfer's (1970). Rehm cites Kanfer's definition of self-control as, "those processes by which an individual alters the probability of a response in the relative absence of immediate external supports" (1977: 789). More simply stated, the self-control model is oriented toward helping a person feel better without an outside source of support or reinforcement.

Rehm (1977) outlines a tripartite paradigm consisting of: (1) self-monitoring, (2) self-evaluation, and (3) self-reinforcement. In the first category, he notes the tendency of depressed individuals to attend selectively to negative events (similar to Beck's selective ab-straction and arbitrary inference). In terms of self-evaluation, Rehm observes a faulty attribution system and a rigid set of standards for themselves in many depressed people. The person either believes he or she is helpless, sensing an independence between behavior and consequences in the environment, or at the other extreme assumes an over-responsibility which stimulates guilt. In the third area, Rehm notes that the rate of self-reinforcement is low while the rate of pun-ishment is high.

In a study devised to test Rehm's model, Fuchs and Rehm (1977) set up three groups consisting of thirty-six moderately depressed women, aged 18 to 60. Self-control therapy was applied to one group, a nonspecific approach to the second group, and the third group remained on a waiting list. A major implication emanating from Rehm's theory is the importance of monitoring pleasant events. Thus, a positive activities schedule was used in the self-control group. In addition, the group members were helped to set realistic goals and were taught basic principles of reinforcement. The groups met over a period of six weeks. At the completion of these sessions, the Beck Depression Inventory and the Minnesota Multiphasic Personality Inventory were administered to determine the effects of the two therapy approaches. Results showed significant decreases of depression in the self-control group. On these post-tests, all self-control scores were in the normal range.

It is quite evident that Rehm's approach is highly similar to the cognitive approach delineated by Beck. Its emphasis, however, on self-control is particularly relevant to our concern with treating depression in the terminally ill. The patient facing death has lost much of his or her sense of control, and potentially many external reinforcers. Rehm's somewhat exclusive focus on the role of self-control in depression may prove to be especially beneficial in facilitating an increased sense of mastery and control for the dying patient.

In more traditional client-centered therapeutic approaches, the dying patient is encouraged to explore feelings of helplessness, lack of control, anxieties, and fears. This may benefit the patient in a cathartic sense, yet it does not necessarily generate a healthier attitude or facilitate positive coping strategies. It may serve, rather, to accentuate the negatives without substituting a viable alternative. In applying Rehm's self-control paradigm, it is possible to redirect the patient's focus to those aspects of life that are in fact controllable. For example, deep muscle relaxation or meditation techniques can easily be taught and can provide patients with an effective method to control pain. There are a myriad of creative therapeutic applications utilizing Rehm's theory. The essential idea is to permit the patient to control as much as possible given the circumstances. Even the very ill person can be given the right to decide when and if to see visitors, whether to have the television on, and so forth. Controlling one's personal environment, where feasible, is critical among the terminally ill and should be maximized in order to balance the pervasive sense of helplessness often observed.

Relaxation Training

An age-old method of reducing muscle tension and promoting pervasive relaxation has recently been revived and restated by Dr. Herbert Benson (1975). Each era of history finds men and women searching for means to combat environmental stress, to decrease tension, and to relax both physically and mentally. A deep sense of relaxation has been gained through such measures as transcendental meditation, yoga, prayer, and in contemporary American society, biofeedback and deep muscle relaxation.

In his excellent and very readable book, *The Relaxation Response* (1975), Benson illustrates the common physiological response that results from the various relaxation methods. The relaxation response has been found useful not only in alleviating emotional stress and anxiety, but also in reducing hypertension, the leading cause of heart attacks and strokes (Benson 1975). The benefits are profound and extensive; the costs are none. Our fast-paced computerized society, however, neither encourages nor ideologically supports the use of these techniques. Instead, our culture condones the uses of alcohol and tranquilizers like Valium, the most widely prescribed medication on the market. The media enjoins us to work hard, get ahead, use our leisure time well, be active and energetic. Doing "nothing" very often carries a pejorative connotation, and yet it is just this—adopting a passive stance—that helps to elicit the relaxation response. For a thorough explanation and illustration of the techniques involved in relaxation training, see the self-help manual, *The Relaxation Book* (Rosen 1977).

There are several reasons for applying relaxation methods to the depressed patient with terminal disease. First, many depressive disorders manifest a large component of anxiety secondary to the depression, but nevertheless painful and debilitating. Deep muscle relaxation methods can be used as part of the overall treatment package to reduce some of this tension.

A second factor relates to medical considerations. Gradually evidence is accumulating that shows that the more stressed an individual is, the more susceptible he or she becomes to disease. Similarly, once having contracted an illness, particularly a life-threatening one, an individual is increasingly vulnerable to stress. Thus, the patient dealing with a fatal disease clearly has a high potential to experience stress as well as to develop additional medical problems, such as high blood pressure or tension headaches. In teaching the technique of deep muscle relaxation, the clinician affords the dying patient an ability to lower tension levels and at the same time to raise a sense of self-efficacy (Bandura 1977). The patient is indirectly helped to engage in other behaviors that increase reinforcer effectiveness. Relaxation can be a significant preventative intervention.

One of the virtues of relaxation training is its simplicity and the ease with which people can learn it and practice on their own. In terms of self-control, one can clearly imagine the beneficial and therapeutic effects of teaching relaxation methods to the depressed and terminally ill patient. The technique may be learned quickly; it is entirely under the patient's control; it represents a pro-active way of alleviating physical discomfort; it can be executed in a comfortable chair or in bed (thus suited even to the very ill patient); and finally, it promotes feelings of peace and well-being, so important to everyone, but even more so for the patient suffering from a terminal illness.

The behavioral intervention of deep muscle relaxation training can be useful in many ways and applicable to patients even at a stage of impending death. In concentrating exclusively on the systematic processes of relaxing muscle groups, a depressed patient is diverted momentarily from both negative cognitions and depressed affect. It is time-out, during which the individual focuses on a personal and attainable goal. The relaxation period is a time for clearing the mind of distractions, a time exclusively devoted to attaining peace, comfort, and a feeling of inner calmness (Sobel and Worden 1981). In a psychosocial sense, deep muscle relaxation represents an activity detached from other people, an active measure separate from doctors, nurses, even family, something uniquely for oneself. Relaxation techniques in combination with cognitive therapy can be used as an anti-pain agent as well. (See Chapter 4).

Benson (1975) remarks on the universal capability of eliciting the relaxation response:

> Throughout this book we have tried to show you that the Relaxation Response is a natural gift that anyone can turn on and use. By bridging the traditional gaps between psychology, physiology, medicine, and history, we have established that the Relaxation Response is an innate mechanism within us (1975).

CONCLUSIONS AND SUMMARY

Within the confines of a relatively brief chapter, I have attempted to discuss the need for accurate diagnosis of depression and to present a rationale for the application of behavioral approaches to reactive depression among the terminally ill. The issue of self-control has been important throughout and has been a theme underlying the several treatment modalities presented. The concept of multidimensional dynamics operative in a depressive illness is another significant theoretical perspective I have wished to convey. Having examined depression—the causative factors, target symptoms, and treatment—from the eyes of several behaviorists, we begin to understand the complicated nature of depression and its multifaceted structure. Craighead (1980) elaborates on this concept: ". . . depression may best be viewed as a label or construct for a complex pattern of overt somatic-motor, cognitive, and physiological responses . . . the construct is polydimensional, with a potential multiplicity of causes" (1980: 126).

There is a need to evaluate, in any given depression, which deficits are operating. For example, is the depression emanating from a distorted cognition (Beck), or from an inadequacy in the patient's self-evaluative ability (Rehm)? The theorists reviewed in this paper have developed concise systems that go far in expanding our comprehension of depression. For the more eclectic health-care practitioner, however, I believe that it behooves us to learn and assimilate the information from all the systems when we attempt to evaluate patients. The systems need not be mutually exclusive. There is no reason why we cannot diagnose a learned helplessness problem as well as a faulty cognitive style in the same individual. The essential goal is to maintain clinical openness, and to choose the appropriate treatment strategy for the specific coping deficit.

In light of the dearth of research on behavior therapy for depression in the terminally ill, caution must be exercised in its actual practice. Its prospective value is apparent, but research must be undertaken to determine its true efficacy. In addition, I do not propose a blanket prescription of behavior therapy for depression in the terminally ill. For many patients a more existential or client-centered approach may be the treatment of choice. A patient may simply need someone to talk with, someone with whom to discuss critical issues of personal meanings or fears. Clearly, one must listen to the patient. It is crucial to comprehend the needs of the patient and to respond with a treatment that matches those needs maximally. Behavioral and existential approaches can function together as long as the therapist is flexible and sensitive to the patient's illness plight.

Much of this chapter has dealt with alleviating depression in the terminally ill patient, and enabling a person to cope while attempting to maintain a personally meaningful existence. Our focus has been largely on living with a fatal disease rather than on confronting death. It has been my contention that this aspect of terminal care merits attention and ought not to be excluded from the literature.

Weisman (1972) describes what he considers to be an "appropriate death:"

> An appropriate death, in brief, is a death that someone might choose for himself—had he a choice. The central idea, of course, is that to foster an appropriate death, one must realize that death is not an ironic choice without an option, but a way of living as long as possible (41).

Coming from a psychoanalytic-existential viewpoint, Weisman proposes that choice, or the ability to express one's will and to exert personal control, is the central ingredient in an appropriate death. This is where the behaviorists and the more analytic or existential thinkers join together in essential agreement. In some significant ways their philosophical positions reveal a basic consistency. It is within the realm of technique and therapeutic style that the primary differences emerge.

Perhaps in no other area of human services does behavior therapy manifest its potential humanism as in its application to the terminally ill. In preventing serious depression via cognitive and behavioral techniques, the helper facilitates quality time for the dying. The sense of living more autonomously, while in fact dying, is brought to consciousness and enhanced. It is vital that the dying person be given this chance to live to the fullest capacity. The opportunity to engage in a therapeutic verbal interchange can provide the necessary arena in which the patient may examine feelings and attitudes, make appropriate choices, and ultimately accept a dignified and graceful death.

REFERENCES

Alberti, R.E. and Emmons, M.L. *Your perfect right: A guide to assertive behavior* (2nd ed.). San Luis Obispo, California: Impact Press, 1974.

Bandura, A. Self-efficacy: Toward a unifying theory of behavior change. *Psychological Review*, 1977, *84*, 191–215.

Beck, A. *Depression—clinical, experimental, and theoretical aspects.* New York: Harper & Row, 1967.

Beck, A., Rush, A., Shaw, B., and Emery, G. *Cognitive therapy of depression.* New York: Guilford Press, 1979.

Benson, H. *The relaxation response.* New York: Avon Books, 1975.

Cautela, J., and Kastenbaum, R. A reinforcement survey schedule for use in therapy, training, and research. *Psychological Reports*, 1967, *20*, 1115–1130.

Craighead, W.E. Away from a unitary model of depression. *Behavior Therapy*, 1980, *11*, 122–128.

Ellis, A. *Reason and emotion in psychotherapy*. New York: Stuart, 1962.

Fuchs, C.Z., and Rehm, L.P. A self-control behavior therapy program for depression. *Journal of Consulting and Clinical Psychology*, 1977, *45*, 206–215.

Kanfer, F.H. Self-regulation: Research issues and speculations. In C. Neuringer and J.L. Michael (Eds.), *Behavior modification in clinical psychology*. New York: Appleton–Century–Crofts, 1970.

Klerman, G.L. Clinical research in depression. *Archives of General Psychiatry*, 1971, *24*, 305–319.

Lange, A.J., and Jakubowski, P. *Responsible assertive behavior*. Champaign, Ill.: Research Press, 1976.

Lazarus, A. *Behavior therapy and beyond*. New York: McGraw–Hill, 1971.

Mahoney, M.J. *Cognition and behavior modification*. Cambridge, Mass.: Ballinger, 1974.

McFall, R.M., and Marston, A.R. An experimental investigation of behavior rehearsal in assertive training. *Journal of Abnormal Psychology*, 1970, *76*, 295–303.

Meichenbaum, D. *Cognitive-behavior modification: An integrative approach*. New York: Plenum, 1977.

Mendelson, M. *Psychoanalytic concepts of depression*. New York: Spectrum Publications, Inc., 1974.

Ram Dass. *The only dance there is*. Garden City, New York: Anchor Books, 1970.

Rebok, G.W., and Hoyer, W.J. Clients nearing death: Behavioral treatment perspectives. *Omega*, 1979, *10*, 191–201.

Rehm, L.P. A self-control model of depression. *Behavior Therapy*, 1977, *8*, 787–804.

Rimm, D.C., and Master, J.C. *Behavior therapy: Techniques and empirical findings*. New York: Academic Press, 1974.

Robinson, L. *Psychological aspects of the care of hospitalized patients*. Philadelphia: F.A. Davis Company, 1968.

Rosen, G. *The relaxation book: An illustrated self-help program*. Englewood Cliffs, N.J.: Prentice–Hall, Inc., 1977.

Sachar, E. Evaluating depression in the medical patient. In J. Strain and S. Grossman (Eds.), *Psychological care of the medically ill*. New York: Appleton–Century–Crofts, 1975.

Secunda, S.K., Katz, M.M., Friedman, R.J., and Schuyler, D. *Special report: 1973—the depressive disorders*. Washington, D.C.: U.S. Government Printing Office, 1973.

Seligman, M.E.P. *Helplessness: On depression, development, and death*. San Francisco: W.H. Freeman, 1975.

Sobel, H.J., and Worden, J.W. *Helping cancer patients cope*. New York: BMA and Guilford Press, 1981.

Weisman, A. *On dying and denying.* New York: Behavioral Publications, Inc., 1972.

Wolpe, J., and Lazarus, A.A. *Behavior therapy techniques.* New York: Pergamon Press, 1966.

4 PAIN AND THE TERMINALLY ILL CANCER PATIENT
A Cognitive-Social Learning Perspective

Dennis C. Turk
Karen Rennert

For many people a diagnosis of terminal illness generates concerns not only about death but also about the process of dying and, in particular, the presence and intensity of pain. In addition, many patients are especially anxious regarding their own ability to cope with intense and prolonged noxious sensations.

We have decided to focus our discussion on the cancer patient for several reasons. First, cancer is a prevalent disease. Bonica (1979) estimated that internationally there are approximately 5 million cancer deaths each year, with 20 percent of all deaths in the United States and other Western countries attributed to cancer. In the United States alone, there are 700,000 newly diagnosed cases of cancer, and 400,000 cancer deaths annually (American Cancer Society 1978). Cancer is the second leading cause of death in the United States. Epidemiological studies show that one out of every four Americans will contract some form of neoplastic disease during their lifetime (Sobel 1980).

The prevalence of pain in neoplastic disease is the second reason for targeting our discussion on cancer. Malignant disease is the most common cause of intractable pain seen in patients with terminal disease (Swerdlow 1973). There are a number of physiological bases for the presence of pain in cancer including bone destruction, luminal

Support for this project was provided by Biomedical Research Support Grant NIH 5-507-RR07015.

obstruction, infiltration or compression of nerves, and infiltration or distension of the integument or organ capsules. Additionally, the symptomatic treatments employed with cancer patients, perhaps more than with any other disease, often create a multitude of discomforts, pain, and suffering.

Finally, despite evidence that psychological factors contribute to pain (Chapman 1979; Melzack 1973; Turk 1978a; and Weisenberg 1977), there are only a handful of papers that address the utility of psychological interventions in relieving the pain and suffering accompanying cancer. We believe this is an important dimension of behavioral medicine and terminal care.

CONCEPTUALIZATIONS OF PAIN

By alerting the individual to some injury or disease, pain is generally viewed as serving an important function essential for survival. However, in the patient with chronic pain, the pain is meaningless and may in itself become debilitating and demoralizing. The pain serves as a constant reminder of the disease. For the terminally ill, it is often a sign of impending death.

Philosophers, religious leaders, health-care providers, and the lay population in general have speculated as to the nature, cause, and treatment of pain. Philosophers from earliest times saw pain as caused by either cognitive activity, dysphoric emotions, or physical stimuli. Theologians have suggested that pain is imposed by God or the gods as a test of faith or a form of punishment for original or other sins.

The conceptualization of pain we adopt will determine the nature of the strategies employed to alleviate it. The range of approaches extends from prayer, stoicism, and ingestion of esoteric substances (e.g., moss scraped from the skull of a person who died a violent death, ground gallstones obtained from sheep and goats, and leeching) to heat, cold, surgery, and so forth (Meichenbaum and Turk 1976; and Turk 1975, 1978a).

Developments in sensory physiology and psychophysics during the late 1800s provided the first physiological explanation for the experience of pain, relegating cognitive and affective factors to the status of reactions to pain and thus of secondary importance (Melzack 1973; Turk 1978a; and Turk and Genest 1979). The conceptualization of pain as a function of direct sensory-input remains the basis of contemporary medical practice. The sensory-input model postulates a direct causal relationship between physical aspects of the stimuli that are transmitted first from the pain receptors to the spinal cord and components of the nervous system. This transmission line conceptualization leads to the assumption that pain can be eliminated or reduced by either removal of the source of physical stimulation (e.g., excision of a tumor compressing a nerve), blockage of the pain pathways by analgesic agents, or severing the pain pathways (e.g., sympathectomy, rhizotomy, cordotomy). All of the medical and surgical procedures currently employed are designed to remove the offending stimulus or to block transmission of pain impulses.

Surgeons have shown great ingenuity in developing procedures designed to relieve intractable pain, and the physician's pharmacopia has greatly expanded to include a variety of natural and synthetic narcotics. However, no procedure is presently available that consistently and permanently relieves pain in all circumstances. In a recent report, Toomey, Ghia, Mao, and Gregg (1977) note that approximately 50 percent of chronic pain patients are unresponsive to purely somatic modes of treatment. Physicians frequently note that procedures designed to cut or block pain pathways for patients manifesting a given syndrome are differentially effective; there are frequent recurrences of pain among those patients who at first appeared responsive to treatment (Melzack 1973). Moreover, patients with ostensibly the same pain syndrome often are quite varied in their reports of pain. For example, in the terminal stage of cancer substantial proportions (30 to 50 percent) of patients do not report pain even though at autopsy there are no differences in the extent of tissue damage between those who complained of severe pain and those who did not (Aitken–Swan 1959; Bonica 1979; and Turnbull 1979). Thus, even in neoplastic disease, tissue pathology and pain do not necessarily correspond in an isomorphic relationship. In addition to being ineffective or only partially effective in reducing pain for some patients, surgical treatment may produce iatrogenic effects (e.g., painful neuromas at the site of surgical lesions, presence of anesthesias and parasthesias, loss of bowel or bladder function).

These observations, as well as a number of other puzzles, are now leading many health-care providers to question the adequacy of the sensory-physiological conceptualization of pain. For example, Beecher (1946) noted that soldiers receiving extensive wounds in battle did not report experiencing much pain. Beecher (1959) concluded that "there is no simple direct relationship between the wound per se and the pain experienced. The pain is in very large part determined by other factors, and of great importance here is the significance of the wound" (1959: 165). Freeman and Watts (1960) describe the effects of prefrontal lobotomies on the pain experience as follows: "Prefrontal lobotomy changes the attitude of the individual toward his pain, but does not alter the perception of pain. Patients report that the pain is still present but that it is no longer bothersome to them" (1960: 354). Barber (1959) concludes:

> It appears that some procedures that are said to reduce pain actually reduce anxiety, fear, worry and other emotions that are usually intermingled with pain. For instance, the pain relief that follows the administration of morphine and other opiates may be closely related to the reduction of anxiety or fear. Although the patient who has received an opiate may still experience pain sensations, the reduction in anxiety, fear, or other emotions apparently leads him to report that pain is reduced (453).

Of particular relevance for the present chapter are the results of a study reported by Byron and Yonemoto (1975). In this study the authors found that 77 percent of patients with advanced cancer obtained complete pain relief for four hours or more from placebos (i.e., pharmacological preparations that include no active analgesic medication).

Examinations of such observations and research data led Melzack and Casey (1968) to conclude:

> The surgical and pharmacological attacks on pain might well profit by redirecting thinking toward the neglected and almost forgotten contribution of motivational and cognitive processes. Pain can be treated not only by trying to cut down sensory input by anesthetic blocks, surgical intervention and the like, but also by influencing the motivational-affective and cognitive factors as well (435).

What Melzack and Casey are suggesting is a multidimensional conceptualization of pain as an alternative to the unidimensional sensory-physiological view. According to their perspective, there are three components of pain: sensory, affective, and cognitive (the individual's appraisal of situations, sensations, and coping resources).

TREATMENTS FOR CANCER PAIN

Discussions of pain and terminally ill cancer patients have taken one of several tracks. The most common approach includes discussions of the relative efficacy of different surgical and pharmacological regimens as symptomatic or palliative treatments to control or eliminate pain. Surgical procedures include rhizotomies, cordotomies, medullary tractomies, thalamotomies, and lobotomies. In fact, almost every site from the periphery to the central nervous system has been attacked in the quest to eliminate pain. Pharmacological attacks on pain include the systemic use of various narcotic and non-narcotic analgesics, psychotrophic medications (antidepressants and tranquilizers), and combinations of narcotic and non-narcotic analgesics with psychotrophic medications (especially, the Brompton Mixture — an oral narcotic preparation combined with phenothiazines). In addition, the physician's armamentarium includes analgesic nerve blocks, transcutaneous nerve stimulation, hyperthermia, and radiation therapy (for a detailed discussion of each of these techniques, their relative utility, and side effects, see the recent volume on treating pain of advanced cancer edited by Bonica and Ventafridda 1979).

Although each of the symptomatic medical treatments is effective in selected cases, none of the treatments are efficacious with all patients. Moreover, there appears to be a group of terminally ill cancer patients for whom none of the medical treatments provide adequate pain relief. Even combinations of potent narcotic agents, such as morphine and heroin combined with major tranquilizers, are not universally effective in controlling pain. For example, in one study in which cancer patients were given the Brompton Mixture, approximately 10 to 25 percent of the patients continued to report experiencing unbearable pain (Melzack, Ofiesh, and Mount 1976).

Another limitation associated with medical treatments is that the effectiveness of various procedures diminishes over time. For example, it has been suggested that with early tolerance to narcotic analgesics the patient may not be able to derive adequate relief from pain in the late stages of the disease (Murphy 1973). Laboratory studies demonstrate that tolerance does occur rapidly and that increasingly larger doses are required to obtain the same analgesic effects, with increasing dosages eventually clouding the cognitive processes and blunting affect (e.g., Houde 1974; and Siegel 1975, 1977). While others state that tolerance does not present a problem when sufficient narcotics are administered orally on a regular schedule rather than PRN (Mount 1976; and Saunders 1976), this remains a controversial issue. Procedures involving interruption of pain pathways may produce only temporary relief, with the pain recurring within weeks or months (Black 1979). Similarly, the benefit of transcutaneous electrical stimulation tends to wear off in most patients, so that it is not generally effective for long-term relief.

The decision to use a particular medical procedure requires careful consideration of the associated risks and negative side-effects, as well as the benefits and limitations. For example, complications from the spinothalamic tractotomy, one of the most widely used neurosurgical operations for cancer, include weakness or paralysis of the lower extremities or of the bowel and bladder sphincters, abdominal disturbances, girdle pains and parasthesia above the level of anesthesia, orthostatic hypotension, and loss of sexual function (Murphy 1973). Side-effects of narcotic analgesics include nausea and vomiting, constipation, respiratory depression, and sedation (Black 1979). Although treatments are available to counteract some of the side-effects, these medications may have undesirable side-effects of their own. For instance, phenothiazines, which are frequently used to control nausea and vomiting, may produce sedation and constipation.

A second approach to the terminally ill patient, one that is often seen as a supplement to more conventional medical treatments, is that taken by traditional mental health workers. The emphasis of this approach is on supportive psychotherapy to assist patients in coming to terms with a terminal illness. The psychiatric approach seeks to reduce or alleviate the distress of either the patient or the family (Bond 1979; and Weisman, Worden, and Sobel 1980). In addition to counseling the patient, the psychiatric approach often employs psychotrophic medications to reduce anxiety and depression. Much less attention is paid to the pain per se. However, it is frequently observed that emotional distress can produce or exacerbate pain (Chapman 1979; Turk 1978a; and Weisenberg 1977). Thus, indirectly, by reducing emotional distress, the psychiatric approach may reduce pain and suffering. We will return to this point in more detail later.

In addition to providing supportive counseling, some psychologically based interventions are specifically employed to alleviate the pain accompanying neoplastic disease. For example, hypnosis has been used to control pain in cancer (Barber and Gitelson 1980; and Hilgard and Hilgard 1975). More recently, biofeedback techniques have been used with cancer patients (Fotopoulos, Graham, and Cook 1979). Although both hypnosis and biofeedback appear to be promising interventions, carefully controlled investigations are unavailable and thus we cannot draw any firm conclusions regarding the efficacy of such techniques in the management of cancer pain.

The limited effectiveness of each of the medical and psychological treatments cited above may be, in part, a reflection of the fact that each approach considers only one aspect of the patient's pain experience. If pain is viewed as a multidimensional experience, then any treatment program should incorporate cognitive, affective, and sensory components.

The Holistic Approach

A third approach to pain in terminal illness is a comprehensive or holistic approach. This approach, which is characteristic of the hospice movement, emphasizes the all-consuming nature of chronic pain and addresses both its physical and psychological components (Saunders 1967). The hospice program incorporates pharmacological therapy and social, spiritual, and emotional support for the patient and the family. The hospice approach is concerned primarily with patients in the *terminal stage* of a terminal illness.

The distinction between a terminal illness and the terminal stage of an illness is particularly important. Terminal illness is an illness that cannot be cured by means of present day medical technology and generally leads to death within a specified period of time (years or months). During the period of terminal illness, medical treatments may be undertaken in order to prolong life even though the disease cannot be cured. In contrast, the terminal stage of an illness is the time between the cessation of medical treatment beyond palliative care and death (usually weeks or a few months).

In the remainder of this chapter we will describe a cognitive-social learning perspective on treating pain in individuals with terminal illnesses. We will consider the application of the theoretical model and specific cognitive-behavioral techniques to pain both in the early stages and in the terminal stage of the illness. Although the focus of our discussion will be on the pain concurrent with neoplastic disease, the approach described can be generalized to pain associated with other terminal illnesses.

THE COGNITIVE-SOCIAL
LEARNING PERSPECTIVE

Any event, whether an environmental situation or a physical sensation, can be described in essentially two ways. First, in objective terms of the event, and second, in terms of the psychological significance of the event for the individual. The psychological significance or personal meaning of an event is particularly important to cognitive-social learning theorists and practitioners (Turk 1979, 1980a). Personal meanings are related to an individual's appraisals of both the event and his or her own coping resources. These appraisals are based, in turn, on the beliefs and attitudes that have developed thoughout an individual's entire social learning history.

An individual's appraisals influence emotional arousal and the behavioral response to a situation or sensation. The manner and degree of success in responding will lead to reappraisals of both the event and personal competency. This newly acquired information will contribute to an individual's appraisals when similar or novel events occur in the future. Much of the diversity in people's responses to threatening events or ambiguous sensations is related to variations in the appraisal process. Thus, from the cognitive-social learning perspective, people are viewed as active agents rather than as passive respondents to impinging stimuli, whether the source of the stimuli is internal or external.

The rationale of cognitive-social learning approaches rests on the assumption that individuals can be taught new patterns of thinking, fantasizing, planning, and initiating adaptive behavior. The cognitive-social learning counselor serves as an instigator or motivator and collaborator, helping the patient change conceptions of self and his or her situation. The responsibility for carrying out the program, and for maintaining its effectiveness, ultimately rests with the individual. The counselor works in a collaborative relationship with the patient to help the patient gain a sense of control over his or her emotional state and behavior. The counselor helps the patient feel like an active contributor to his or her own experience and not like a helpless victim. Thus, the ultimate aim of the cognitive-social learning approach is humanistic rather than deterministic. (See Chapter 1.)

Cognitive-social learning approaches can be contrasted with more traditional behavioral approaches that emphasize the direct treatment of specific symptoms. Behavioral approches are usually geared toward actions taken by the individual to avoid, escape, attack, or overcome the situational event and subsequent arousal. The orthodox behavioral approach is unconcerned about what the individual thinks, or what his or her attitudes are regarding the symptoms. In short, patients' cognitions are irrelevant to successful intervention. In contrast, cognitive-behavioral approaches are designed to induce changes in perception, attitudes, sense of control, and helplessness about emotional states, behavior, and presenting problems (Turk 1980a, 1980b).

THE COGNITIVE-SOCIAL LEARNING PERSPECTIVE AND CANCER

As noted by Lazarus (1966), " . . . the more ambiguous are the stimuli cues, the more important are general belief systems in determining the appraisal process" (134). Cancer is, by its very nature, an ambiguous disease. The disease is of unknown origin, its course is unpredictable and erratic, the likelihood of arresting the disease is uncertain, and the physical sensations created by both the disease and the treatments are often vague. In addition to its ambiguity, cancer is a particularly frightening disease and the commonly held beliefs about cancer are overwhelmingly negative. For example, the term cancer quickly brings to mind thoughts of death, pain, disfigurement, incapacity, loneliness, helplessness, and hopelessness.

Since cancer patients often withdraw and become introspective, they are likely to become preoccupied with bodily sensations. The beliefs and attitudes of patients regarding cancer may lead them to interpret ambiguous sensations as pain and to overestimate the intensity of their pain. Such appraisals may result in further increases in anxiety. Anxiety, uncertainty, and unpredictability all lead to misinterpretations of sensations and to exacerbations of pain (Averill 1973; Beecher 1959; Bowers 1968; and Hill et al. 1952). It is in fact possible that some patients will continue to suffer even when the physical cause of pain is eliminated (Black 1979).

The Informational Component

In order to respond adaptively to the diagnosis of neoplastic disease patients require appropriate information. Certain information is needed to appraise events accurately, yet in most human affairs, especially those involving threat, information is frequently unclear or insufficient. In some countries (e.g., Great Britain) even the diagnosis of cancer is often withheld from the patient (Bond 1979) and here in the United States, there is some debate as to whether patients want to be informed of a diagnosis of cancer. When information is provided, the patient is often told about the nature of his or her tumor, how cancer cells proliferate, and the types of treatments available to attack the cancer cells. However, if pain is mentioned at all, the patient is often told only that drugs are available to control pain if it should arise. Patients are rarely informed as to whether their cancer is likely to produce any pain or what it might feel like. This is so despite the fact that pain is consistently reported as being one of the major fears and concerns of cancer patients. Failure to obtain information is likely to result in inaccurate expectations regarding pain and may even exacerbate mild levels of pain.

The amount and quality of information that patients have about the nature and seriousness of their illness, problems likely to be encountered, and the potential effects of the disease on all aspects of their lives, appears to influence the adaptive process across a diversity of diseases, including cancer (Turk 1979; Turk, Sobel, Follick, and Youkilis 1980; and Weisman and Sobel 1979). There is some debate in the literature regarding the relative utility of objective information on the impact of stress (for reviews of this issue, see Cohen 1979; Turk 1978a; and Turk and Genest 1979). It appears that objective information about one's illness will have an effect on the process of adaptation only if it (1) results in a more accurate assessment of the potential harm (i.e., corrects a previously unrealistic appraisal of threat), (2) reduces uncertainty and hence anxiety, or (3) suggests a certain mode of coping with the adjustive demands (Averill 1973).

Health-care providers working with terminally ill cancer patients often wonder whether or not patients should be told about the possibilities of pain. Since the likelihood of pain is on the mind of many cancer patients, rather than asking the question, "Should pain be discussed with patients?," a more appropriate question would be, "How should information about pain be presented to patients?" We inform patients that, on some occasions, they might experience bodily sensations as a result of their own emotional arousal and that they can be taught to employ different coping strategies to alleviate their arousal and consequently their pain. When sensations are perceived as painful and there is a physiological basis, patients can then use coping techniques that, if not capable of totally eliminating the pain, can at least reduce the intensity of the sensations and distress. Patients are also told that, at certain times, a combination of medications and coping techniques may be used to minimize their experience of pain. The important point is that ambiguous information and the fear of the unknown may be increasing the amount of suffering. Consider the case of the character Rubashov in Arthur Koestler's book *Darkness at Noon*:

> Rubashov has been beaten up repeatedly during his last imprisonment, but of this method (of torture) he only knew of hearsay. He had learned that every known physical pain was bearable; if only one knew beforehand exactly what was going to happen to one. . . . Really bad was only the unknown, which gave no chance to foresee one's reactions and no scale to calculate one's capacity of resistance. . . . He called to memory everything he knew about the subject 'steambath' (the name of the torture procedure). He imagined the situation in detail and tried to analyze the physical sensations to be expected, in order to rid them of their uncanniness. The important thing was not to let oneself be caught unprepared (1961: 56).

In short, the unknown is worse than the known, anticipation may be worse than reality. Providing patients with realistic information may reduce their emotional distress and thereby lessen their experience of pain.

Anticipatory Coping and Control

A second point evident from the Koestler quotation is that much of the coping process is anticipatory in nature. It has been suggested that preparations completed before pain actually materializes might short-circuit the negative emotions which exacerbate the perception of pain (Janis 1958). Even though many cancer patients do not report the presence of pain early in the progression of the disease, we have found that early intervention produces the best results. Finer (1979) comes to a similar conclusion regarding the efficacy of hypnosis to control the pain accompanying metastatic disease.

The cognitive-social learning approach is designed to address pain on a preventative basis, early in the course of the disease, by helping patients modify any thoughts, beliefs, or behaviors that produce anxiety and depression. In addition, the cognitive-social learning approach trains patients in the use of various coping skills that can be employed during episodes of recurrent pain. These skills include techniques designed to modify the sensory as well as the cognitive and the affective aspects of the pain experience. Through the use of a variety of cognitive and behavioral techniques, the cognitive-social learning approach enhances patients' perceptions of control and self-confidence. Increasing an individual's perception of control tends to reduce anxiety (Houston and Holmes 1974), decrease discomfort, and increase pain tolerance in laboratory studies (Bowers 1968; Glass et al. 1973; and Staub, Tursky, and Schwartz 1971). The cognitive-social learning approach has been successfully employed in the treatment of depression (Rush et al. 1977), anxiety-based dysfunction (see review in Meichenbaum 1977), and both laboratory (Horan et al. 1977; and Turk 1975, 1977) and clinical pain (Holroyd, Andrasik, and Westbrook 1976; Khamati and Rush 1978; Rybstein–Blinchik and Grzesiak 1977; Turk and Genest 1979; Turner 1979; and Wernick and Taylor 1979).

The research investigations of Project Omega (Weisman, Worden, and Sobel 1980; and Weisman and Sobel 1979) examine the utility of a cognitive-social learning approach in the reduction of emotional distress with vulnerable, at-risk cancer patients; that is, patients who appear likely to become particularly distressed at any time (Weisman and Worden 1977). The regimen employed by the Omega team emphasizes both problem-solving and tension reduction. Although the results of these studies are preliminary, they do demonstrate the utility of the cognitive-social learning perspective in reducing emotional distress. The authors did not directly attempt to enhance coping with intense physical sensations (although the inclusion of relaxation exercises may have been of some utility in this regard), nor did they assess the impact of their program on any indicators of pain. However, a specific pain management component could readily be incorporated into the program developed by these investigators (Sobel and Worden 1981).

In addition to its effect on the patient's feelings of distress and discomfort, perceptions of competence or self-efficacy also influence the willingness to cope in an adaptive fashion. For example, although a cancer patient might believe that relaxation exercises can help alleviate pain, the patient may not believe that he or she can successfully employ such exercises. If patients believe that psychological techniques are irrelevant or beyond their capabilities they may not even attempt to use them, and consequently, they never learn of the potential utility of such techniques (Turk 1980a). Therefore, the first step in any treatment program will consist of facilitating a patient's motivation and reducing resistance to participation (Meichenbaum and Gilmore 1980; and Turk, Meichenbaum, and Genest in press). We will have more to say about patient motivation when we describe the details of our cognitive-behavioral treatment regimen.

Our application of the cognitive-social learning approach and the specific cognitive and behavioral techniques for treating cancer pain will be described in the next section. However, a more detailed presentation of the specific techniques is available in a recent book completed by Turk and his colleagues, entitled *Pain and Behavioral Medicine* (Turk et al. in press) and in a set of audiotapes (Turk 1980c).

A COGNITIVE–SOCIAL LEARNING TREATMENT FOR CANCER PAIN

As noted earlier, cognitive-behavioral therapy is based on the rationale that affect and behavior are largely determined by the way individuals construe their world. Cognitive-behavioral therapy is designed to help patients identify, examine, and correct maladaptive thoughts and dysfunctional beliefs. In addition, it is a form of therapy that is directed at increasing the adequacy of a patient's behavioral repertoire. These two components of cognitive-behavioral treatment increase a patient's sense of self-mastery and control.

The techniques employed to bring about change include rational restructuring (see Chapter 6), coping-skills training, problem-solving training, and self-regulation training. These techniques are not mutually exclusive and overlap substantially. Rational restructuring is directed at helping patients identify maladaptive patterns of thinking, thus encouraging them to recognize the deleterious impact of such thinking. It also involves teaching patients how to supplant maladaptive thinking with more appropriate thought patterns and training them to become aware of environmental cues or internal cues that could be triggers for self-generated coping behaviors (Mahoney and Arnkoff 1978; and Turk 1981). Coping-skills training emphasizes the development of a flexible repertoire of cognitive and behavioral coping skills (relaxation, attention diversion, and so on.) (Goldfried 1971). Problem-solving training is designed to help patients learn how to specify problems, generate alternative solutions, tentatively select a solution, and then test the effectiveness of the solution (D'Zurilla and Goldfried 1971; and Sobel and Worden 1981). Self-regulation training consists of essentially three phases: self-monitoring, during which patients identify their typical pattern of responding; self-evaluation, when patients compare their performance to some personally established goal; and self-reinforcement, a phase of self-reward for achieving goals (Kanfer 1970). We have developed a cognitive-behavioral regimen for terminally ill patients that makes use of all of these techniques.

Cognitive-behavioral interventions are active, time-limited, structured forms of treatment. The cognitive-behavioral treatment protocol that we currently use is comprised of four general and overlapping phases: (1) pretreatment preparation; (2) conceptualization-translation; (3) coping-skills training; and (4) rehearsal.

It should be noted that, in addition to increasing a patient's ability to cope with the pain symptoms per se, the cognitive-behavioral regimen is designed to help patients cope with environmental factors that may prevent them from optimal functioning in general. As in the treatment approach described by Sobel and Worden (1981), and Weisman, Worden, and Sobel (1980), general problem-solving skills and cognitive restructuring techniques are woven into the fabric of the treatment. However, for the purposes of the present chapter, we will be focusing specifically on coping with emotional distress as it is related to the experience of pain.

Phase 1: Pretreatment Preparation

Many cancer patients believe that there is little they can do to alter the course of their disease, to improve the quality of their lives, or to control pain. This view of patient helplessness may be subtly fostered by those health-care providers who focus only on symptomatic treatment of the disease or palliation of pain. Often no suggestion is made that there may be much a patient can do to improve the quality of his or her life. Although there may be relatively little patients can actually do to control the progression of the disease (and even this has been challenged by Simonton, Matthews–Simonton, and Sparks 1980), there is a good deal they can do to control the emotional distress that may exacerbate pain. The cognitive-behavioral treatment protocol is designed to increase a patient's sense of control and resourcefulness, and thereby decrease a sense of helplessness (Weisman and Sobel 1979).

The absence of patient motivation is a major concern and must be addressed at two levels. First, health-care providers must understand the multidimensional conceptualization of pain on which the cognitive-behavioral approach is based. They must have some belief in the utility of this treatment approach and then convey this positive attitude to the patient (Meichenbaum and Gilmore 1980; and Turk et al. in press).

The second level on which motivation must be addressed is that of the patient. One initial concern of cancer patients is the fact that they are referred to a psychologist, social worker, or psychiatrist. Patients often perceive this as a suggestion that they are "crazy." The perception may then inhibit their willingness to engage in a cognitive-behavioral program. The cognitive-behavioral counselor must address this concern from the outset even if it is unstated. We address this issue in a forthright manner stating that all patients with serious diseases are confronted with many stresses and that experiencing distress (e.g., anxiety or depression) is normal and to be expected. We then note that the presence of various threats and problems can create pain or exacerbate mild levels of discomfort. We continue by providing some general orientation to the role of thoughts and feelings in the experience of pain. When we first contact patients we tell them the following:

> Pain seems to be an inevitable aspect of life, but few of us pay much attention to it until it strikes. We have all experienced it, and we fear it, but by and large we accept the idea that there is nothing we can do but endure it. Further, when we do encounter pain, we automatically turn to the physician and the pharmacist for relief. Tradition has taught us that pain is an involuntary sensation but we now know that this is incorrect, and we do ourselves a serious disservice if we continue to regard pain sensations as just automatic bodily functions. We now know that pain involves more than just automatic

bodily functions and physical sensations; it is influenced by our beliefs, attitudes, and emotions. Since you have some control over your own thoughts and feelings you may be able to do more than anyone else to reduce your pain and discomfort.

You have been referred to the cognitive-behavioral program because your physician believed that it would be useful in helping you control stress and pain. The techniques you will be taught have been found to reduce the stress and discomfort of many cancer patients treated. Many cancer patients never experience severe pain. Thus, the cognitive and behavioral skills may even short-circuit or prevent the development of significant amounts of pain.

One question that we are frequently asked by cancer patients is why they need to learn coping techniques when they can achieve reductions of pain simply by taking narcotics. We usually respond to this question by explaining that, although narcotics can be useful at certain times, many patients interpret relatively low intensities of discomfort as being severe pain because of emotional distress rather than physiological effects of the cancer itself. Reducing physiological arousal by using the techniques included in the training often leads to reduced needs for potent narcotics. We also inform patients that the body does build up a tolerance for narcotics and too frequent usage of these medications, when not essential, may require excessively high doses during the later course of the disease. Moreover, massive doses of narcotics may lead to undesirable side-effects such as drowsiness and confusion and thus make it difficult for the patient to have a satisfying and meaningful life. We hasten to add that should narcotics be required, they will be readily available.

At this point we ask patients to examine their own thoughts and feelings about cancer, particularly their feelings of frustration and helplessness. We proceed by describing how such negative thoughts and feelings can exacerbate pain. We acknowledge that it would not be surprising if they held some skepticism about the cognitive-behavioral treatment, but encourage them to hold this in check and at least give the treatment a try, as they really have nothing to lose and much to gain.

During this pretreatment stage, we lay the groundwork for the later stages of the intervention. We try to educate both health-care providers and patients about the nature and utility of the approach. Our best success with health-care providers, as well as patients, is obtained when they hear positive comments about the approach from patients who have gone through the training.

Phase 2: Conceptualization–Translation

A key feature of the cognitive-behavioral treatment is to facilitate the emergence of a new conceptualization of pain. The second phase of the treatment is designed to provide the patient with a framework for understanding the nature of the pain experience and, thereby, prepare the patient for subsequent therapeutic techniques. The conceptualization of pain described is based on the multidimensional model of pain outlined earlier in this chapter (Melzack 1973; and Melzack and Wall 1965). This multidimensional conceptualization is contrasted with the unidimensional model of pain held by most patients (that is, pain is a function of physical stimuli or tissue damage). The interactions of cognitive, affective, and sensory aspects of the pain experience are discussed and various examples are used to clarify this reconceptualization. For instance, the therapist might note the lack of pain reported by soldiers wounded in battle, or the ability of athletes to play despite pain and even without awareness of pain during competition. Many examples are available and the counselor tries to use those that are relevant for the particular patient.

Patients are encouraged to consider episodes in their own lives when feelings and cognitions may have exacerbated pain (e.g., waiting to receive an injection, sitting in the dentist's office). An important point to emphasize here is that the counselor makes every effort to involve the patient in treatment. Information and examples are not presented in a didactic fashion but in a Socratic dialogue. If the patient has experienced any pain since the diagnosis of cancer, then the counselor attempts to determine if the patient's thoughts and feelings might have contributed to exacerbations. The patient is asked to describe the feelings during the pain episode (e.g., "The tumor is growing," "The disease is spreading," "I feel helpless," "Nobody understands"), and the impact that these thoughts and feelings had on the pain intensity. We have found it useful to ask the patient to close his or her eyes and try to imagine the episode in as much detail as possible so that we can identify any maladaptive thoughts and affects. Often this is helpful in making the new conceptualization concrete and personally relevant.

Although cancer patients may initially report that their pain is always severe and uncontrollable, careful monitoring often shows that while it may be present most of the time, the intensity varies.

The patient is encouraged to view mild and moderate levels of pain as problems that he or she can prepare for and deal with. We inform patients that during the remainder of the training they will be learning skills that affect each of the three components of pain: they will be taught relaxation to control some of the sensory and affective aspects of pain, and cognitive techniques to control the cognitive and other affective components. An analogy we employ is that of an athletic team developing game plans during intergame periods. We find that learning and practicing coping skills, prior to the presence of pain episodes, lowers the risk of a patient becoming overwhelmed when recurrent pain appears.

During the second phase of treatment, patients are also encouraged to reconceptualize nonpain specific problems. Patients are taught to translate vague, undifferentiated, and overwhelming problems, both pain related and nonpain related, into difficulties that can be pinpointed and therefore viewed as solveable or modifiable.

Phase 3: Coping-Skills Training

During this phase the patient is taught a variety of coping skills that can be used to reduce pain and minimize stress. Both cognitive and behavioral strategies are employed. In teaching a patient skills for coping with situations more effectively, this training serves to enhance a sense of control.

Relaxation. In her observations of terminally ill patients at St. Christopher's Hospice, where three-fourths of the chief complaints are pain, Saunders (1976) observed that there was a direct correspondence between analgesic medication requirements and the patient's state of relaxation. Thus we usually begin the coping-skills training stage with relaxation exercises. These techniques are especially useful at this point in the skills-training phase because they can be readily learned by almost all patients and have a good deal of face validity.

The relaxation exercise that we use involves systematically tensing and relaxing various muscle groups, both general and specific to the particular area of pain reported by patients. To facilitate relaxation, patients are also instructed to visualize a pleasant scene (e.g., lying on the beach or walking through the forest) or to focus their attention on a word such as "calm" or "serene." By repeatedly pairing the same pleasant scene or word with the experience of relaxation, the scene or word itself elicits feelings of relaxation. We also incorporate controlled breathing into our treatment since research has demonstrated that the amplitude and frequency of respiration has an effect upon heart rate and the accompanying experience of anxiety.

Relaxation training serves several purposes. First, relaxation exercises can be used to reduce emotional arousal and, thereby, inhibit the production of pain. There are two ways this can happen. Emotional arousal frequently leads to physiological arousal or tension that either may be misinterpreted as pain or that can, itself, produce pain. Second, relaxation exercises may be employed by patients in reducing the intensity of pain once it is present. Finally, practice in the use of relaxation and controlled breathing strengthens a patient's belief that one can indeed exert some control during periods of stress and pain, and that one is not helpless or impotent.

A variety of relaxation training techniques are available (e.g., autogenic training, meditation, Jacobsonian relaxation). The counselor may want to become familiar with several so that patients can select the technique that is the most effective for them. Common problems that arise during relaxation training include mind-wandering, falling asleep, and intrusive disturbing thoughts. We find it useful to tell patients, at the outset, that such problems may occur and that it is not unusual. They are also told that, like any skill, relaxation requires practice. Should mind-wandering occur or intrusive thoughts become prevalent, patients are encouraged to use this event as a cue to try to clear their minds and to focus on their pleasant image or cue words. For some patients we find it helpful to provide audiotapes of relaxation for home use. Finally, we encourage patients to practice the relaxation exercise at home, at least twice a day, and to use relaxation whenever they feel anxious or experience pain.

Attention Diversion. One cancer patient described the pain in his jaw as a "little island of pain floating in a sea of indifference." The patient had received thirty operations and lived in pain for thirty years. The prosthesis he wore was awkward and painful, distorting his face and speech, but he took no analgesic medications and only in the terminal stage did he consent to taking aspirins. The patient was Sigmund Freud. Many similar cases can be found in the literature where, by employing a set of attentional, behavioral, and interpersonal coping skills, an individual is able to function in spite of pain and may even avoid pain.

The value of diversional activities is noted by several authors who treat cancer patients (Saunders 1979; Shawver 1977; and Twycross 1975, 1979). Saunders (1979) suggests that diversion of attention may be one of the best painkillers.

Before teaching patients various attention-diverting strategies we explain the important role of attention in pain and coping. Patients are told that attention is necessary for the perception of pain. We explain that people can only fully focus their attention on one thing at a time. Moreover, and although it requires considerable effort, they can control, to some extent, what they attend to. Various examples of the selective and amplifying functions of attention are discussed. We might point out that it is difficult to concentrate on completing income tax forms while rock music is playing in the background. Another example is the practice of counting sheep in order to become drowsy and fall asleep. Here the intention is to distract one's attention from thoughts or feelings that are interfering with sleep. Our objective is to communicate to the patient that people commonly employ various methods to acquire some degree of control.

A useful exercise is to have the patient close his or her eyes while the counselor directs attention to different sounds and sensations that the patient was unlikely to be aware of until called to attention (e.g., the humming of a florescent light, the conversation between people down the hall, the pressure of a watch on his or her wrist). We emphasize that their minds are like searchlights that can only fully focus light on one thing at a time.

Distraction or diversion can be operationalized in many ways, but for our purposes we will consider just two. The first is comprised of environmental stimulation techniques. These include participating in social events or occupational therapy, watching television, listening to music, or talking to someone. The environmental stimulation measures are self-evident and so we will not spend time elaborating on them. We encourage our patients to make lists of various environmental stimulation techniques that are relevant for them and we often give homework assignments designed to involve them in some of the activities that they generate.

The second category of diversional techniques consists of cognitive-coping strategies. These strategies involve having patients use their own cognitive processes to divert attention. These techniques are particularly useful for patients in the terminal stage, when energy is at a low level. One patient who had gone through our treatment program described these techniques as particularly useful when he woke up in the middle of the night, was too tired to read, and no one was available for conversation.

Attention-diverting cognitive-coping strategies probably have been employed since people first experienced pain (Meichenbaum and Turk 1976). A great deal of research focuses on the relative efficacy of various attention-diverting cognitive-coping strategies (Turk 1978b; and Wack and Turk 1980). Since no one type of coping strategy has been proven universally effective, we provide patients with training in the use of several types of strategies (e.g., focusing attention on different aspects of the environment, focusing on non-painful sensations, focusing on positive thoughts, and imagining oneself in a pleasant situation (Turk 1980c, 1980d).

It is important to underscore the point that patients take an active role in the selection of the specific cognitive-coping strategies they will employ. A variety of different strategies are discussed and patients are asked to generate lists of those that are personally relevant. Some patients find it helpful to write these out on 3 × 5 cards, thus carrying them along wherever they go.

Since some of the cognitive-coping strategies incorporate visual images, patients are given training in the use of imagery. We are now using guided imagery in which certain images are suggested to the patient. We encourage patients to employ as many senses as possible, since vividness and involvement in imagery have been shown to be important in distraction from noxious sensations in the laboratory (Turk 1977). An example of a guided image is that of a lemon on a white plate. We direct patients to imagine themselves slicing and smelling the lemon, feeling the sticky juice on their fingers, and tasting the lemon. It is the inclusion of various senses rather than the quality of the particular image that is critical. Sometimes we use images that patients suggest and then guide them through this patient-derived image.

This concludes the skills training phase of the treatment program. A major goal of this phase is to provide patients with a variety of skills that can be used to control physiological arousal, maladaptive thoughts, and maladaptive behaviors. We also attempt to foster a sense of resourcefulness to combat the pervasive sense of helplessness.

Phase 4: Rehearsal

In an attempt to consolidate the skills acquired to this point, and to reinforce a patient's sense of self-efficacy (Bandura 1977), we begin a practice phase. Two techniques are part of this treatment phase. In the first, we ask patients to imagine themselves in a situation in which they have experienced pain and to see themselves coping with the noxious sensations by using the various coping techniques. We ask them to provide a continuous monologue of their thoughts and feelings as well as of their behavior in the imagined situation. We acknowledge negative thoughts, but suggest that they use these as cues to switch to more adaptive modes of thinking. In addition, and since the effectiveness of a given technique is variable across situations, we encourage patients to experiment with different strategies.

A second technique used during the rehearsal phase is role-reversal. In this exercise, the patient and counselor reverse roles. The patient takes the role of a counselor who is going to teach the various coping techniques to a new patient. This enables the counselor to observe whether the patient has learned the skills adequately and to identify any area of confusion.

HOMEWORK

Homework assignments form an integral part of our treatment program, accompanying each phase of the protocol. Encouraging a patient to practice different coping strategies at home increases proficiency in the use of these skills. In addition, the homework tasks give a patient the opportunity to discover, while still in treatment, any problems that might arise in real life situations. We can then address these difficulties in treatment, help a patient to generate alternative solutions, and thereby reduce the likelihood that he or she will give up before mastering the coping skills. This is particularly important during the early stages of treatment when self-efficacy is low (Bandura 1977).

We assign homework that consists of graded tasks gradually increasing in difficulty over the course of treatment. For example, we begin by encouraging patients to use the relaxation exercises when pain is at a low level or not present, rather than when the pain is most intense. This enables patients to experience some success using these techniques and thus increases their sense of competence. As they master various coping techniques, we suggest that they employ them when the pain or distress is more severe.

In summary, we are finding the cognitive-behavioral treatment to be an effective method for reducing a patient's experience of pain. Moreover, this approach increases the patient's sense of control and mastery over life. This increased sense of control seems to enhance a patient's self-esteem and improve the quality of life, even when pain is not completely eliminated.

COPING WITH PAIN IN THE TERMINAL STAGE

Whenever possible we try to work with patients prior to the terminal stage of their illness. There are three major reasons for this. First, physical factors associated with the disease process may interfere with patients learning and using some of the techniques we have described. Second, many patients in the terminal stage have been given massive doses of analgesics and psychotrophic medications and may be heavily sedated. Finally, proficiency in the use of coping skills requires practice and there may be insufficient time for this to be achieved during the terminal stage. Despite these limitations, relaxation training and various cognitive-coping strategies have proven to be of some use even at the final stage of life. Much to some physicians' surprise, patients seem less distressed and require smaller doses of analgesics following relaxation training.

CONCLUSIONS AND SUMMARY

In the beginning of this chapter, we alerted the reader to the importance of psychological factors in pain. We discussed some of the inadequacies in viewing pain as simply a function of tissue damage.

We then, very briefly, reviewed the most frequently employed approaches to pain management in cancer. These include medical and surgical techniques, psychologically oriented approaches, and the more comprehensive hospice approach.

In the third part of the chapter we provided an overview of the cognitive-social learning perspective that emphasizes the importance of an individual's thoughts and feelings on the perception of both sensory phenomena and environmental situations. We suggested that the cognitive-social learning perspective was analogous to the multidimensional model of pain (Melzack and Wall 1965). We reviewed the reasons why the cognitive-social learning approach is particularly relevant for cancer patients. As emphasized, the approach was designed to train patients in the use of self-control techniques and thereby enhance perceptions of resourcefulness and competence.

In the final section of the chapter, we provided a detailed description of a cognitive-social learning regimen that we developed for use with cancer patients. The treatment protocol includes training in the use of a number of cognitive and behavioral coping skills that are designed to enhance the cancer patient's sense of control and competence, and thus reduce emotional distress and pain. We described several cognitive and behavioral procedures that are used to increase the likelihood that patients will employ these coping skills in their natural environment, even after treatment sessions have ended. Additionally, we emphasized the importance of educating health-care providers and increasing patient motivation.

We do not intend the cognitive-social learning regimen to be viewed as a rigid program. The content of the training should be developed in collaboration with the patient. The counselor must be flexible in the use of various phases of the training. Furthermore, we do not view the treatment protocol as a panacea nor do we see it as divorced from traditional pain-management approaches. Rather, we view this approach as a valuable addition to the health-care provider's pain-management armamentarium. We believe that helping the patient acquire new coping skills will result in increased perception of competence and reductions in pain intensity. Thus it is our hope that the cognitive-social learning approach will lead to an improvement in the quality of a patient's remaining days and months.

REFERENCES

Aitken–Swan, J. Nursing the later cancer patient at home: The family's impression. *Practitioner*, 1959, *183*, 64–69.

American Cancer Society. *Cancer facts and figures.* New York: American Cancer Society, 1978.

Averill, J.R. Personal control over aversive stimuli and its relationship to stress. *Psychological Bulletin*, 1973, *80*, 286–303.

Bandura, A. Self-efficacy: Toward a unified theory of behavioral change. *Psychological Review*, 1977, *84*, 191–215.

Barber, J., and Gitelson, J. Cancer pain: Psychological management using hypnosis. *CA*, 1980, *30*, 130.

Barber, T. Toward a theory of pain: Relief of chronic pain by prefrontal leucotomy, opiates, placebos, and hypnosis. *Psychological Bulletin*, 1959, *56*, 430–460.

Beecher, H. Pain in men wounded in battle. *Annals of Surgery*, 1946, *123*, 96–105.

Beecher, H. *Measurement of subjective responses.* New York: Oxford University Press, 1959.

Black, P. Management of cancer pain: An overview. *Neurosurgery*, 1979, *5*, 507–518.

Bond, M. Psychological and emotional aspects of cancer pain. In J. Bonica and V. Ventafridda (Eds.), *Advances in pain research and therapy*, vol. 2. New York: Raven Press, 1979.

Bonica, J. Importance of the problem. In J. Bonica and V. Ventafridda (Eds.), *Advances in pain research and therapy*, vol. 2. New York: Raven Press, 1979.

Bonica, J., and Ventafridda, V. *Advances in pain research and therapy*, vol. 2. New York: Raven Press, 1979.

Bowers, K. Pain, anxiety, and perceived control. *Journal of Consulting and Clinical Psychology*, 1968, *32*, 596–602.

Byron, R., and Yonemoto, R. Pain associated with malignancy. In B. Crue, Jr. (Ed.), *Pain research and treatment.* New York: Academic Press, 1975.

Chapman, C. Psychologic and behavioral aspects of pain. In J. Bonica and V. Ventafridda (Eds.), *Advances in pain research and therapy*. New York: Raven Press, 1979.

Cohen, F. Personality, stress, and the development of physical illness. In G. Stone, F. Cohen, and N. Adler (Eds.), *Health psychology*. San Francisco: Jossey–Bass, 1979.

D'Zurilla, T., and Goldfried, M. Problem-solving and behavior modification. *Journal of Abnormal Psychology*, 1971, *78*, 107–126.

Finer, B. Hypnotherapy in pain of advanced cancer. In J. Bonica and V. Ventafridda (Eds.), *Advances in pain research and therapy*, vol. 2. New York: Raven Press, 1979.

Fotopoulos, S., Graham, C., and Cook, M. Psychophysiologic control of cancer pain. In J. Bonica and V. Ventafridda (Eds.), *Advances in pain research and therapy*, vol. 2. New York: Raven Press, 1979.

Freeman, W., and Watts, J. *Psychosurgery in the treatment of mental disorders and intractable pain*, 2nd ed. Springfield, Ill.: Charles C. Thomas, 1950.

Glass, D., Singer, J., Leonard, H., Krantz, D., Cohen, S., and Cummings, H. Perceived control of aversive stimulation and the reduction of stress responses. *Journal of Personality*, 1973, *41*, 577–595.

Goldfried, M. Systematic desensitization as training in self-control. *Journal of Consulting and Clinical Psychology*, 1971, *37*, 228–234.

Hilgard, E., and Hilgard, J. *Hypnosis in the relief of pain*. Los Altos, Calif.: William Kaufman, Inc., 1975.

Hill, H., Kornetsky, C., Flanary, H., and Wikler, A. Effects of anxiety and morphine on discrimination of painful stimuli. *Journal of Clinical Investigation*, 1952, *31*, 473.

Holroyd, K., Andrasik, F., and Westbrook, T. Cognitive control of tension headache. *Cognitive Therapy and Research*, 1977, *1*, 121–134.

Horan, J., Hackett, G., Buchanan, J., Stone, C., and Demchik–Stone, D. Coping with pain: A component analysis of stress-inoculation. *Cognitive Therapy and Research*, 1977, *1*, 211–221.

Houde, R. The use and misuse of narcotics in the treatment of chronic pain. In J. Bonica (Ed.), *Advances in neurology*, vol. 4. New York: Raven Press, 1974.

Houston, B., and Holmes, D. Effect of avoidant thinking and reappraisal for coping with threat involving temporal uncertainty. *Journal of Personality and Social Psychology*, 1974, *30*, 382–388.

Janis, I. *Psychological stress: Psychoanalytic and behavioral study of surgical patients*. New York: John Wiley and Sons, 1958.

Kanfer, F.H. Self-regulation: Research, issues and speculation. In C. Neuringer (Ed.), *Behavior modification in clinical psychology*. New York: Appleton–Century–Crofts, 1970.

Khatami, M., and Rush, A. A pilot study of the treatment of outpatients with chronic pain: Symptom control, stimulus control and social system intervention. *Pain*, 1978, *5*, 163–173.

Koestler, A. *Darkness at noon*. New York: New American Library, 1961.

Lazarus, R. *Psychological stress and the coping process*. New York: McGraw–Hill, 1966.

Mahoney, M., and Arnkoff, D. Cognitive and self-control therapies. In S. Garfield and A. Bergin (Eds.), *Handbook of psychotherapy and behavior change*, 2nd ed. New York: John Wiley and Sons, 1978.

Meichenbaum, D. *Cognitive-behavior modification: An integrative approach*. New York: Plenum Press, 1977.

Meichenbaum, D., and Gilmore, J. Resistance: From a cognitive–behavioral perspective. In P. Wachtel (Ed.), *Resistance in psychodynamic and behavioral therapies*. New York: Plenum Press, 1980.

Meichenbaum, D., and Turk, D. The cognitive-behavioral management of anxiety, anger, and pain. In P. Davidson (Ed.), *The behavioral management of anxiety, depression and pain*. New York: Brunner/Mazel, 1976.

Melzack, R. *The puzzle of pain.* Hammondsworth, England: Penguin Books, 1973.

Melzack, R., and Casey, K. Sensory, motivational, and central control determinants of pain: A new conceptual model. In D. Kenshalo (Ed.), *The skin senses.* Springfield, Ill.: Charles C. Thomas, 1968.

Melzack, R., Ofiesh, J., and Mount, B. The Brompton mixture: Effects on pain in cancer patients. *Canadian Medical Association Journal,* 1976, *115,* 125–129.

Melzack, R., and Wall, P. Pain mechanisms: A new theory. *Science,* 1965, *150,* 971.

Mount, B. The problem of caring for the dying in a general hospital: The palliative care unit as a possible solution. *Canadian Medical Association Journal,* 1976, *115,* 119.

Mount, B., Ajemian, I., and Scott, J. Use of the Brompton mixture in treating the chronic pain of malignant disease. *Canadian Medical Association Journal,* 1976, *115,* 122–124.

Murphy, T. Cancer pain. *Postgraduate Medicine,* 1973, *53,* 187–194.

Rush, A., Beck, A., Kovacs, M., and Hollon, S. Comparative efficacy of cognitive therapy and pharmacotherapy in the treatment of depressed outpatients. *Cognitive Therapy and Research,* 1977, *1,* 17–38.

Rybstein–Blinchik, E., and Grzesiak, R. *Cognitive strategies in the treatment of chronic pain: A preliminary study.* Paper presented at the 11th Annual Convention of the Association for the Advancement of Behavior Therapy. Atlanta, December, 1977.

Saunders, C. *The management of terminal illness.* London: Hospital Medicine Publications, Ltd., 1967.

Saunders, C. Control of pain in terminal cancer. *Nursing Times,* 1976, *72,* 1133–1135.

Saunders, C. The nature of terminal pain and the hospice concept. In J. Bonica and V. Ventafridda (Eds.), *Advances in pain research and therapy,* vol. 2. New York: Raven Press, 1979.

Shawver, M. Pain associated with cancer. In A. Jacox (Ed.), *Pain: A source book for nurses and other health professionals.* Boston: Little, Brown and Company, 1977.

Siegel, S. Evidence from rats that morphine tolerance is a learned response. *Journal of Comparative and Physiological Psychology,* 1975, *89,* 498–506.

Siegel, S. Morphine tolerance acquisition as an associative process. *Journal of Experimental Psychology: Animal Behavior Processes,* 1977, *3,* 1–13.

Simonton, O., Matthews–Simonton, S., and Sparks, T. Psychological intervention in the treatment of cancer. *Psychosomatics,* 1980, *21,* 226–233.

Sobel, H. J. Review of the current literature: Coping with cancer. *Behavioral Medicine Newsletter,* 1979, *1,* 6–9.

Sobel, H. J., and Worden, J.W. *Helping cancer patients cope.* New York: BMA and Guilford Press, 1981.

Staub, E., Tursky, B., and Schwartz, G. Self-control and predictability: Their effects on reactions to aversive stimulation. *Journal of Personality and Social Psychology*, 1971, *18*, 157–162.

Swerdlow, M. Relieving pain in the terminally-ill. *Geriatrics*, 1973, 100–103.

Toomey, T., Ghia, J., Mao, W., and Gregg, J. Acupuncture and chronic pain mechanisms: The moderating effects of affect, personality, and stress on response to treatment. *Pain*, 1977, *3*, 137–145.

Turk, D. *Cognitive control of pain: A skills training approach.* Unpublished master's thesis, University of Waterloo, Ontario, Canada, 1975.

Turk, D. *A coping-skills training approach for the control of experimentally-induced pain.* Unpublished doctoral dissertation, University of Waterloo, Ontario, Canada, 1977.

Turk, D. Cognitive-behavioral techniques in the management of pain. In J. Foreyt and D. Rathjen (Eds.), *Cognitive behavior therapy: Research and application.* New York: Plenum Press, 1978a.

Turk, D. *Coping with pain: A review of cognitive control techniques.* Unpublished manuscript, Yale University, New Haven, Connecticut, 1978b.

Turk, D. Factors influencing the adaptive process with chronic illness. In I. Sarason and C. Spielberger (Eds.), *Stress and anxiety*, vol. 6. Washington, D.C.: Hemisphere Publishing Corporation, 1979.

Turk, D. *The role of metacognition in health and illness.* Paper presented at the annuel meeting of the American Psychological Association, Montreal, September, 1980a.

Turk, D. *A cognitive-behavioral approach to pain management.* Paper presented at the 2nd annual meeting of the American Pain Society, New York, September, 1980b.

Turk, D. *A cognitive-behavioral approach for the management of pain.* New York: Biomonitoring Audiocassettes, 1980c.

Turk, D. Cognitive behavioral techniques for the control of pain: A skills training manual. *JSAS Selected Documents in Psychology*, 1980d, *10*, 17 (MS. 2002).

Turk, D. Cognitive learning approaches: Applications in health care. In D. Doleys, R. Meredith, and A. Ciminero (Eds.), *Behavioral medicine: Assessment and treatment strategies.* New York: John Wiley and Sons, 1981.

Turk, D., and Genest, M. Regulation of pain: The application of cognitive and behavioral techniques for prevention and remediation. In P. Kendall and S. Hollon (Eds.), *Cognitive-behavioral interventions: Theory, research, and procedures.* New York: Academic Press, 1979.

Turk, D., Meichenbaum, D., and Genest, M. *Pain and behavioral medicine.* New York: Guilford Press, in press.

Turk, D., Sobel, H., Follick, M., and Youkilis, H. A sequential criterion analysis for assessing coping with chronic illness. *Journal of Human Stress*, 1980, *6*, 35–40.

Turnbull, F. Pain and suffering in cancer. *The Canadian Nurse*, 1971, *67*, 28.–30.

Turner, J. *Evaluation of two behavioral interventions for chronic low back pain.* Unpublished doctoral dissertation, University of California at Los Angeles, 1979.

Twycross, R. Disease of the central nervous system: Relief of pain. *British Medical Journal*, 1975, *4*, 212–214.

Twycross, R. The Brompton cocktail. In J. Bonica and V. Ventafridda (Eds.), *Advances in pain research and therapy*, vol. 2. New York: Raven Press, 1979.

Wack, J., and Turk, D. *Discovering latent structures in strategies for coping with pain.* Paper presented at the 2nd annual meeting of the American Pain Society, New York, September, 1980.

Weisenberg, M. Pain and pain control. *Psychological Bulletin*, 1977, *84*, 1008–1044.

Weisman, A., and Sobel, H. Coping with cancer through self-instruction: A hypothesis. *Journal of Human Stress*, 1979, *5*, 3–8.

Weisman, A., and Worden, J. *Coping and vulnerability in cancer patients.* Boston, Mass.: Research report of Project Omega, 1977.

Weisman, A., Worden, J., and Sobel, H. *Psychosocial screening and intervention with cancer patients.* Boston, Mass.: Research report of Project Omega, 1980.

Wernick, R., and Taylor, P. *Pain management in severely burned patients.* Paper presented at the 25th annual meeting of the Southeastern Psychological Association, New Orleans, Louisiana, March, 1979.

5 SOME OBSERVATIONS ON BEHAVIORAL APPROACHES TO THE TREATMENT OF GRIEF AMONG THE ELDERLY

James R. Averill and
Patricia A. Wisocki

In this chapter we will discuss briefly six related topics: (1) the importance of grief from a public health and from a humanitarian point of view; (2) characteristic reactions during grief; (3) the origins of grief—biological, psychological, and sociocultural; (4) grief reactions among the elderly; (5) anticipatory grief; and (6) the application of behavioral techniques to the treatment of normal and pathological grief reactions.

A separate chapter could be devoted to each of these issues, and hence our treatment of them must be cursory. However, we have not sacrificed depth for breadth of coverage without reason. Our overriding concern in this chapter is how grief can best be alleviated among the aged. A more specific concern is the application of behavior therapy to assist the elderly following bereavement. Unfortunately, little empirical research is available that is directly relevant to either of these concerns; most research on grief focuses on younger populations, and behavior therapy is not widely applied to the sequelae of bereavement. Our goal, therefore, is not to prescribe a particular mode of treatment, but to place the relevant issues in

Preparation of this chapter was supported, in part, by a grant from the National Science Foundation (BNS-7924471) to Dr. Averill for work on the social foundations of emotional behavior. The behavioral assessment strategies and clinical recommendations contained in the chapter are primarily the result of the work of Dr. Wisocki with elderly patients. However, all of the ideas expressed are the product of the collaboration of both authors.

perspective in the hope that further research will soon be forth-coming.

GRIEF AS A PUBLIC HEALTH AND AS A HUMANITARIAN PROBLEM

Most of us can think of first-hand examples of an elderly person who died shortly after bereavement, the death apparently hastened by the trauma of loss. Such episodes, because they are especially dramatic and poignant, may influence our theorizing. But how common are they? To what extent is bereavement a public health problem, especially for the aged, as well as an obvious humanitarian concern?

In addition to numerous case histories and anecdotal reports, two main types of studies have been used to assess the impact of bereavement on the health of the survivor. Retrospective or cross-sectional studies have compared the morbidity and mortality rates of bereaved persons with the corresponding rates for married persons of a similar age. Prospective or longitudinal studies have identified persons who have suffered a loss, and have followed their course of development during the first few years of bereavement. After reviewing the results of both types of research, Epstein et al. (1975) conclude that "the risk of dying is at least twice as great for widows and widowers at all age levels for a great variety of diseases" (541).

However, there are major methodological difficulties with the types of studies on which the above conclusion is based. For example, cross-sectional studies using morbidity statistics typically fail to take into account factors that might have affected the health of both the deceased and the bereaved. An illustration of this is the case of an accident in which one spouse is killed immediately and the other dies from injuries six weeks later. Longitudinal studies are better able to control for such potential artifacts, but longitudinal studies are rare, they generally employ small and not necessarily representative samples of subjects, and most importantly, they have yielded inconsistent results.

When potentially confounding factors and negative findings are taken into account, Stroebe et al. (in press) conclude that there is little direct evidence that bereavement increases the risk of mortality. They qualify this conclusion, however, by noting that indirect evidence is sufficient to warrant continued research in this area. Even if there were no evidence for increased mortality, there is reason to believe that grief often contributes to a wide variety of minor somatic and psychological disorders.

Based on her own longitudinal studies and on the research of others, Clayton (1979) draws the following tentative conclusions regarding the effects of bereavement on health. First, during the first year of bereavement, young widows and widowers tend to have more hospitalizations for somatic complaints and receive more psychoactive drugs (tranquilizers, sedatives, and so on) than their married counterparts. Second, older widows and widowers differ little from control subjects in this respect, unless they were already ill before bereavement. Third, there does not appear to be any difference between widowed and control subjects in the amount of psychiatric care and hospitalization during the first year of bereavement. Fourth, there is probably no increase in mortality rates for young widows and widowers; however, older widowers, but not older widows, may be at a greater risk.

For certain groups (e.g., older men, persons who are already ill), then, bereavement may increase the chance of morbidity. For the most part, however, bereavement does not pose as great a risk to health as has sometimes been assumed. Moreover, even in cases where bereavement is followed by a deterioration in health, the specific etiology may be difficult to identify. Bereavement is a time of great stress, and stress may exacerbate existing health problems and lower resistance to pathogens (e.g., by suppression of the immune system). Also, the loneliness and social isolation following the death of a spouse may lead to alcohol abuse and other behavior patterns detrimental to health. But is grief a disease, as Engel (1961) and Frederick (1976–77) propose?

Grief is a normal response and not a form of pathology. Only in the sense that it is the source of great anguish can it be considered truly a *dis*-ease. It is difficult to imagine a world without grief. A parent who does not mourn the loss of a child, a spouse who does not grieve at the death of a mate, a friend who is not saddened by the departure of a companion—such persons are to be pitied, not envied. The problem, then, is not to eliminate grief, but to understand it; and, with understanding, to alleviate some of the anguish of grief.

CHARACTERISTIC REACTIONS DURING GRIEF

Since Lindemann's (1944) classic description of grief, the sequelae of bereavement and loss have been investigated in great depth by a number of authors, including Bowlby (1980), Gorer (1965), and Parkes (1972). Typically, grief is depicted as developing in four stages:

1. *Shock.* This is a common first reaction to any disaster, not just bereavement. It is characterized by a dazed sense of unreality or numbing that may last from a few hours to a few days.

2. *Protest and yearning.* In this stage, the loss is recognized but not entirely accepted. There is protest over the fact of loss and attempts are made to retrieve the lost object symbolically if not actually. Behaviorally, this is a time of agitation and heightened physiological arousal; cognitively, there is a preoccupation with memories of the lost object and a focusing of attention on those aspects of the environment that were associated with past pleasures. There is no exact time limit on any of the stages of grief, but as a very rough guideline, this second stage of protest and yearning typically lasts for several months.

3. *Disorganization and despair.* This is perhaps the most enduring, complex, and difficult stage in the grief process. Although the fact of loss may be accepted and attempts to recover the lost object abandoned, a bitter pining remains. Apathy, withdrawal, and despondency are common during this period, as are a loss of sexual interest, poor eating habits, sleep disturbances, and other behavioral and somatic problems. As if these symptoms were not burdensome enough, despair, hostility, shame, and guilt may be added to the cacophony of dysphoric emotion.

4. *Detachment and reorganization.* The symptoms of the previous stage are ultimately relieved when the bereaved develops new ways of perceiving and thinking about the world and his or her place within it. Most often, this involves the establishment of new object relationships, new roles, and a new sense of purpose in life. Several years may be required before a relatively adequate readjustment occurs, even in cases of normal grief.

The conception of grief as progressing in stages is criticized by Bugen (1977) on the grounds that the presumed stages shade into one another dynamically; that they are not necessarily successive (e.g., disorganization may occur concurrently with or even precede protest); that some stages may be greatly abbreviated or short-circuited entirely; and that the intensity of the stages may vary markedly as a function of individual and situational variables.

Bugen is certainly correct in pointing out the logical and empirical difficulties of a conception of grief in foreordained stages. It is important to recognize, however, that grief is not a grab bag of individual symptoms without internal coherence. Grief is a process, a progression, a way of coming to terms with a new reality. The more disorganized the process, the more difficult its course is liable to be. Ramsay (1979) states the issue well:

> In spite of Bugen's criticisms of the stages model, we feel that in planning and carrying out therapy, it is useful to have a general idea of what a grief process consists of, even though individual differences are great. For example, there is almost invariably a stage of desolation, with uncontrollable crying outbursts. If this has not occurred, we can be fairly sure that the whole process has been delayed or distorted. If there has been no experience of protest and aggression, that lends weight to our hypothesis of pathology. Add to all this, continuing searching behavior long after the death of the loved one, and we can safely say that the process has not yet been worked through (220).

Ramsay (1979) does agree with Bugen, however, that in many instances it might be better to speak of the *components*—rather than stages—of grief, provided we recognize that some components may predominate early in the process and others later (Ramsay and Happée 1977).

THE ORIGINS OF GRIEF

Before considering in greater detail some of the variations that may occur in grief, it might be helpful to view the entire syndrome from a broad perspective. In many respects, grief is a paradoxical reaction. Bereavement calls for action: old responses must be extinguished and new patterns of behavior established. Yet much of the behavior of the bereaved is antithetical to such goals. The withdrawal, apathy, hostility, loss of sexual interest, and so forth are not conducive to the establishment of new object relationships. In Fruedian terms, grief involves a suspension of one of the most fundamental principles of mental functioning—the pleasure principle. Why should this be so? The entire syndrome of grief makes sense only if we consider its origins in the biological, psychological, and social history of the individual.

Biological Origins of Grief

Human beings are a social species. As with other higher primates, group living is one of our primary adaptations. But what bonds hold the group together? Positive rewards (such as sex) are not sufficient. Attachment to other human beings seems to be rewarding; and, conversely, separation is a source of profound distress. It has been hypothesized (by Averill 1968; Bowlby 1969; and others) that grief-like reactions have evolved to help ensure group cohesiveness in species where a social form of existence is necessary for survival. This hypothesis is based on two assumptions: (1) that one way to ensure group cohesion is by making separation from the group, or from specific members of the group, a painful experience and hence one to be avoided; and (2) that in cases where separation cannot be avoided, as in death, the relevant reactions may nevertheless run their biological course, often to the distress and even physical detriment of the bereaved. These two assumptions help to explain the preemptory quality and tenacity of some of the reactions that occur during the protest and despair stages of grief, respectively.

No attempt will be made here to review the evidence in support of the above assumptions (see Averill 1979). Rather, we will simply describe three lines of evidence in support of the general thesis that grief is, at least in part, a biologically based syndrome.

The Universality of Grief. The capacity for grief, and at least some of its symptoms, appears to be universal among human beings. Most of the detailed studies of grief involve Westerners (Europeans and Americans). One study, however, conducted in Japan (Yamamoto et al. 1969) indicates a great deal of overlap in symptomatology between Japanese and Westerners following bereavement. Analyses of the ethnographic records of a wide variety of different cultures (Rosenblatt, Walsh, and Jackson 1976) also suggests that some of the symptoms of grief may be observed universally.

We do not wish to deny the fact that there are major differences in grief, reflecting culture-specific differences in mourning practices. Thus we speak of the *capacity* for grief, and of *some* of the symptoms of grief, rather than of grief per se. Perhaps an analogy will make our meaning clear. All normal human beings have the capacity for language, and some aspects of language may be universal. Nevertheless, any language (e.g., English, Russian, or Chinese) is specific to a given cultural or linguistic group. Similarly, grief may vary considerably from one culture to another and still be universal in some of its aspects.

The Phylogeny of Grief. Grief-like reactions are also observed in infra-human primates. One example of an abnormally severe reaction in an adolescent chimpanzee will illustrate the kind of observations that have been made repeatedly in both laboratory and field settings. The incident occurred at the Gombe Research Center in Tanzania, and is described by Hamburg, Hamburg, and Barchas (1975). Flint (the chimpanzee's name) was eight and one-half years old when his mother died. Although an adolescent, he was very attached to his mother. He shared her nest almost every night and seldom travelled independently of her. Following his mother's death, Flint was observed almost continually until his own death twenty-five days later. Hamburg et al. (1975) describe his behavior during these twenty-five days:

> He became increasingly tense and apathetic. He sat for long periods in a huddled posture and lost interest in the environment. He was largely unresponsive to stimulation by other chimpanzees. He ate very little and lost one-third of his body weight over several weeks. On 16 evenings he nested alone, most in old nests which he probably shared with Flo (his mother). On the five occasions that he nested away from the stream with a group, he was with an older brother. He also moved with his older sister on several occasions. His eyes had a wide, frightened look which never left them. He found it increasingly difficult to travel more than short distances. Most of the remainder of his life was spent in the vicinity of the place where Flo died. Perhaps his cessation of eating and drastic weight loss heightened his vulnerability to infectious agents (247–248).

The Ontogeny of Grief. The relative independence of a response from direct learning experience is another line of evidence that supports the argument of a biological basis of grief. Human infants, after about six months of age, display many of the symptoms of grief if separated from their mothers or other attachment figures. Prior experience is, of course, necessary for the formation of the attachment; but the protest, yearning, and despair that follows separation does not need to be learned. Somewhat similar considerations apply to the reactions of a mother to the loss of an infant. This is a very potent source of grief, even though the loss may have occurred (e.g., shortly after childbirth) before there was occasion to build up a behavioral repertoire focused on the infant.

It is not entirely clear whether the same mechanisms that mediate the reactions of an infant to the loss of a mother, and vice versa, also mediate the reactions of one adult to the loss of another (e.g., conjugal bereavement). There may be different kinds of grief, biologically speaking, depending upon the nature of the loss. However, the simplest hypothesis (and one which is supported by a fair amount of evidence) is that there is considerable overlap and developmental continuity between infant and adult reactions to separation. Indeed, abnormally severe grief reactions in adults can sometimes be traced to traumatic separations during childhood.

The Psychological Origins of Grief

The above considerations do not mean that grief is an invariable response, uninfluenced by situational factors, or that psychological mechanisms do not play an important role in determining the symptomatology of grief. The psychological determinants of grief may be divided into two broad categories which we will call "negative" and "positive."

Negative Determinants. One of the most commonly reported complaints among the bereaved, particularly the elderly bereaved, is a loss of meaning or purpose in life. This theme has been echoed by a number of theorists. For example, Parkes (1971, 1975) attributes grief to the disruption of a person's "assumptive world," and Marris (1975), to the disruption of "structures of meaning." It is not easy, and may not even be possible, to give a completely behavioristic interpretation of these concepts. It may be said that for behavior to be meaningful, three conditions must be met: (1) the occasion for the response must be appropriate; (2) the response must meet socially accepted standards of performance; and (3) the response must be followed by relevant consequences. After bereavement, one or more of these conditions may no longer be fulfilled. For example, (1) the bereaved may continue to respond to situations as though the deceased were still alive; (2) the behavior may be exaggerated, inhibited, or otherwise misguided due to the loss of feedback (social comparison) previously provided by the deceased; and (3) the response may no longer be followed by customary rewards and punishments. All of these deficits may contribute to the symptoms of grief, but we will limit ourselves to a few observations on the loss of reinforcement since it has been the topic of the most research and speculation.

An amazingly wide range of behavior, from the most trivial (e.g., which television program to watch) to the most important (e.g., pursuing a career) may ultimately derive their meaning from day-to-day interactions with another person (e.g., a child or a spouse). Should that person die, many responses are no longer reinforced and hence become extinct. As is well known, extinction can be a painful and frustrating process, even for a rat in a Skinner box, not to mention for a bereaved widow or widower who has built up a repertoire of responses during a lifetime of shared experiences with the deceased.

At first, it might appear that extinction offers a simple explanation for many of the symptoms of grief. The simplicity is somewhat deceptive. Extinction implies a reduction of reinforcement. Following bereavement, reinforcement may be reduced for any of four different reasons: (1) customary reinforcers, for example, those directly dependent on the presence of the deceased, may no longer be available; (2) customary reinforcers, although available, may no longer be effective, as when a previously pleasurable activity becomes affectively neutral; (3) the person may no longer have the desire or ability to make the responses required to achieve reinforcement (e.g., due to apathy); or (4) the person may refrain from responding because of negative consequences (e.g., when the response serves as a painful reminder of the deceased or is a source of guilt or social criticism).

Thus, although a reduction in reinforcement may explain some of the symptoms of grief, the reduction itself must be explained and overcome. Similar observations could be made of other psychological mechanisms that are proposed to account for some, if not most, of the symptoms of grief: for example, learned helplessness (Seligman 1975), the interruption of behavior (Mandler 1975), and negative cognitive appraisals (Beck 1976). Such factors undoubtedly help determine certain components of grief, yet their scope and mode of operation are poorly understood.

Positive Determinants.   Bereavement calls for compassion and support. Moreover, bereavement offers a rationale for behavior that might otherwise be unacceptable (e.g., withdrawal from social obligations, alcohol abuse). It is not surprising, therefore, that people may sometimes use their grief to achieve secondary gains.

Snowdon, Solomons, and Druce (1978) observed twelve cases of feigned bereavement in a London teaching hospital during an eighteen-month period. Several of these patients were evidently motivated by monetary gain (i.e., their bereavement was a deliberate fraud). In the remaining cases, however, the fraud (if one wishes to call it that) was perpetuated by the patients on themselves. These patients showed, in varying degrees of intensity, genuine anguish, depression, and even self-destructive behavior.

Twelve cases is not a large number. However, to feign bereavement and to experience some of the common symptoms of grief, represents only the tip of the proverbial iceberg. How many persons who have actually suffered bereavement cultivate their grief for the rewards it brings, in spite of the intensification of anguish that they also must endure? The answer is probably most people, if only to a very limited extent.

The Social Origins of Grief

Death, like birth, is an event of considerable importance for society as well as for the individual (and the species). It is not surprising, therefore, that most cultures have developed rather elaborate mourning practices. The primary function of these practices is to be found on the social and not the individual level of analysis. Mourning rites allow surviving members of the group to realign commitments, renew allegiances, and reinforce the fabric of society under conditions that are potentially disruptive. From this perspective, grief can be viewed as a *transitory social role* (Averill 1980); like any other social role, grief entails certain obligations as well as benefits.

The obligations imposed by society are not always in the best interest of the bereaved. To cite an extreme example, many societies throughout history have expected the bereaved to follow the deceased in death (i.e., to commit suicide). This obligation has typically been limited to a privileged few, such as the spouse or retainers of a chieftain. More commonly, the bereaved are expected to demonstrate their grief in modest ways: by paying homage to the deceased, by displaying appropriate affect when the occasion demands, by abstaining from certain forms of social interaction, by wearing special clothing as a sign of mourning, and so forth. No matter how costly to the individual, failure to observe socially prescribed practices—to grieve "properly"—may result in censure, if not from others, then from the bereaved him- or herself (e.g., in the form of guilt feelings).

Although sacrifice may be demanded, it is in the interest of society to facilitate recovery from bereavement. Thus the role of the bereaved typically carries certain benefits and privileges as well as obligations. For example, by providing a recognized period of withdrawal, mourning practices allow the symptoms of despair and apathy to run their course without undue interference, while also providing a timetable for recovery and reintegration into society. Socially prescribed ways of mourning also help the bereaved to articulate grief in an acceptable and recognized manner. This is particularly important, since grief that is left unexpressed may prolong the suffering; conversely, grief that is expressed in an exaggerated or inappropriate fashion may be so discomforting to others (e.g., friends and relatives) that interpersonal relations are further disrupted. Finally, by honoring and providing a place for the dead, mourning practices may help the bereaved to integrate his or her loss in a meaningful way without too swiftly or too completely relinquishing ties to the deceased.

As noted in the previous section, some individuals take advantage of the role of the bereaved. But neither this, nor the sometimes burdensome obligations imposed by the role, should blind us to the fact that socially prescribed mourning practices are an integral part of the normal grief process.

In Western industrial societies, mourning practices have become increasingly abbreviated and the process is continuing. The funeral, for example, is a popular topic for exposé as being overcommercialized, ostentatious, and a financial burden on the bereaved. To a certain extent, these criticisms are true. But society's obligation to the bereaved does not stop with disposing of the body of the deceased in the most cost-effective way; and there is evidence (Pine et al.

1976) that people who participate in traditional mourning practices, such as viewing the body of the deceased, may have better recovery than those who forego such formalities.

Summary

The treatment of a condition need not bear a one-to-one relationship to the origins of that condition. A person may suffer the loss of a leg either from disease or as the result of an accident. In either case, the program of rehabilitation may take a similar form. Nevertheless, an understanding of origins or historical causes can often aid in the selection of the most appropriate techniques for treating specific symptoms; and, even when that is not the case, understanding is an important scientific and humanitarian endeavor in its own right.

Grief is an extremely complex syndrome, the origins of which can be found in the biological, psychological, and sociocultural history of the individual and the species. Thus, some of the components of grief (e.g., protest, searching, and depression of activity, with concomitant physiological changes) may reflect biological adaptations, either directly or indirectly. Other components may be the result of psychological factors, such as the extinction and loss of meaning of habits that have been built up over many years of living with another person. Finally, still other components may reflect social privileges and duties. Any therapeutic regimen that seeks to alleviate the suffering of the bereaved must be sensitive to these historical causes, as well as to the aspects of the current situation that together help determine the nature, severity, and duration of the entire syndrome.

Let us now consider some of the contemporaneous factors that help influence the course of bereavement. Our primary concern will be with the age of the bereaved and the timing of death (i.e., whether it was anticipated or not). We shall then make specific recommendations on the application of behavior therapy techniques to the treatment of normal and abnormal grief reactions, especially among the elderly.

GRIEF REACTIONS AMONG THE ELDERLY

There is not a great deal of research on how older people (e.g., beyond 60 years of age) react to bereavement. However, the available data are fairly consistent on at least three points. First, grief tends to be milder in the elderly; second, somatic disturbances (physical symptoms) tend to be more common among the aged; and, third, the elderly bereaved often complain of a sense of uselessness or loss of purpose in life. Other features of grief that may be exaggerated in the elderly are apathy, self-isolation, and idealization of the deceased (cf. Ball 1976–1977; Heyman and Gianturco 1973; Parkes 1964; Skelskie 1975; and Stern, Williams, and Prados 1951).

The above effects are open to a variety of interpretations, from the optimistic (e.g., emphasizing the ability of the elderly to adapt to the role of widow or widower) to the pessimistic (e.g., emphasizing the weakened ego resources of the elderly, and hence the self-isolation and the channeling of affect into somatic complaints). Heyman and Gianturco (1973) suggest that the elderly often adapt to bereavement with emotional stability, a stable social network of family and friends, and relatively few changes in lifestyle. If this optimistic picture is true, then the somatic complaints frequently observed among the elderly might be due more to the cumulative effects of chronic illnesses and the natural deterioration of functioning than to bereavement.

Like most studies of grief in the aged, Heyman and Gianturco base their observations on relatively few subjects: forty-one people who were bereaved during the course of a longitudinal study at the Duke University Center for the Study of Aging and Human Development. Heyman and Gianturco report that most of the subjects held deep religious convictions and that they did not suffer severe disruptions in their social or financial condition as a result of bereavement. This is not the situation with many elderly bereaved. In spite of their generally good adjustment, it is significant to note that a major complaint of the people studied by Heyman and Gianturco was a feeling of uselessness following bereavement. Retired from a job, with few family responsibilities, and with the loss of a spouse, the elderly bereaved in even the most favorable circumstances may have little to look forward to except the inocuous pleasures of the moment, and their own ultimate demise.

Other investigators paint a gloomier picture of grief in the elderly than do Heyman and Gianturco. Skelskie (1975) suggests that the flattened affect often observed among the elderly bereaved is more a sign of inhibited grief than of good adjustment. In addition, for many elderly persons bereavement may mean more than the loss of a spouse. The survivor may have to move to smaller, more manageable quarters; children and other family members may be living at a distance, and thus be unable to provide continuing social support; financial resources may be inadequate to sustain a comfortable lifestyle, and so forth. Perhaps the major point to keep in mind is that the elderly do not form a homogeneous group—economically, socially, or even in terms of age, and certainly not in terms of reactions to bereavement.

ANTICIPATORY GRIEF

Lindemann (1944) was not only among the first to give a detailed description of normal grief as a coherent syndrome, he was also the first to note the importance of anticipatory grief:

> A common picture hitherto not appreciated is a syndrome which we have designated *anticipatory grief*. The patient is so concerned with her adjustment after the potential death of a father or son that she goes through all the phases of grief—depression, heightened preoccupation with the departed, a review of all the forms of death which might befall him, and anticipation of the readjustment that might be necessitated by it (147).

In this case, Lindemann was referring primarily to the reactions of the wife of a serviceman who faced a real possibility of death in World War II. Lindemann cites several instances in which the anticipatory grief was so complete (i.e., reaching the stage of detachment and reorganization) that the husband was met with a demand for immediate divorce upon his return. Lindemann also noted, however, that anticipatory grief could assuage the suffering of actual bereavement.

Since Lindemann's initial and rather cursory description, anticipatory grief has been the topic of much discussion. (For a good introduction to the topic, see the volume by Schoenberg et al. 1974.) Unfortunately, the concept of anticipatory grief is not well-defined. In the above quotation by Lindemann, for example, two distinct notions may be discerned: (1) grieving in anticipation of a probable or certain loss; and (2) anticipation of one's own grief following a loss. The former involves working through some of the protest, despair, and detachment that normally accompanies bereavement, but before the fact. The latter involves preparing oneself for the events that lie ahead, for example, by cognitively rehearsing how one will react to the loss when it actually occurs.

There is little doubt that the second of these mechanisms—anticipating and preparing for one's own grief—can have major beneficial effects. Because death has been a taboo subject in our society, and with the abandonment of formal mourning practices, many bereaved persons do not know what to expect or how to behave following the death of a loved one. The pain, despair, apathy, and other symptoms of normal grief may then be interpreted as signs of pathology ("I must be going crazy"). Or, not knowing whom to blame for the suffering, the bereaved may take on an added burden of guilt ("God must be punishing me") or lash out in anger at others ("you are not doing enough").

But what about anticipatory grief per se? It is commonly assumed that the opportunity to engage in grief work before the actual bereavement may ease the impact of the loss and facilitate long-term recovery. In support of this assumption, several studies (Clayton 1975: and Parkes 1972) found that young widows grieve less and remarry sooner following an anticipated as opposed to a sudden bereavement. A cautionary note must be added, however. Anticipatory grief can often do more harm than good. This appears to be especially true for the elderly.

Gerber et al. (1975) found that elderly widows had a better prognosis if their husbands died suddenly rather than after a lingering illness. Similar results were obtained by Vachon et al. (1977). These investigators compared the widows of cancer patients with the widows of men who suffered from chronic cardiovascular disease. The deaths of the cancer victims were generally anticipated; in the case of the chronic cardiovascular patients, the deaths were sudden, but still not completely unexpected. One to two months after bereavement, 38 percent of the widows whose husbands had died of cancer reported that they felt worse than they did immediately following the death. The corresponding figure for the widows whose husbands died of cardiovascular disease was 23 percent, a statistically significant difference. The cancer widows were also more likely to feel that they were in poor health following bereavement.

Why should an anticipated loss, as opposed to sudden bereavement, be more debilitating for older than for younger people? There are at least four reasons. First, death seldom comes as a complete surprice to the elderly. For American men between the ages of 65 and 74, the death rate is approximately 4 percent a year, and between the ages of 75 and 84, it is about 9 percent a year. (The corresponding figures for women are 2 percent and 6 percent.) These figures are low enough not to be a source of constant anxiety, but high enough to encourage anticipation by a prudent person. Consequently, some of the value a forewarning might provide to the young may be superfluous to the aged.

A second point is that the anticipation of a threatening event can be a potent source of stress in its own right. For an older person, knowing that his or her spouse will die within a limited period of time can add to the stress of bereavement without necessarily conferring compensating benefits. This is especially true if, as is often the case among the elderly, the surviving partner is suffering from chronic ill health or some other pre-existing condition that might be exacerbated by the stress of caring for a dying spouse.

Caring for a dying spouse is not *just* a source of added stress. It can also provide a purpose to life. Ironically, this is a third reason why an anticipated bereavement may be particularly hard on the elderly. In the absence of an extended family, many older couples have only one another to rely upon for support. Therefore, when one becomes gravely ill, the other must assume the role of caretaker. Bereavement under such circumstances can be especially severe, especially if other forms of social reinforcement have been relinquished during the course of the illness.

A fourth reason why anticipatory grief can be a complicating rather than a beneficial factor for the aged is related to the above. A person cannot make the personal sacrifices that are often demanded by a dying spouse without experiencing some ambivalence. This is especially true if the illness proceeds through a series of remissions, increasing the risk of premature detachment (of the reactions of the potential war widows described by Lindemann 1944). An ambivalent relationship prior to bereavement is frequently implicated as an etiological factor in pathological grief (Aldrich 1974; Maddison 1968; and Parkes 1972).

The above points do not mean that anticipatory grief is necessarily detrimental to the aged. Rather, they serve as a warning that anticipatory grief is not the panacea that some believe it to be. Furthermore, the hopes, fears, loneliness, and suffering of the dying patient cannot be ignored in an attempt to ease the way for the surviving partner. Anticipatory grief, if it is to have any benefits, must be carefully timed and coordinated with the actual course of the patient's illness. This is often very difficult to do, especially for someone not intimately involved with the medical treatment of the dying person.

In the remainder of this chapter, we will discuss the applications of behavioral techniques to the treatment of normal and abnormal grief reactions. Our primary focus will be on post-mortem bereavement, although many of the same considerations also apply to anticipatory grief.

BEHAVIOR THERAPY WITH THE ELDERLY BEREAVED

In a behavioral approach, grief is not the focus of therapy. The various components of grief, although occasioned by the loss of a loved one, cannot be attributed to any single cause and hence cannot be alleviated by any single procedure. Goals and procedures should be established depending on the component reactions that are presenting difficulties. Thus, the assessment process is the most important part of designing a treatment strategy for grief. During assessment the therapist determines the *quality* of the grief (e.g., whether it has elements of pathology, has been prolonged, is following a normal progression, and so on) and the *functional extent* of the problem (i.e., how the grieving behavior may be affecting other life conditions). A thorough assessment should also include cultural, generational, and personal values about grief so that these may be incorporated into treatment.

The Treatment of Normal Grief Reactions

In assessing the quality of the grief, the therapist first determines who has been responsible for bringing the client into therapy and, therefore, who has defined the grieving behavior as needing treatment. For example, some elderly clients enter therapy at the urging of family members who are bothered by the bereavement and believe that "it's time (the client) got back to normal"; or the client may enter therapy on his or her own initiative, seeking support and a possible resolution of the pain that is being experienced. Next, the therapist should provide the necessary information about what might be expected in the grieving process, give assurance and support, and establish him- or herself as a contact person if further problems arise. At this time, suggestions might be made about restructuring the environment to increase social support and maintain adaptive behaviors. Also, the client might be trained in specific techniques for the alleviation of distress. (The choice of appropriate techniques will be discussed in a subsequent section.)

It is clear that much can be done in a few therapeutic sessions to help place normal grief in a meaningful perspective for the client, to begin the process of restructuring the environment to meet new realities, and to train the client in techniques for alleviating specific symptoms. Nevertheless, an intensive treatment program is not recommended. Following bereavement, there is a dearth of normally available reinforcers. The client can easily become dependent upon the therapist, and the therapist, if not cautious, may reward the very responses that are proving troublesome outside of the therapeutic relationship.

In recommending therapeutic restraint, we do not deny the importance of allowing the client to express his or her grief openly. The inhibition of normal grief can be seriously pathogenic. A distinction must therefore be made between the expression of normal grief, which should be encouraged, and the reward of certain symptoms (e.g., self-blame, social withdrawal) that, if prolonged, can lead to further difficulties. It is a fine line to draw, but an important one. Therapeutic restraint, coupled with sympathetic understanding, conveys to the bereaved that grief is normal, that it will end in due time, and that life will continue. For elderly clients in particular, it is important to avoid the suggestion that psychotherapy is necessary, for they may interpret this as meaning that their grief is abnormal or that the things they fear may indeed be forthcoming.

The Treatment of Pathological Grief Reactions

The application of a behavioral model to the treatment of pathological grief reactions consists of three essential parts: (1) a thorough assessment; (2) the establishment of goals for the therapeutic operations; and (3) the selection of effective procedures.

Behavioral Assessment. Among the symptoms of abnormal grief listed by Wahl (1970) are profound feelings of irrational despair and hopelessness; inability to accept or to deal with feelings of ambivalence toward the person who has died; loss of self-esteem; self-blame for the death; inability to proffer affection to others; loss of interest in planning for the future; and protracted apathy, irritability, or hyperactivity without appropriate affect. This is only a partial list, but it illustrates an important point. Most of the symptoms of pathological grief are also common during normal grief. They become pathological only if unduly prolonged or if they are expressed in such a manner that they lead to other forms of maladaptive behavior (e.g., alcoholism, the threat of suicide, alienation from others).

The therapist must make a careful assessment of the specific responses that are causing difficulties—their frequency of occurrence, intensity, duration, and latency, and the schedule on which they occur. Such measures are important for determining the client's progress during treatment and for evaluating the efficacy of the change procedures.

The therapist also must determine the events that set the occasion for the behaviors (antecedents) and the events that maintain them (consequences). Antecedents and consequences may be identified at both proximal and distal points in time. Proximal events immediately precede or follow the responses identified as troublesome. Distal antecedents and consequences occur at more remote times.

The most important distal antecedents are those concerning the manner of bereavement. As already described, grief reactions may vary depending upon whether the death was anticipated or sudden, and whether or not the client's relationship with the bereaved was ambivalent.

Regarding distal consequences, the therapist must ascertain what it would mean for the client or the family if the grieving behaviors were alleviated. It may be that certain aspects of grief have become the client's primary mode for interaction with others. For example, the role of widow or widower may have become a source of meaning and self-esteem. If this has occurred, grief reactions may not be tied to any particular proximal stimulus, but may have become semi-autonomous—a client's mission in life.

Finally, in addition to the specific problem behaviors, and their antecedents and consequences, the therapist must assess the client's coping skills and resources. This is particularly important in the case of the elderly, where failing health, diminished psychological capacities, and inadequate financial and social support may place severe limitations on the goals that realistically can be achieved and on the selection of appropriate techniques of treatment.

Goals of Treatment.   From a behavioral point of view, the goals of treatment must be tailored to the specific responses that are presenting difficulties. Such goals may be divided into five broad categories, depending on the target behavior.

1. *Physiological complaints.*   Goals may be set for reducing specific somatic symptoms, such as insomnia or migraine headaches; for increasing physical activity; for increasing the client's compliance to medical regimens and self-care programs; and so forth.

2. *Subjective (private) events.*   Goals are set to change self-concepts, specific emotional experiences and desires (e.g., the urge to commit suicide), disturbing fantasies, and maladaptive thought patterns.

3. *Overt behavior.*   Goals are set to change specific observable responses, including behavioral excesses (e.g., the overuse of alcohol and drugs), compulsions, avoidance reactions, and so on.

4. *Interpersonal relationships.*   Goals are set to reduce isolation and improve the quality of social interaction.

5. *Environmental support.*   Goals are set to change environmental structures (physical as well as social) to support or facilitate therapeutic gains.

These last two categories are of special importance for elderly clients. In contemporary American society, old age means a loss of status, money, and environmental control. These difficulties may be greatly exacerbated following bereavement. The bereaved may need to learn money management skills; ways of negotiating business; efficient use of public transportation or the family car; or household tasks previously managed by the deceased. On a more personal level, bereavement may mean the loss of a primary source of reinforcement; and with declining health and sensory acuity, even those simple activities that can be enjoyed alone—reading, watching television, eating—may lose much of their reinforcing value.

Whatever the category or nature of the problem, goals should be established through a discussion with the client. The goals should be spelled out in operational terms so that both the client and therapist have a clear idea of the direction of the therapy.

Choice of Procedures for Treatment. A great many techniques are available to the behavior therapist: relaxation, systematic desensitization, covert conditioning, cognitive rehearsal, role-playing, contingency contracting, and various kinds of skills training, to mention a few. In many instances, the application of these techniques to the symptoms of grief is a relatively straightforward extension of ordinary clinical practice. For example, relaxation procedures may be used to help the bereaved overcome general feelings of anxiety and, on a more specific level, to alleviate such symptoms as insomnia. The thought-stopping procedure described by Cautela and Wisocki (1978) can also be used to reduce the stress associated with bereavement. This procedure consists of targeting a stress-inducing perseverative thought pattern and training the client to interrupt the pattern with distracting stimuli.

The experienced clinician can easily extend the list of techniques to include his or her preferred modes of treatment. However, a caveat should be noted. Because of their complex origins, the symptoms of grief may not yield to treatment as readily as other forms of distress. Indeed, it is not always easy to decide which symptoms of grief should be treated, and at which point in time. Consider again the technique of thought-stopping. This procedure should be used only for thoughts that are troublesome to the client because they are impeding recovery (e.g., negative self-references which add to the person's feelings of guilt, anxiety, or depression). The client should not be encouraged to shut out all thoughts of the deceased, even if those thoughts are sometimes quite painful.

To our knowledge, there have been no controlled studies designed explicitly to test the efficacy of behavioral techniques for the treatment of grief reactions, although there are a number of field studies and case reports. Ramsay (1979) describes the successful treatment of 23 clients by a combination of flooding and prolonged exposure to the stimuli that arouse undesirable emotional reactions. During two-hour periods, three days a week, clients were forced to confront situations that evoked anxiety, guilt, shame, jealousy, and so on, and to remain until the undesirable reactions were extinguished. A variety of techniques, including modeling, prompting, and fantasy, were used to facilitate the flooding process. However, as Ramsay points out, this form of behavior therapy is hard on both the client and the therapist, and it should not be attempted by an inexperienced therapist. Ramsay also does not recommend it for elderly clients.

Flannery (1974) presented a case report in which an elderly man was treated for agitated depression and grief six months after the death of his sister. After negotiating a specific behavioral contract with the client—setting goals for the therapy—Flannery differentially reinforced the client for positive self-statements, ignored socially aversive statements that the client made, gradually prompted the client to discuss his sister's death, and rewarded him for speaking of his feelings. These techniques were generally successful in achieving the goals.

In addition to reports such as the above, there is a growing literature on the use of support groups (e.g., widow-to-widow programs) and other social networks in the treatment of grief. Walker, McBride, and Vachon (1977) provide an excellent review of the relevant research. We shall therefore limit our own comments to the observation that the therapist who works with the bereaved, and particularly with the elderly bereaved, should be prepared to extend his or her practice into the community, and to render services that are not strictly psychological. For example, one of the greatest needs of an elderly client might entail the establishment of a workable budget. The therapist may have to set aside sufficient time to train the client in a variety of such mundane tasks in order to sustain and complement a program of individual therapy. At the very minimum, the therapist should be aware of relevant support services available within the client's local community, such as financial and legal aid, and be able to serve as a catalyst to assure that such services are properly utilized.

CONCLUSIONS AND SUMMARY

In this chapter, we have sketched in broad outline a behavioral approach to the treatment of grief among the elderly. Many issues have not been thoroughly addressed. For example, what proportion of the elderly bereaved suffer from pathological grief? When grief does take a pathological course, what is the relative contribution of situational (e.g., socioeconomic) and psychological factors? How does the course of grief differ as a function of the nature of the loss (e.g., the death of a grown child as opposed to the death of a spouse)? The lack of adequate research findings prevents us from addressing these questions.

Behavior therapists have not contributed greatly to the literature on grief, either in terms of basic understanding or in terms of therapeutic applications. This lack of involvement may be attributed to several factors. Grief is such a deep and painful experience that the most natural response is to offer unconditional nurturance. Within such an atmosphere, the application of behavioral techniques may appear inappropriate and coldly mechanistic. The appearance is deceptive, but it is nevertheless real. Also real, however, is the pain of grief, and the need for the client to return to a satisfying life. Any barrier that artificially prevents the application of potentially effective techniques to the treatment of grief should be addressed and not ignored because it is deceptive or unjustified.

There are also more substantive reasons for the lack of involvement of behavior therapists in research on grief. As previously described, behavior therapists tend to focus not on grief per se, but rather on the treatment of specific reactions. Since most of the reactions during grief can be observed in other disorders as well, the extension of well-established behavioral techniques to the problems of bereavement might seem relatively straightforward and noncontroversial. For the most part, this is probably true; yet, grief reactions do form a coherent syndrome, and part of the environment of any one reaction is its relationship to other reactions within the syndrome. Hence, it cannot be assumed that a technique effective in treating insomnia in a nongrief context will also be effective in treating the insomnia occasioned by bereavement. Research is needed to determine the effectiveness of various behavioral techniques in treating the symptoms of grief; that research has not yet been done.

Still another reason for the lack of involvement of behavior therapists in the problem of grief is more theoretical than practical; it stems from the fact that the treatment of a phenomenon may bear only an indirect relationship to the explanation of that phenomenon. As described earlier, behavior therapists often focus on the antecedents and consequences of a reaction; but the time perspective is typically limited even when distal events are taken into account. As a complex syndrome, grief cannot be understood without taking into account long-term historical causes, including biological and socio-cultural evolution. Such issues are not always relevant to treatment, usually the primary focus of behavior therapists.

Topics related to death and dying have become very faddish of late. Where is this fad leading? Is it to a pro forma recommendation that everyone who is bereaved (or facing his or her own death) should contract with a therapist to assist in mourning? We hope not, and yet the idea is not entirely farfetched.

Grief presents a tremendous humanitarian problem, one that is being poorly met by contemporary American society. The mental health professions have much to contribute in this area. But at the risk of sounding overly crass, we might also point out that the bereaved represent a fertile field for therapeutic entrepreneurs in search of clients. The danger in this situation is obvious, if not always pleasant to contemplate.

REFERENCES

Aldrich, C.K. Some dynamics of anticipatory grief. In B. Schoenberg *et al.* (Eds.), *Anticipatory grief.* New York: Columbia University Press, 1974.

Averill, J.R. Grief: Its nature and significance. *Psychological Bulletin*, 1968, 70, 721–748.

Averill, J.R. The functions of grief. In C. Izard (Ed.), *Emotions in personality and psychopathology.* New York: Plenum, 1979.

Averill, J.R. A constructivist view of emotion. In R. Plutchik and H. Kellerman (Eds.), *Theories of emotion.* New York: Academic Press, 1980.

Ball, J.F. Widow's grief: The impact of age and mode of death. *Omega*, 1976–77, 7, 307–333.

Beck, A.T. *Cognitive therapy and the emotional disorders.* New York: International Universities Press, 1976.

Bowlby, J. *Attachment and loss*, Vol. 1 *Attachment.* New York: Basic Books, 1969.

Bowlby, J. *Attachment and loss*, Vol. 2. *Separation: Anxiety and anger.* New York: Basic Books, 1973.

Bowlby, J. *Attachment and loss*, Vol. 3. *Loss: Sadness and depression.* New York: Basic Books, 1980.

Bugen, L.A. Human grief: A model for prediction and intervention. *American Journal of Orthopsychiatry*, 1977, 47, 196–206.

Cautela, J.R., and Wisocki, P.A. The thought stopping procedure: Description, application, and learning theory interpretations. *Psychological Record*, 1977, 27, 255–264.

Clayton, P. J. The effect of living alone on bereavement symptoms. *American Journal of Psychiatry*, 1975, *132*, 133-137.

Clayton, P. J. The sequelae and nonsequelae of conjugal bereavement. *American Journal of Psychiatry*, 1979, *136*, 1530-1534.

Engel, G. L. Is grief a disease? *Psychosomatic Medicine*, 1961, *23*, 18-22.

Epstein, G., Weitz, L., Roback, H., and McKee, E. Research on bereavement: A selective and critical review. *Comprehensive Psychiatry*, 1975, *16*, 537-546.

Flannery, R. B. Behavior modification of geriatric grief: A transactional perspective. *International Journal of Aging and Human Development*, 1974, 197-203.

Fredrick, J. F. Grief as a disease process. *Omega*, 1976-77, 7, 297-305.

Gerber, I., Rusalem, R., Hannon, N., Battin, D., and Arkin, A. Anticipatory grief and aged widows and widowers. *Journal of Gerontology*, 1975, *30*, 225-229.

Gorer, G. *Death, grief, and mourning.* London: Crescent Press, 1965.

Hamburg, D. A., Hamburg, B. A., and Barchas, J. D. Anger and depression in perspective of behavioral biology. In L. Levi (Ed.), *Emotions: Their parameters and measurement.* New York: Raven Press, 1975.

Heyman, D. L., and Gianturco, D. T. Long-term adaptation by the elderly to bereavement. *Journal of Gerontology*, 1973, *28*, 359-362.

Lindemann, E. Symptomatology and management of acute grief. *American Journal of Psychiatry*, 1944, *101*, 141-148.

Lopata, H. Z. On widowhood: Grief work and identity reconstruction. *Journal of Geriatric Psychiatry*, 1975, *8*, 41-55.

Maddison, D. The relevance of conjugal bereavement to preventive psychiatry. *British Journal of Medical Psychology*, 1968, *41*, 223-233.

Mandler, G. *Mind and emotion.* New York: John Wiley, 1975.

Marris, P. *Loss and change.* Garden City, N.Y.: Anchor Press/Doubleday, 1975.

Parkes, C. M. The effects of bereavement on physical and mental health: A study of the case records of widows. *British Medical Journal*, 1964, *2*, 274-279.

Parkes, C. M. Psychosocial transitions: A field for study. *Social Science and Medicine*, 1971, *5*, 101-115.

Parkes, C. M. *Bereavement: Studies of grief in adult life.* London: Tavistock Publications, 1972.

Parkes, C. M. What becomes of redundant world models? A contribution to the study of adaptation to change. *British Journal of Medical Psychology*, 1975, *48*, 131-137.

Pine, V. R., *et al. Acute grief and the funeral.* Springfield, Ill.: Charles C. Thomas, 1976.

Ramsay, R. W. Bereavement: A behavioral treatment of pathological grief. In P. O. Sjöden, S. Bates, and W. S. Dockins (Eds.), *Trends in behavior therapy.* New York: Academic Press, 1979.

Ramsay, R.W., and Happée, J.A. The stress of bereavement: Components and treatment. In C.D. Spielberger and I.G. Sarason (Eds.), *Stress and anxiety*, Vol. 4. New York: John Wiley and Sons, 1977.

Rosenblatt, P.C., Walsh, R.P., and Jackson, D.A. *Grief and mourning in cross-cultural perspective*. New Haven: HRAF Press, 1976.

Schoenberg, B., Carr, A.C., Kutscher, A.H., Peretz, D., and Goldberg, I.K. *Anticipatory grief*. New York: Columbia University Press, 1974.

Seligman, M.E.P. *Helplessness: On depression, development, and death*. San Francisco: Freeman, 1975.

Skelskie, B.E. An exploratory study of grief in old age. *Smith College Studies in Social Work*, 1975, *45*, 159–182.

Snowdon, J., Solomons, R., and Druce, H. Feigned bereavement: Twelve cases. *International Journal of Psychiatry*, 1978, *133*, 15–19.

Stern, K., Williams, G.M., and Prados, M. Grief reactions in later life. *American Journal of Psychiatry*, 1951, *108*, 289–293.

Stroebe, M.S., Stroebe, W., Gergen, K.J., and Gergen, M. The broken heart: Reality or myth? *Omega*, 1980, in press.

Vachon, M.L.S. Grief and bereavement following the death of a spouse. *Canadian Psychiatric Association Journal*, 1976, *21*, 35–44.

Vachon, M.L.S., Freedman, K., Formo, A., Rogers, J., Lyall, W.A.L., and Freeman, S.J.J. The final illness in cancer: The widow's perspective. *Canadian Medical Association Journal*, 1977, *177*, 1151–1154.

Wahl, C.W. The differential diagnosis of normal and neurotic grief following bereavement. *Psychosomatics*, 1970, *11*, 104–106.

Walker, K.N., MacBride, A., and Vachon, M.L.S. Social support networks and the crises of bereavement. *Social Science and Medicine*, 1977, *11*, 35–41.

Yamamoto, J., Okonogi, K., Iwasaki, T., and Yoshimura, S. Mourning in Japan. *American Journal of Psychiatry*, 1969, *125*, 1660–1665.

6 THE RATIONAL-EMOTIVE APPROACH TO THANATOLOGY

Albert Ellis

This chapter outlines the rational-emotive therapy (RET) approach to thanatology; it could well be subtitled, How to Teach People to Stubbornly Refuse to Disturb Themselves Emotionally about Any-thing—Including Death and Dying. For RET, although it aims to be a highly practical form of cognitive-behavior therapy (CBT) and is intrinsically wedded to empiricism and to the scientific method, is also a theory and a philosophy. Its basic view is that humans largely (not completely) choose to disturb themselves emotionally and that they have the (relatively little used) ability to refuse to do so. Fur-thermore they can choose to feel appropriately sad, concerned, and frustrated when assailed with tragedies such as a terminal illness instead of feeling inappropriately panicked, horrified, depressed, and self-pitying.

Does this mean that RET teaches people how to eliminate their intense feelings and to emote only in a calm and detached manner, as the Zen Buddhists sometimes espouse, or to feel only tranquil and serene, as Epictetus (1898) and the ancient Stoics often advocated? Not at all. RET often encourages and abets intense feelings—particu-larly feelings of strong determination to change adverse conditions, of vibrant awareness and aliveness, of passionate sexuality and love, and of intense interest in a cause, ideal, goal, or long-range value which people find (or make) important. It also encourages, when people are seriously frustrated or deprived, powerful negative emotions of sorrow, disappointment, regret, annoyance, and (at times) of grief or mourning. So RET is hardly a non-feeling type of psychotherapy; it is not called rational-*emotive* for nothing!

Nonetheless, RET is highly philosophic as well as empirical, always trying to be both humanistic and efficient (Ellis 1977a, 1977b, 1980)—which is often rather difficult but hardly impossible. It therefore holds that almost all humans, as long as they are not in dire physical pain or psychotically or organically unable to think clearly, have the capacity to look at the highly undesirable, and consequently "grim," events of their lives and to accept them without liking them. If they choose to do so in a strong, determined manner, then they can largely eliminate (or, at the very least, minimize) what we normally call "emotional disturbance"—that is, needless feelings of severe anxiety, depression, hostility, and low frustration tolerance. This chapter will outline the RET approach to thanatology and show how rational-emotive practitioners can significantly help people live successfully (though not necessarily happily) with death and dying.

BACKGROUND OF RET

I originated rational-emotive therapy (RET) in 1955, after I had practiced psychoanalysis for several years and then had experimented with other forms of psychotherapy, such as that of Ferenczi (1950) and Rogers (1951, 1961) and found them all, especially psychoanalysis, quite inefficient. Fortunately, my hobby had always been philosophy as much as psychology, and the more disillusioned I became with traditional methods of therapy, the more I began incorporating philosophic principles into my work, and the better results I started to get (Ellis 1962, 1972a, 1973d, 1977c, 1981b). At the same time, I realized from the clinical experience I was having with my clients, as well as from the experimental literature in psychology, that humans hold on to their self-defeating views with extreme tenacity and that they rarely surrender them unless, behaviorally, they act and think against them. In the few years, therefore, that I was experimenting with nonanalytic therapy and using other methods, I incorporated more and more behavioral thinking into my work and used *in vivo* desensitization as well as philosophic disputation to show my clients how they were disturbing themselves and what they could do to think, feel, and behave more appropriately to their basic desires.

Although RET has sometimes been wrongly accused of being originally heavily cognitive and later getting on the behavior therapy bandwagon (Lazarus 1979; and Wolpe 1979), this is not true. It was always both cognitive and behavioral. I think it can be safely said that it is the major school of psychotherapy that has pioneered the welding of cognitive reconstruction to behavior modification and that, because of the therapy research it inspired in the 1960s and 1970s, it essentially started and remains at the very core of the present cognitive-behavior revolution in therapy (Beck 1976; Mahoney 1974; and Meichenbaum 1977).

On both theoretical and practical grounds, RET is uniquely multimodal. Although some cognitive-behavior therapists, notably Lazarus (1971, 1976, 1981), espouse technical eclecticism and advocate for many clients the use of several different kinds of techniques, RET has a basic theoretical stance out of which flows the recommended use, with almost all clients, of a number of selected cognitive, emotive, and behavioral methods. It assumes that cognition, emotion, and behavior are never really separate: that they invariably interact and can hardly be defined accurately without reference to each other (Ellis 1981; Ellis and Abrahms 1978; Ellis and Grieger 1977; and Ellis and Whiteley 1979).

What we usually call "emotional disturbance" is really a compound of ideational, feeling, and action disturbance; and in order for it to be elegantly or profoundly changed, it requires that afflicted individuals significantly modify many of their beliefs, passions, and acts. Although, RET holds that humans, unlike lower animals, are uniquely philosophic and that it is their *view* of what happens to them rather than the *events* that occur in their lives that largely disturbs them (Epictetus 1898). RET tries to help individuals change this view by having them assign to themselves a variety of cognitive, emotive, and behavioral exercises, and by having them repetitively *practice* these exercises on a day to day basis, particularly in their regular lives rather than primarily in the therapy sessions.

More specifically, RET hypothesizes that it is "rational," "healthy," and "self-actualizing" for most humans to have strong or intense *desires, wishes,* and *preferences* — such as the desire to stay alive and live happily when (1) by themselves; (2) relating gregariously to other people; (3) intimately relating to a few selected individuals; (4) productively engaging in a trade or profession; and (5) enjoying recreational pursuits, such as art, music, science, dance, gardening, sports, and so forth. At the same time, RET holds that when people unrealistically turn their desires and preferences for almost anything, including life itself, into absolutistic demands or commands that they *must*—yes, completely *have to*—get what they want, they almost always think, feel, and behave dysfunctionally and bring on "emotional" disturbance.

Although people's absolutistic *shoulds, oughts,* and *musts* are theoretically variegated and endless, there appear to be three major headings under which these disturbance-creating absolutes invariably seem to fall: (1) "I MUST act competently and MUST be approved or loved by significant others!"; (2) "Other people MUST treat me kindly, considerately, and fairly!"; and (3) "The conditions under which I live MUST be easy and rewarding and MUST NOT provide me with highly undesirable hassles or inconveniences!" The first of these three MUSTurbatory irrational beliefs leads people to create their own feelings of anxiety, depression, guilt, shame, and worthlessness; the second leads to hostility, anger, resentment, homicide, and genocide; and the third leads to dysfunctional behaviors (such as addictions, procrastination, and inertia) and to feelings of self-pity, depression, anger, and hyper-irritability.

Once humans devoutly believe in the ideas that they MUST do well and be loved, HAVE TO be treated nicely by others, and ABSOLUTELY NEED easy and enjoyable conditions of living, they almost always deduce three major additional irrationalities from these MUSTS: (1) *Awfulizing*—"When I don't do as well as I MUST or you don't treat me as nicely as you ABSOLUTELY SHOULD, it is AWFUL, TERRIBLE, and HORRIBLE!" (2) *I-can't-stand-it-itis*—"When conditions are not as good as they MUST BE, I CAN'T STAND IT, CAN'T BEAR IT, CAN'T TOLERATE IT! Either I will die of these TERRIBLE conditions; or will live but can't really be happy at all while they exist!"; and (3) *Worthlessness or self-downing*—"Because you don't love me as well as you MUST or because I haven't done as well as I HAVE TO to win your approval, I am a ROTTEN PERSON, a HOPELESS SLOB, who doesn't really deserve any goodness in life!" These three major irrational thoughts and self-defeating feelings may possibly exist in their own right; but it seems likely that they are deductions or conclusions that follow from basic MUSTurbatory premises.

One of RET's basic hypotheses is that when people are panicked, depressed, angry, or self-pitying about death and dying (or just about anything else), the philosophic core of their disturbance stems from their absolutistic commands or demands, their shoulds, oughts, and musts that they (consciously or unconsciously) foist on themselves, on others, and on the universe. If, therefore, they are shown that they actually choose to think this way; if they take full responsibility for their own self-disturbing, irrational beliefs; if they use the scientific (logico-empirical) method of ripping up their own self-sabotaging way of thinking; and if they practice anti-disturbing ways of emoting and behaving, they then have the power to stop upsetting themselves about virtually anything and to live as happy a life as they are capable of living when faced with real deprivations and frustrations. RET in particular, like cognitive-behavior therapy (CBT) in general, devotes itself to showing them how to do this.

RET APPLIED TO THANATOLOGY

Let me specifically begin to apply RET to thanatology. Suppose you, as a physician, a nurse, a counselor, or a therapist, have a patient or client who is faced with the death of a much-loved child, mate, or friend; and suppose that this person nastily dies after much pain, and at a relatively young age. Because your client's loved one is a human, is particularly well-loved, and is a real contributor to the client's life and happiness, the loss is a great one—is really tragic. For people with this kind of loss to be happy about it, is highly inappropriate and almost unthinkable. For them to be calm and serene or detached about it, is conceivable—since they can make themselves feel just about any way they want to feel when a tragedy like this strikes— but still inappropriate. Deep feeling is a good, not a bad, part of human nature; and calmness, serenity, and detachment will hardly help people cope with their genuine feelings of loss; in fact, they will tend to deny them and hide them. If people are only calm and detached when a loved one is dying, what will they do about getting the best possible attention and care for the stricken person? Or about urging themselves and others to ward off deadly ailments? Or about building a new life for themselves without the companionship of the dead person?

Strong feelings or emotion *moves* people—motivating them to minimize their tragic losses and to replace them with substitute gains. Keen sorrow or disappointment about losing a child or a mate enables deprived ones to recognize fully what they are lacking and to try to replace it—by begetting, if they can still do so, another child or a new mate. Mere detachment or serenity are emotions of a sort, but what do they appropriately move one to do when faced with a serious loss or tragedy? Very little.

Let us consider a serious illness, even a fatal illness, of your own. If you only stoically accept this illness, and make yourself feel serene and detached about it, are you likely to have high hopes of conquering it? Will you then make every possible effort to get the best available medical diagnosis and treatment, and to follow your physician's prescriptions to overcome your illness, however slim your chances may be? Hardly.

RET, let me repeat, teaches people to be distinctly emotional, even highly emotional—but appropriately instead of inappropriately so. It helps them to feel beneficially cautious, vigilant, and concerned about illness and death (of themselves and others) but not unbeneficially overconcerned, anxious, and panicked. It shows them how to be hopefully determined to cope with physical and mental problems rather than hopelessly horrified about their existence. It helps them to feel *very* sorry and irritated about pain and suffering, without adding to those feelings the gratuitous *surplus* and self-damaging reactions of terror, depression, and despair. It favors, when disease and morbidity are to be combatted, strong feelings such as protest and courage rather than bland feelings of resignation and withdrawal, or powerful (and often self-paralyzing) emotions of terror and madness.

COGNITIVE METHODS OF RET

RET holds that "emotions" and "emotional disturbances" are largely (but not exclusively) created by irrational, absolutistic, *must*-urbatory thinking; and it consequently uses a large number of cognitive or philosophic methods to show people who are dying, or who have dying or recently dead loved ones, how to overcome their feelings of anxiety, depression, despair, hostility, self-pity, and the concomitant dysfunctional behaviors (such as withdrawal and inertia) that frequently accompany these feelings. Full details of its main cognitive methods are presented at length in many articles and books (Ellis 1962, 1971, 1973, 1974; Ellis and Abrahms 1978; Ellis and Grieger 1977; Ellis and Harper 1975; Ellis and Whiteley 1979; Goldfried and Davison 1976; Grieger and Boyd 1980; Hauck 1972; Lange and Jakubowski 1976; Maultsby 1975; Morris and Kanitz 1974; Lembo 1976; Walen, DiGiuseppe, and Wessler 1980; Wessler and Wessler 1980; and Wolfe and Brand 1977). Let me summarize here some of the main RET cognitive approaches for people who are beset with the tragedies of death or dying.

Detection of Irrational Beliefs

RET teaches people to look for, and usually quickly find, their irrational beliefs (iBs) that are mainly causing their depressed and angry feelings. As noted above, these almost invariably seem to include an absolutistic *should, ought,* or *must* and derivatives from these *musts* that involve awfulizing, I-can't-stand-it-itis, and self- and/or other-downing. Typical *musts* to look for are: (1) "I (or So-and-So) MUST not die (or MUST not die so young or MUST not die so painfully)!"; (2) "Because I have led such a good life, I SHOULD not suffer!"; (3) "It is terribly unfair that I (or So-and-So) should die; and things MUST not be so unfair!"; and (4) "This treatment for my serious illness MUST NOT be so gruesome!"

Based on these kinds of absolutistic MUSTS, many people who are dying or watching friends or relatives die derive a good many other irrational beliefs, such as: "It is AWFUL for anyone to die so young!"; "I CAN'T STAND my (or my loved one's) dying!"; "If I am suffering like this, I must DESERVE to suffer and must be a ROTTEN PERSON!"; "The world is a TERRIBLE PLACE for making anyone die like this!"; "I can have NO PLEASURE WHATEVER in life now that So-and-So has died!"

If you will teach your clients that when they are extremely upset about death or dying they almost certainly have some irrational beliefs, some absolutistic MUSTS, and if you will show them how to look for these demands and comments, then they will soon have little trouble in detecting them and acknowledging that they really believe them.

Distinguishing Rational from Irrational Beliefs

RET assumes that virtually all irrational beliefs by which people upset themselves are held along with equally rational beliefs or desires, and that the former can be fairly easily distinguished from the latter (Phadke 1976). Thus in the case of a 48-year-old woman who had recently lost her husband of twenty-six years, she was clearly able to see, after talking with me for a few therapy sessions, that she was first telling herself a set of rational beliefs (rBs):

> I really miss the companionship of Harry, and I am very sorry about being alone every night. I don't like going out with men who want to get me into bed quickly, without any relationship, and I wish I could find one who truly cares for me first, and not mainly for my body. I relied too much on Harry taking care of me financially, and now I have to take care of myself, and it's very hard to do so, and I wish I had someone to handle the finances, as he used to do so well. Many of the couples I know now seem to look upon me as a fifth wheel, and I think the women particularly find me a threat and don't want me around. That's really bad that they feel that way!

These rational beliefs all took the form of strong desires, on her part, to have things differently. She wanted to return to the companionable, sexual, and financial state she was in when her husband was alive. The rational beliefs led to pronounced feelings of sorrow, regret, and frustration at her loss.

But this woman also had an accompanying set of irrational beliefs (iBs):

> I CAN'T BEAR the loneliness of not having Harry around any more and of having to go out with other men for whom I have little real feeling and with whom I feel alone even when I am talking to them. It's AWFUL to date men who mainly look upon me as a piece of ass and who are not really interested in ME as a person! It's not only hard to take care of my own finances, now that Harry is gone; it's TOO hard! It SHOULDN'T BE that hard! How HORRIBLE that some of my women friends now look at me as a fifth wheel and are very uneasy when their husbands pay any attention to me! They SHOULD NOT be jealous of their husbands' attentions to me and want to get rid of me!

When this woman was able to see *both* her rational and her irrational beliefs about the loss of her husband and about the present conditions of her life, and to see how the latter differed significantly from the former, she was able to focus on her desires and wishes and stop escalating them into dire needs. Thus she could feel mainly sad and sorry about her loss and only rarely angry and depressed about it.

Disputing Irrational Beliefs

The main or most elegant cognitive method of therapy used in RET is to help clients to challenge, question, and vigorously (and steadily) dispute their irrational beliefs. This consists of using the scientific method to see that these beliefs are really only hypotheses or theories, and not facts, and then to ask where the evidence is to back up these hypotheses, see that such evidence does not exist, and finally surrender the beliefs. In the case of the 48-year-old woman who had recently lost her husband, she was shown how to dispute her irrational beliefs (iBs) as follows:

Question: "Where is the evidence that I CAN'T BEAR the loneliness of not having Harry around any more and of having to go out with other men for whom I have little real feeling and with whom I feel alone even when I am talking to them?"

Answer: "There is no evidence that I CAN'T BEAR this loneliness? I don't think that I'll ever LIKE being alone, without an ongoing emotional relationship with a man; and I certainly don't PREFER talking to the men I date with whom I have little going emotionally. But I CAN stand what I don't like; and being lonely won't KILL ME. Now let me continue to look for another relationship and see if I can't finally find one."

Question: "Why is it AWFUL to date men who mainly look upon me as a piece of ass and who are not really interested in ME as a person!"

Answer: "It isn't! It's highly inconvenient and sometimes obnoxious. But it's not TOTALLY bad—and therefore AWFUL. And anything that's really AWFUL would be MORE THAN bad—at least 101 percent bad. And being lonely right now, or being viewed mainly as a piece of ass, certainly isn't in that category! If it were really AWFUL, moreover, it would mean that this undesirable state of affairs MUST NOT exist and that it is AWFUL that it does. But it MUST exist, if it does; that is the way it is. Tough!"

Question: "Where is it writ that it's TOO HARD for me to take care of my own finances, now that Harry is gone. Why SHOULD it not be that hard?"

Answer: "It's written in my nutty head! Sure it's hard, but it's definitely not TOO hard, since it's quite possible for me to go to the trouble of handling my own finances. And it SHOULD BE hard if it's really hard! Again, whatever hardness exists MUST right now exist. Too damned bad that it's this hard; but I'd better face it, handle it, and thereby make it LESS hard!"

Question: "In what way is it HORRIBLE if some of my women friends now look upon me as a fifth wheel and are very uneasy when their husbands pay any attention to me? Why MUST they not be jealous of their husbands' attention to me?"

Answer: "It's NOT horrible—only damned disadvantageous and annoying. Not all of them are that uneasy; and those that are, I can live without. And there is no reason why they MUST not be jealous of their husbands' attention to me. If they are, then they *must* be! Too bad!—but it's hardly the end of the world!"

Choosing One's Feelings

One of the most important ideas that RET tries to convey to people who are dying or are suffering over the death of a loved one is that they really have the power to choose their feelings, and that they are foolishly choosing to feel anxious, depressed, and hostile. Many of them, particularly at first, will not buy this reality. They devoutly believe either that they *have* to feel depressed when, say, they are dying; or that they would be "unnatural" and "inhuman" if they were only sorrowful and not depressed; or that if they make themselves feel undepressed they are repressing their true feelings, and that it is "natural"—meaning easy and exceptionally human—to feel depressed about death or dying. However, with a great deal of work and effort, they can "unnaturally," and much more healthfully, choose to feel very sad and frustrated but *not* depressed.

A favorite technique of RET in this connection is the one I used recently with a 50-year-old woman who may well have only a few years to live with a cancerous condition and who is normally very alive and creative but is now severely depressed. Part of my dialogue with her went as follows:

Therapist: "Of course, it's very painful and sad to know that you may only live a few years more, but why do you *have to* depress yourself about this sad condition?"

Client: "Wouldn't anyone feel depressed if they were in my state?"

Therapist: "No, obviously not. Suppose a thousand women, all your age and education, and with a husband and children like yours, all had the same kind of cancerous condition as you, would every single one of them feel as depressed as you do?"

Client: "I don't know. I would think so."

Therapist: "Think again! Now, would they *all* feel very depressed?"

Client: "Well, uh, I guess not."

Therapist: "Some of them, albeit few, would probably feel very sorrowful and disappointed — but not seriously depressed. Right?"

Client: "Uh, yes, I guess so."

Therapist: "You're right! Some of them definitely would. In fact, a few, for their own reasons, might even feel happy about it."

Client: "Happy?"

Therapist: "Yes, a few of them who might have been depressing themselves about other things and might not have had the courage to kill themselves might even feel happy or relieved that they now have a way out. But most of them, as you imply, would be quite miserable or depressed. How about, however, the few who wouldn't be? What would they probably be saying to themselves?"

Client: "I really don't know."

Therapist: "You *do* know! Now, think for a moment. What would *they* be telling themselves?"

Client: "Well, uh, something like, uh, 'I guess I've lived long enough and had it pretty good. And my children don't really need me any more. And once I'm dead, I won't have this pain any longer. Uh —'"

Therapist: "Right! Something like that. Or some other philosophy of acceptance that would make them still sad and unhappy, but resigned to their cruel fate, and not depressed about it. See! They *do* have a choice. And so do you. We *always* pick, choose, select our own feelings when bad things like dying happen to us. And you are now *choosing* to depress yourself. Now why not work at *choosing* to make yourself sad and disappointed but *not* depressed. It's your choice!"

Pointing Out Disadvantages of Disturbance

Some people believe that feeling disturbed is not only natural and inevitable when serious problems like death impend, but that such a feeling is actually good or advantageous. They believe, for example, that being depressed and withdrawn will save them from hurt and pain; or that it will ward off worse feelings (such as anxiety); or that they can handle this disturbance but might not be able to handle some worse, unknown feeling that might possibly replace it. Perhaps they may even believe that some fate or god will punish them if they do not make themselves miserable about death—particularly about a friend or a relative's death. RET shows these people that making themselves panicked or depressed about death will almost always do much more harm than good. For example, as I said to a 30-year-old mother whose infant child had recently died:

> You may think that feeling depressed will do you or others some good. But will it? I doubt it! Much more likely, it will make you feel much more pain than your natural grief would make you feel. It will first of all focus you on gruesome things and predictions—like the prediction that nothing good will ever happen to you. It will keep you preoccupied, and make it almost impossible for you to figure out and do more enjoyable things. It will keep you thinking that you *should* have done more for your child, when she was alive, and that you are a thorough louse because you didn't. It will gain you some pity from others, but also encourage people to avoid you because of your depressed state. It will distract you from taking good care of your other two children, and will encourage them to upset themselves more about the loss of their sister than they otherwise would probably do. It may get on your husband's nerves, and alienate him from you instead of encouraging him to be more supportive. It will help reindoctrinate you with the depression-creating philosophy, 'Things *must* not be this bad! I *can't stand* them when they are!" If you continue to depress yourself, you may then down yourself and depress yourself more about being depressed. So you see that indulging in your depression will harm you and your family in several ways and do virtually no good. Why indulge in it then?

Showing that the Worst Things that Might Happen are Still Only Inconvenient

People who make themselves terribly anxious or depressed over death and dying are almost always imagining that something can be *more than* inconvenient or disadvantageous, when of course it cannot be. They awfulize in their heads about 101 percent or 150 percent inconvenience—which obviously does not exist. To help them over this, it is often effective to escalate, deliberately, their predictions of pain into the worst thing that could possibly happen to them, and to show them that even this thing is bearable and leaves room for quite a good degree of human happiness. Here, for example, is part of my dialogue with a 25-year-old male who is extremely anxious about the likelihood of his young wife dying of cancer:

Therapist: "It certainly would be a tragedy for you, and to others as well, if your wife cannot be cured and if she dies of cancer. But why would that be terrible, if it happened?"

Client: "I wouldn't be able to take it. I don't know how I could live without her."

Therapist: "Obviously, you could; though you might choose not to. But don't you really mean that you couldn't live *happily* if she were dead?"

Client: "Yes, I know I couldn't."

Therapist: "Why couldn't you?"

Client: "I just couldn't."

Therapist: "Yes, but why?"

Client: "Well, I just could never find anyone else like her. It took me almost ten years to find her; and now, at my age, I'd never find anyone like her again."

Therapist: "That's very dubious! If you really looked, I'm sure you could find someone else, not exactly like her, of course, but someone who would make you a fine mate. But let's suppose the worst. Let's suppose your wife dies and that you never do find another woman to live with. Why would you then have to be utterly miserable?"

Client: "I don't know. I just would be."

Therapist: "No, you would insist, perhaps, on *making* yourself miserable. But you wouldn't have to. Even if you *never* found a suitable woman to love again, couldn't you do other enjoyable things—tennis, for example, or listening to music, or being absorbed in your work?"

Client: "Yes, I guess so."

Therapist: " 'But I really *couldn't*!' That's what I hear you saying underneath. But think, now! Suppose your wife died and no other

good woman ever crossed your path again—which is highly unlikely. Why *couldn't* you enjoy many things, even including dat-
ing and sex. Why *couldn't* you enjoy tennis, work, etc.?"

Client: "Well, I, uh, wouldn't want to!"

Therapist: "Oh, that's different. You *could*, you see; but you would foolishly choose not to. But think about it, again; really give it some
thought! If worse came to worst and you never had a good, lasting relationship with a woman again, you would certainly be
deprived and frustrated. You would never be *as* happy as you are
now. But you still, if you *chose* to do so, could be happy. In many
ways! On a desert island, with no people around whatever, you
could find something to make yourself happy. Or in solitary confinement in prison—as some people have done. Even at the worst,
you could stubbornly look for some degree of happiness and find
it. If you stop whining about the possible loss of your wife and if
you stop demanding, in a Jehovian fashion, that you *only* can be
happy with her!"

Detecting and Disputing Symptoms
about Symptoms

Most people, when they are seriously disturbed or when they are
emotionally upset for quite a period of time, develop a secondary
symptom, or a symptom about their symptom. In RET terms, they
first experience loss or failure at point A (Activating experience),
such as the loss of a close friend or relative. At point B (Belief system), they rationally tell themselves that they deplore this loss and
wish it hadn't occurred, and feel at point C (emotional Consequence)
sad, regretful, or grief-stricken. But at point B they also irrationally
tell themselves that this loss MUST not occur and that it is AWFUL
that it has happened. At point C they feel the disturbed Consequence
of panic, despair, or anger.

Being human—for this is one of their fundamental natures and has
biological as well as sociological roots—they then frequently take
point C, their disturbance, and make it into another A (Activating
experience). They then undergo the following sequence:

1. A (Activating experience)—"I see that I am panicked and de-
    sparing about the loss of my loved one."

2. rB (rational Belief)—"I don't like these feelings; and I'd better do something to change or eradicate them."
3. deC (desirable emotional Consequence)—Feelings of frustration and sorrow.
4. iB (irrational Belief)—"I must not have these feelings; it's TERRIBLE that I have them; what an INADEQUATE PERSON I am for feeling so panicked and despairing!"
5. ueC (undesirable emotional Consequence)—Anxiety about having anxiety; depression about feeling depressed.

In RET, we almost invariably inquire about people's secondary symptoms and then show them how to deal with them. Thus, I saw a 55-year-old man who was terribly depressed about the death of his two brothers, both of whom had heart attacks in their late forties. He was anxious about his own high blood pressure and about possibly having a fatal heart attack. Because he had been anxious for five years, I asked him how he felt about his being anxious. "Very foolish!" he replied, "I know that my anxiety is doing me no good, and my doctor tells me to relax and take it easy or else I'll affect my blood pressure; and I see that I can't relax, so I feel like a fool." "So you're anxious about your anxiety?" I asked. "Very much so!" he replied.

I then showed him that, in regard to his brothers' dying, he was awfulizing: "It's terrible for them to have died so young. I may have the same predisposition as they had, and it would be awful for me to die so young!" And about his anxiety he was awfulizing: "How awful for me to be so anxious! It only does me harm to feel this way. I shouldn't be anxious, I shouldn't be so foolish as to make myself so anxious! What an idiot I am for needlessly making myself so anxious!" When I got him to be fully in touch with his anxiety about his anxiety (about which he was only dimly aware) and to dispute his awfulizing beliefs that were causing this secondary symptom, he lost much of this anxiety, accepted the fact that it was too bad (but not AWFUL) to feel anxious, and then was in a much better mood to tackle his original anxiety and finally conquer it. In RET, we almost always probe to discover anxiety about anxiety or depression or guilt about anger, and work on this secondary symptom first—and then get back to working on the primary symptom.

Uprooting Guilt About Death and Dying

A great many people make themselves feel exceptionally guilty or self-downing when a loved one dies or is in the process of dying. They upset themselves about not having paid enough attention to this person before; or not having done something to detect his or her poor health before it became fatal; or not being nice enough to this person during his or her dying days; and so forth. RET particularly specializes in helping such people rid themselves of this kind—or any other kind—of guilt or self-flagellation. For RET teaches them to distinguish between (1) doing a wrong, immoral, or harmful act (e.g., neglecting a dying person) and (2) being a "louse" or "worm" for performing this act. It holds that a sense of responsibility or wrongdoing is generally right and proper, but that any kind of self-downing for immorality or irresponsibility is itself irresponsible and will rarely lead to anything but needless, additional harm.

In the case of the 55-year-old man mentioned in the previous section whose two brothers had died in their forties, he often felt very guilty because he had not taken their symptoms too seriously and had not been too close to them for a decade or so before they died. At one point, I strongly said to him:

> There is no evidence that you even did a wrong thing by neglecting your brothers for years before they died. For even if they wanted closer contact with you at this time, you are entitled to want less intimate contact with them. They have one set of desires and you have another; and who is to say whose desires are 'right' or 'good' in any absolute sense? But let's even suppose that you were wrong: that you could have easily taken a little trouble, called them more often, and been closer to them, thereby helping them live happier lives before they died. Even if we could prove your iniquity in this respect—which we will still have one hell of a time doing!—why MUST you be right? Where is it writ that you HAVE TO do the correct or desirable thing and to help your brothers thereby? And why are you *a worm—rather than a person who sometimes acts wormily*—if you did the wrong thing with your brothers? Prove your wormhood to me!

Of course, this man could not prove that he was rotten or worthless, even if it were provable that he acted rottenly with his brothers before their death. When he saw this, and stopped downing himself for his behavior (which he still felt was poor), he lost his guilt and was able to concentrate on becoming less anxious and (as noted above) less anxious about being anxious. While he was guilty, he was so absorbed in his self-defamation that he was able to do little about working on his primary and secondary symptoms of anxiety.

Using Rational or Coping Statements

In its elegant form, RET invariably tries to get people to see their own irrational beliefs (iBs) and actively and persistently to dispute and give them up. Various individuals are not too able to do this, for a variety of reasons. Some children are too young to do good disputing; other individuals are not smart enough to do so; some are so disturbed that they are temporarily incapable of doing so. For individuals such as these (who may well include the majority of people who are exceptionally anxious, depressed, and hostile about death and dying), RET provides a set of suitable rational or coping statements that they can write on 3×5 cards and continually go over and indoctrinate themselves with. These include self-coping statements or rational philosophies that they can partly learn by rote—and then, perhaps, later think through. Here, for example, are such statements: "Although I loved So-and-So very much, I *can* lead a happy life without him or her"; "No matter how desirable it is for me to live to a ripe old age, it is not *necessary* for me to do so"; "It's going to be very hard for me to accept the loss of my child but I definitely *can* do so"; "Dying may be a very painful process but once you are dead you have no feeling whatever and are completely without pain."

Teaching a Nondisturbed Philosophy

RET holds that people had better be, at times, quite sad, sorry, frustrated, annoyed, regretful, and determined to change undesirable conditions in their lives, but that they virtually never have to upset themselves (that is, make themselves panicked, depressed, self-hating, hostile, or self-pitying) about *anything*—yes, *anything*. It is hard for physicians and therapists to prove this to their patients and clients, but if you thoroughly believe this yourself, you may be able to teach some of your counselees, particularly those who are smart and educated, the following basic philosophies by which they can stubbornly refuse to depress or panic themselves about just any aspect of death and dying, including their own impending death:

1. No matter what happens to people, or how unfortunate life may sometimes be, this is the way it is—tough! Nobody promised us a rose garden; and if one's personal life is much worse than it once was, or even worse than most other people's, that is still tough— but never AWFUL, HORRIBLE, or TERRIBLE.

2. The world is often unfair and most probably will always be. Justice is highly preferable but doesn't HAVE TO exist. Misery mainly stems not from injustice but from one's whining and screaming about that injustice—from childishly demanding that it SHOULD NOT, MUST NOT exist. But it MUST exist—when it does!

3. The only thing that can really happen to a person is serious inconvenience or unpleasantness. Horror or terror are fictions— demons that really do not exist—unless we stupidly *think* that they do. The worst that can happen to anyone is extreme pain— and that rarely occurs. But if it does, it is *only* painful and never *more than* painful. When we grandiosely think that pain SHOULD NOT, MUST NOT exist when it unfortunately DOES exist, we then *make it* into a "holy horror" instead of a great inconvenience.

4. Although we will never like what we don't want, we can still STAND, still BEAR what we don't LIKE. Very few conditions are truly INTOLERABLE or UNBEARABLE. If truly "intolerable" conditions exist—if, for example, we are in constant acute pain that nothing will alleviate—then our existence may not actually be "living" or be worth living. Under such conditions, when we are not likely to obtain virtually any present or future pleasure, rational suicide may well be a good—or lesser evil—solution; and we had better seriously consider it. Not cavalierly, as a cop-out when we are facing temporary or moderate pain, but as a viable option to continued ceaseless physical suffering.

5. The state of death, in the light of all our available knowledge, is a completely insensate condition, involving no thought, no feeling, and no behavior of any kind. It is a thorough void, a true nothingness; as far as living and knowing is concerned, a zero. When we die, we are really dead, dead, dead—with no knowledge

of our past and present and no anxiety about the future. Death, consequently, is a harmless, unnoxious, unfeeling state, not to be feared at all and in no way unnatural or bad. It is exactly the state we were in just before we were conceived—and in what way was that state unpleasant or fearful (Ellis 1972b)?

6. Death, at the present time, is also inevitable. The mere fact that we are born and continue to live means that, like all forms of contemporary life, we will definitely die. To be accorded the boon of life, we have to (until the fountain of youth is some-day—perhaps!—discovered) suffer the fate of dying. Some of us will die sooner, some later, but we all (yes, all!) will die.

7. Worrying about how or when our demise will occur can hardly aid our living or prolong our dying. The more certainly we de-mand the exact date of our death, the more panicked we will make ourselves—thereby often facilitating a quicker and more gruesome departure! Demanding that we *know* how and when we will go will only give us the near-certainty of a horrified, more troublesome "life!"

8. Even when things go very badly, we can almost always, if we do not focus on poor conditions, find *some* ways of enjoying our-selves. Crippled, blind, and iron-lung-restricted individuals can still thrill to music. Deaf and dumb people can relish reading, writing, and loving. Long-term prisoners can paint, write books, train birds, and enjoy a hundred other things. Dying men and women can talk to their friends, fantasize, and dream about pleasures they can no longer actively pursue. Almost everyone who is still alive and kicking can discover, with determination and effort, several distractions and pleasures to comfort them in their most trying hours. They can if they stop wailing and whin-ing, to themselves and others, that they MUST not suffer what they are indubitably suffering (Spivack, Platt, and Shure 1976).

Other Cognitive Methods

RET uses several other cognitive therapy methods with people who upset themselves about death and dying. Thus, they are taught cog-nitive distraction, for example, Edmund Jacobsen's (1942) muscle relaxation technique or additional distraction methods to focus on

things other than worry and horror. They are shown how to use imagining methods (Lazarus 1979) and particularly (as noted below)
rational-emotive imagery. Almost always, they are given bibliother-
apy materials to read, such as *A New Guide to Rational Living* (Ellis
and Harper 1975), *Humanistic Psychotherapy: The Rational–Emotive
Approach* (Ellis 1973a), and *How to Master Your Fear of Flying*
(Ellis 1972b), which has a special chapter on how to overcome the
fear of dying. They are offered lectures and workshops that are
offered regularly by the Institute for Rational–Emotive Therapy in
New York; and cassette recordings and other audio-visual aids are
made available to them by the Institute (Ellis 1973b, 1973c, 1976).
They are taught some of the principles of general semantics (Korzybski 1933) to help them stop overgeneralizing and to give up thinking
in terms of necessity and allness. They are shown how to do practical problem-solving in connection with problems about death and
dying (D'Zurilla and Goldfried 1971; Ellis and Knaus 1977; and
Platt, Spivack, and Shure 1976).

EMOTIVE METHODS OF RET

Because RET holds that human cognitions, emotions, and behaviors
are interactional and that changing affects and behaviors can significantly modify irrational thoughts (just as changing thoughts can
significantly modify dysfunctional affects and behaviors), it employs
a number of emotive, evocative, dramatic techniques with most
clients, including those who are suffering with death and dying. For
example:

1. It teaches clients how to use rational–emotive imagery (Maultsby
    1975; and Maultsby and Ellis 1974), in which they let themselves
    implosively think about dreadful events, such as impending
    death, get fully in touch with their disturbed feelings of depres-
    sion or despair when they do so, and then work at changing these
    feelings to appropriate ones of sorrow and keen disappointment.

2. It uses role-playing to help people enact scenes that they are
    avoiding (e.g., informing a child that his or her father has a fatal
    illness), to experience, deeply, the emotions they feel when they
    are enacting a scene, and to work through it, emotionally and be-
    haviorally, and show themselves that they can truly handle the
    situation and their feelings about it.

3. It employs rational humorous songs (Ellis 1977d) to convey, in a forceful and dramatic manner, the message that they need not whine about anything, including death and dying, and that they can surrender feelings of anger, depression, and self-pity.

4. It encourages some clients to write down and carry with them rational statements—for example, "I do NOT need what I want and I CAN survive frustration and loss!"—and to say these to themselves many times a day very vigorously and powerfully until they sink into their minds and hearts and are truly believed and felt (Ellis and Whiteley 1979).

5. It uses shame-attacking exercises (Ellis 1972c), in the course of which clients are urged to do, in public, various foolish, ridiculous, or "shameful" acts (such as yelling out the stops in the subway or yelling out the time in a department store) and to get themselves to feel unashamed when doing so. In this manner, they are helped to overcome their feelings of inadequacy and self-downing—especially when they blame themselves for the death of a beloved or for not treating that individual "well enough" when he or she was alive.

BEHAVIORAL METHODS OF RET

RET, as noted above, has been exceptionally behavioral right from the start and has employed certain kinds of desensitization, such as *in vivo* desensitization, more than many of the other kinds of behavior therapy. In this regard, it frequently utilizes the following methods with people who are angry or depressed about death or dying:

1. Activity homework assignments are usually given to clients who are fearful of some "dangerous" situation (such as attending a funeral) and who keep their fears alive by continually avoiding these "dangers." People with low frustration tolerance—who, for example, will not attend a funeral because they think that they "can't stand" the pain they would feel if they did so—are often encouraged to do the thing that they view as "too" painful in order to show themselves that they definitely *can* bear it.

2. Although gradual desensitization is often used in RET, it is sometimes found more advisable to use flooding techniques and to have individuals continually and rapidly undergo "fearful" ex-

periences, so that they can more quickly and more intensively surrender their ideas that these events are "horrible" or "awful" and that they can hardly survive them (Ellis and Abrahms 1978).

3. Operant conditioning is used with many RET clients to help them do unpleasant homework tasks (such as refrain from certain enjoyments during a mourning period, out of deference to their relatives). They are shown how to reinforce or reward themselves with something pleasant (e.g., food) contingent upon their doing these tasks and to forego this reward when they do not do their homework. Operant conditioning is also used to encourage them to do cognitive homework, such as regularly filling out the Self-Help Report Form (Ellis 1977d) published by the Institute for Rational–Emotive Therapy.

4. Stiff penalties, in addition to reinforcements, are sometimes used in RET. Thus, if a client refuses to visit his dying mother, even though he has promised himself and others to do so, he may agree to do something obnoxious (e.g., burning a hundred-dollar bill or talking for an hour to a boring acquaintance) every time he avoids this self-contracting.

5. Skill training is often done in RET, in which clients or workshop participants are taught how to assert themselves, to communicate with others, to engage more adequately in love or sex activities, and to do other things that they would like to do but are, usually for neurotic reasons, avoiding.

CONCLUSIONS AND SUMMARY

RET normally takes a very hardheaded, philosophic approach to people who needlessly panic and depress themselves over problems of death and dying, showing them how they may *choose* to feel appropriately sad, griefstricken, and frustrated rather than inappropriately horrified, angry, and self-pitying. It consequently uses many cognitive, emotive, and behavioral methods; and uses them not simply because they work but because they may lead to the elegant philosophic result of clients seeing that nothing is truly upsetting and that they can always—yes, always—stubbornly refuse to upset themselves about anything.

But what of those who won't listen to science, to reality, and to reason? What of those who will consider the rational–emotive message too "hardhearted," too "cold" to take? Can we offer these recalcitrant misery-amassers any relief?

Why not? RET has several levels of solutions to emotional problems, ranging from the highly elegant one of radical philosophical restructuring to several less elegant levels of tender loving care, reassurance, distraction, and even (where nothing else seems to work) more pollyannaish modes of hope, faith, and charity. When maimed and dying people cannot—or will not—work at acquiring a sensible scientific philosophy, there is no reason why a flexible, kindly RET practitioner cannot palliate and offer them anything from positive thinking to religious hokum. Whatever works obviously works; and even though antiscientific twaddle has great dangers when employed in psychotherapy—especially the danger of comprising, itself, a distinct kind of delusion and hence disturbance—if that is all people will accept, then that is all they will accept. So be it. A physician whose patient will not tolerate a plaster cast for a seriously sprained ankle may compromise by giving him or her a set of crutches. A psychotherapist with a client who will not accept reality may compromise by providing this individual with a semi-shamanistic unreality. Too bad that the patient, in each case, will not do what would work best; but it is hardly *awful* or *terrible!*

So RET, which is the one main method of therapy that not only uses but teaches clients the scientific method, may (ironically) sometimes resort to magic, mysticism, and palliation. This will not be used by choice and not often, but if a grim and painful living or dying situation calls for it, it can serve as a last resort.

Let us, however, put first things first and last things last. Most dying individuals are not complete babies. They *can* grow and mature—mentally as well as emotionally and physically. They can be shown and persuaded how to be more logical, empirical, and scientific than they "naturally" are. This, perhaps, is the main goal of RET: to try to help everyone who can think straighter and less absolutistically to do so with great frequency and strength. Humans are clearly human—not subhuman or superhuman. Along with their strongly inherent *and* socially learned tendencies to be absolutistic and self-defeating, they also have the capacity to apply the flexible, empirical, and experimental rules of science to themselves and their disturbances. If they work hard at using their scientific potentialities, they are often able to achieve the most elegant, and humanistic, RET solutions and to train themselves, philosophically and behaviorally, to refuse to upset themselves emotionally about *anything*—yes, even about death and dying!

REFERENCES

Beck, A.T. *Cognitive therapy and the emotional disorders.* New York: International Universities Press, 1976.

D'Zurilla, T. and Goldfried, M. Problem-solving and behavior modification. *Journal of Abnormal Psychology*, 1971, *78*, 109–126.

Ellis, A. *Reason and emotion in psychotherapy.* Secaucus, N.J.: Lyle Stuart and Citadel Press, 1962.

Ellis, A. *Growth through reason.* Palo Alto: Science and Behavior Books and Hollywood: Wilshire Books, 1971.

Ellis, A. Psychotherapy and the value of a human being. In J.W. Davis (Ed.), *Value and valuation.* Knoxville, Tenn.: University of Tennessee Press, 1972. Reprinted: New York: Institute for Rational Living, 1972a.

Ellis, A. *How to master your fear of flying.* New York: Institute for Rational Living, 1972b.

Ellis, A. *How to stubbornly refuse to be ashamed of anything.* Cassette recording. New York: Institute for Rational Living, 1972c.

Ellis, A. *Humanistic psychotherapy: The rational-emotive approach.* New York: Crown Publishers and McGraw-Hill Paperbacks, 1973a.

Ellis, A. *Conquering low frustration tolerance.* Cassette recording. New York: Institute for Rational Living, 1973b.

Ellis, A. *Conquering the dire need for love.* Cassette recording. New York: Institute for Rational Living, 1973c.

Ellis, A. My philosophy of psychotherapy. *Journal of Contemporary Psychotherapy*, 1973d, *6*, 13–18.

Ellis, A. *Solving emotional problems.* Cassette recording. New York: Institute for Rational Living, 1976.

Ellis, A. How to be efficient though humanistic. *Dawnpoint*, 1977a, *1*, 38–47.

Ellis, A. *How to live with—and without—anger.* New York: Reader's Digest Press, 1977b.

Ellis, A. *RET abolishes most of the human ego.* New York: Institute for Rational Living, 1977c.

Ellis, A. *Rational self-help report.* New York: Institute for Rational-Emotive Therapy, 1977d.

Ellis, A. *A garland of rational songs.* Songbook and cassette recording. New York: Institute for Rational Living, 1977e.

Ellis, A. The value of efficiency in psychotherapy. *Psychotherapy*, 1980, *17*, 414–419.

Ellis, A. *Rational-emotive therapy and cognitive behavior therapy.* New York: Springer, 1981.

Ellis, A. and Abrahms, E. *Brief psychotherapy in medical and health practice.* New York: Springer, 1978.

Ellis, A. and Grieger, R. *Handbook of rational–emotive therapy.* New York: Springer, 1977.

Ellis, A. and Harper, R.A. *A new guide to rational living.* Englewood Cliffs, N.J.: Prentice–Hall, 1975.

Ellis, A. and Knaus, W. *Overcoming procrastination.* New York: New American Library, 1977.

Ellis, A. and Whiteley, J.M. (Eds.). *Theoretical and empirical foundations of rational–emotive therapy.* Monterey, Calif.: Brooks/Cole, 1979.

Epictetus. *Works of Epictetus.* Boston: Little, Brown, 1898.

Ferenczi, S. *Sex in psychoanalysis.* New York: Basic Books, 1950.

Goldfried, M.R. and Davison, G. *Clinical behavior therapy.* New York: Holt, Rinehart, and Winston, 1976.

Grieger, R. and Boyd, J. *Rational–emotive therapy: A skills-based approach.* New York: Van Nostrand Reinhold, 1980.

Hauck, P.A. *Reason and pastoral counseling.* Philadelphia: Westminster, 1972.

Jacobsen, E. *You must relax.* New York: McGraw–Hill, 1942.

Korzybski, A. *Science and sanity.* Lakewood, Conn.: Institute for General Semantics, 1933.

Lange, A. and Jakubowski, P. *Responsible assertive behavior.* Champaign, Ill.: Research Press, 1976.

Lazarus, A.A. *Behavior therapy and beyond.* New York: McGraw–Hill, 1971.

Lazarus, A.A. *Multimodal therapy.* New York: Springer, 1976.

Lazarus, A.A. *In the mind's eye.* New York: Rawson, 1978.

Lazarus, A.A. *The practice of multimodal therapy.* New York: McGraw–Hill, 1981.

Lembo, J. *The counseling process.* New York: Libra, 1976.

Mahoney, M.J. *Cognition and behavior modification.* Cambridge, Mass.: Ballinger, 1974.

Maultsby, M.C., Jr. *Help yourself to happiness.* New York: Institute for Rational Living, 1975.

Maultsby, M.C., Jr. and Ellis, A. *Technique for using rational emotive imagery.* New York: Institute for Rational Living, 1974.

Meichenbaum, D. *Cognitive behavior modification.* New York: Plenum, 1977.

Morris, K.T. and Kanitz, J.M. *Rational–emotive therapy.* Boston: Houghton Mifflin, 1975.

Phadke, K.M. *Bull fighting: A royal road to mental health and happiness.* Bombay: Author, 1976.

Rogers, C.R. *Client–centered therapy.* Boston: Houghton Mifflin, 1951.

Rogers, C.R. *On becoming a person.* Boston: Houghton Mifflin, 1961.

Spivack, G., Platt, J., and Shure, M. *The problem-solving approach to adjustment.* San Francisco: Jossey–Bass, 1976.

Walen, S., DiGiuseppe, R., and Wessler, R. *A practitioner's guide to rational-emotive therapy.* New York: Oxford, 1980.

Wessler, R. and Wessler, R. *The principles and practice of rational-emotive therapy.* San Francisco: Jossey–Bass, 1980.

Wolfe, J.L. and Brand, E. (Eds.). *Twenty years of rational therapy.* New York: Institute for Rational Living, 1977.

Wolpe, J. Cognition and causation in human behavior and its therapy. *American Psychologist*, 1978, *33*, 437–446.

7 BEHAVIORAL FAMILY SYSTEMS INTERVENTION IN TERMINAL CARE

Martin S. Cohen and
Elizabeth Keating Cohen

Clinical studies of the dying process focus largely on the experience of the individual, with far less attention devoted to the impact of death on the family unit. Yet the dying and death of a family member create tremendous stress within a family and often necessitate major changes in family organization. The diagnosis of terminal illness in a family member hurls the family into an acute crisis situation, disrupting normal patterns of interaction and behavior. The living–dying phase is described as a "physical and psychosocial limbo" for the family (Cohen and Wellisch 1978). Normal plans are suspended and routine functions are interrupted as the family searches for a new equilibrium in the face of impending loss.

Family adaptation to terminal illness requires numerous adjustments that, in themselves, can be disruptive to the structure and function of the family unit. Changes are required on many levels. Family roles and responsibilities must be renegotiated, thus requiring alterations in the family's transactions with society. Physical, emotional, and financial resources are highly taxed and, all too frequently, a supportive network outside the nuclear family is lacking.

The impending loss of a family member represents more than just the loss of a significant relationship for family members; it threatens the very *integrity* and *identity* of the family unit. The individual death is compounded by the sense that the family structure itself is

This chapter represents the joint effort of both authors.

disintegrating and that the usual sources for deriving meaning and support within the family system will be annihilated.

Given the magnitude of the crisis for a family, it is not surprising to discover that clinical studies indicate family members are at high risk for emotional difficulties following the loss of a loved one (Binger et al. 1969; Bowen 1976; and Raphael 1977). Such findings underscore the importance of extending our concern for the dying person to include the entire family system.

The mental health clinician can provide a crucial service to families undergoing the crisis of terminal illness. In this chapter we will discuss the contribution of a behaviorally oriented, family systems approach in facilitating adaptive coping behavior in families with a terminally ill member. Our approach focuses on the interaction of a family's structural organization and preferred coping style with the particular adaptive tasks required of the family in resolving the crisis of terminal illness.

Before discussing family evaluation techniques and the specific family readjustment tasks involved in the grieving process, we will first provide a detailed explication of a behavioral family systems model of intervention.

BEHAVIORAL FAMILY SYSTEMS THERAPY

Behavioral family therapy is sometimes understood as a method of instructing one or more family members in behavior management techniques in order to alter problem behavior in an identified member (Berkowitz and Graziano 1972; Christensen et al. 1980; Johnson and Katz 1973; and Patterson et al. 1975).

Lieberman (1976) expands this concept to include helping family members to change their modes of dealing with one another. In behavioral terms, this means changing the consequences of behavior or the contingencies of reinforcement operating in the family system. Using the principles of operant conditioning in the interpersonal context, adaptive behaviors can be increased at the same time that maladaptive behaviors are extinguished. For example, instead of rewarding deviant behavior with attention and concern, family members learn to give each other recognition and praise for desired behaviors.

Our perspective has much in common with Lieberman's approach since we consider the premises underlying our treatment strategies to be grounded in the principles of a humanistic behavior therapy; our method is an application of behavioral theory to systems of interpersonal interaction. However, our thinking has also been strongly influenced by the systems-oriented schools of structural family therapy (Minuchin 1974), and problem-solving or strategic family therapy (Haley 1976; and Watzlawick, Beavin, and Jackson 1967).

Within our framework, the family is viewed as a dynamic interpersonal system composed of various alliances or subsystems and organized around complex, predictable, and relatively enduring patterns of interaction. Each family, over time, develops a system of family rules (Jackson 1959) that govern interactions and maintain equilibrium. Family members are usually unaware of these rule-oriented sequences of interaction. Stated in more traditionally behavioral terms, each family unit develops a system of reinforcers that elicit and maintain certain behaviors in each of its members. Changes occur when this pattern of interaction is interrupted and the family system is thrown into a state of disequilibrium. In trying to reinstate homeostasis, the family will search out and establish a modified interactional pattern. This is precisely why the crisis situation creates so much stress for the family. The family is temporarily without an adequate response repertoire.

The Family Context of Problems

Disturbed, deviant, or difficult behavior is viewed as essentially a social phenomenon, occurring as one aspect of a system and reflecting some dysfunction in that system. Problem behaviors or pathological reactions in one or more family members are understood, therefore, as manifestations of maladaptive interactional strategies which the family develops while coping with conflict and stress. It is a fundamental premise of all family therapy approaches that the problems which people bring to psychotherapists are embedded in the context of a unique family system, and that such problems persist only if they are maintained by ongoing behavior of the individual and other family members with whom he or she interacts (Weakland et al. 1974). It follows that if the problem-maintaining behaviors are altered or eliminated, the problem will be resolved or disappear. The task of the family therapist is to observe the family's structure and the pattern of behavioral interaction in order to determine the feedback loops (von Bertalanffy 1956) that maintain symptomatic or maladaptive behavior. Once these data are available, the therapist actively intervenes to interrupt the feedback loop, and thus deliberately alters poorly functioning patterns of interaction. The choice of therapeutic intervention is determined by an understanding of the family's structural organization as well as by a functional analysis of problematic behaviors.

The behavioral family systems approach discussed here is well-suited for helping families cope with terminal illness since it offers the clinician a framework in which to conceptualize problems and design practical interventions. Such interventions can help therapists modify maladaptive structures and interactional patterns sufficiently to maximize the family's capacity for effective coping. For example, a family whose equilibrium is disrupted by the terminal illness of a child who previously had assumed many parental functions in the family will need help either in finding another family member to assume that child's role or in developing an entirely new pattern of caretaking functions. What follows is a discussion of how to evaluate family behavioral systems and intervene effectively to help families deal with the inevitable crises that will beset them in the course of adapting to a terminal illness.

FAMILY ASSESSMENT

Although the diagnosis of a terminal illness and the subsequent decline of a family member create a crisis of monumental proportion for any family, the family's response will be more predictable if the clinician obtains a history of how that family responded or failed to respond to crises in the past. Families' habitual problem-solving styles are automatically employed while attempting to cope with the trauma of terminal illness. Therefore the clinician will want to garner as much information as possible about a family's normative coping patterns in response to stress. The response to a terminal illness is seen not as a singular, unilevel and unprecedented reaction in the life of a family, but rather as a derivation of the customary patterns of problem resolution.

Our approach to evaluating families incorporates structural (Minuchin 1974), problem-solving (Watzlawick, Beavin, and Jackson 1967), and behavioral concepts. Data are collected by joining and accommodating to the style of the family (Minuchin 1974) and observing the regulation of family boundaries, repetitive behavior patterns, and the contingencies of reinforcement which maintain them. Of particular interest are the ways in which individuals communicate to one another and the alliances which these patterns of communication betray. For example, does mother talk directly to father, does she talk to the father indirectly by saying things to the children, or does she communicate to the father nonverbally? In contrast, does father listen to mother (regardless of her method of communication) or does he ignore her? Finally, how do these patterns of communication maintain the family homeostasis?

It is particularly important to note the patterns that involve the terminally ill member to determine whether the individual or his or her illness is ignored or overly emphasized. In cases where the ill member is being isolated, one might observe family members referring to the sick individual in the third person, successfully interrupting or usurping him conversationally, physically leaving him or her out of the family's seating arrangement, or even, upon occasion, leaving him or her at home. The sick member can become so isolated that even a coughing attack in the middle of a session will not elicit attention from the family. On the other hand, some families are able to focus only on the terminally ill member. This type of family interrupts its process for every cough, sneeze, and sigh which that individual utters, with the result that no discussion or interaction is ever completed unless it involves the dying patient or the illness.

Specific Role Assessment

A clinician should attempt to gain an understanding of the role which the ill member currently plays and formerly played in the family system. This is important for the following reason: the ill member is no longer able to assume his or her typical position in the daily routine of the family and thus inevitably disrupts family equilibrium. The need to establish a new homeostasis can be so stressful for the family that symptoms develop that, under more benign circumstances, might not have expressed themselves. For example, the illness of a father in a traditionally patriarchal and close-knit family — where that father acted as both breadwinner and emotional stabilizer — can be devastating since that family will need help in deciding who will take over his responsibilities, but will have to do so without the chief executive. Similarly, the illness of the wife in that same family would remove other role enactments that are equally important to family homeostasis and which also would have to be replaced for effective family functioning. In both cases, the therapist must evaluate the role of the dying patient and then consult with the family to help them with the actual and anticipated loss of the patient's routine contributions.

In addition to the roles enacted by the ill member, the clinician evaluates the roles assigned to other family members. This is a necessary step because the evaluator wants to make an early assessment of whether or not the roles assigned to each individual promote adaptation of that individual and the family unit. This can be accomplished through interaction with and observation of the family during the initial sessions and may occur in the hospital room.

As family roles often change dramatically during the course of a member's terminal illness, it is crucial to find out how, or if, the current roles contrast with previous roles and whether each member is more or less comfortable with his or her new role. While some modifications resulting from family reorganization may be adaptive, they also may be maladaptive. Adaptive role changes are alterations which are based on a realistic understanding of present and future realities, are fully supported by all family members, and are likely to have a positive effect on an individual's intra- and extrafamilial adjustment. Maladaptive role changes foster a denial of reality, placing an undue amount of stress on one or all of the family members.

A brief example of a maladaptive response to terminal illness in a family which had previously functioned well would be that a child, whose father is dying, becomes prematurely burdened with many adult responsibilities. As a result the child is denied the opportunity to work through the grief surrounding the father's death as well as to cultivate age-appropriate peer relationships. In contrast, an adaptive role alteration would be one that allowed this same child to grieve for the dying father and to maintain appropriate peer relationships, while encouraging participation in some family and household responsibilities.

Family Flexibility

Another consideration when evaluating a family's structure is the family system's flexibility or capacity to adapt itself to the myriad of new stimuli with which it has been bombarded. Of particular interest is how well the family has been able to comprehend and to cope with the reality of the terminal illness and how open it has been to the interventions of outsiders such as health-care personnel. The latter factor is important because an extremely rigid family will have a difficult time accepting any stranger into its family context. In the extreme, such a family will deal with terminal illness by hiding data from the physician, shopping around until they find a doctor who will not threaten to change the family homeostasis (i.e., will tell them what they want to hear), or behaving in ways indicating a reluctance to let anyone penetrate the family boundary. In fact, even if such a family accepted a referral to a therapist, it is unlikely that they would be comfortable sharing reactions to the illness. While few families are so rigid that they are unable to allow professionals any access to the system, many families are at least moderately so and thus require time to become comfortable with the notion of sharing their plight with a helper.

Related to the issue of rigid extrafamilial boundaries is that of inflexible informational boundaries, a type of family cognitive coping style. The family with overly rigid informational boundaries can be identified by such characteristics as a reluctance to secure information regarding the course of the terminal disease or the various treatment strategies that might be employed. Significantly, these boundaries can be rigid with regard to the transmission of information *within*, as well as *without*, the family unit. In fact, the former difficulty is more common, manifesting itself in situations where family members do not know how others are responding to the illness or what others would like to do in order to cope with it— psychologically or logistically—and yet do know that it is not permissible to discuss the problem.

Such informational and interpersonal rigidities are indeed problematic because they compromise a family's ability to feedback the new information into its matrix, a crucial factor for adapting to stress. It is only through the feedback process that a family can evaluate whether old strategies have been successful and, if not, what new ones are necessary.

The Enmeshed–Disengaged Continuum

The initial family evaluation must also examine how reactive specific family members are to one another, or where they fall on an "enmeshed-disengaged continuum" (Minuchin 1974). An extremely enmeshed family is one in which family members are likely to be highly affected by another's terminal illness. In this type of family, everyone will be greatly disrupted by the illness, anticipating its every turn and reacting in ways that interfere with the dying patient's ability to adjust to the condition. On the other hand, families on the extremely disengaged end of the continuum will often react to a terminal illness by not responding. Taken to its pathological extreme, this family style will isolate the patient so that dying becomes a lonely and dehumanized experience.

Such overly enmeshed or overly disengaged family styles are extreme, and are not necessarily representative of the families that will be referred to most clinicians. Most frequently, families will fall somewhere in the middle of the continuum, needing help either in firming-up boundaries that have weakened in reaction to the stress or in loosening-up boundaries that have become too rigid. The appropriate modulation or modification of boundaries is helpful since it facilitates conversation and interaction relevant to the terminal illness. It helps family members to share their sense of sadness, to make decisions regarding how they are going to cope with everyday life during the living–dying process, and to develop behavioral and cognitive strategies for dealing with medical personnel.

Developmental Staging

Finally, the clinician needs to be aware of the stage in the family life cycle to which the presenting family belongs, since needs and expectations of family members differ at various phases of the life cycle. This is often ignored by many orthodox behaviorists and seems to preclude a multidimensional assessment of coping and adaptation (Sobel 1981). For example, the needs and cognitions of a relatively young family unit with small children are different from both those of a group with adolescents preparing to leave home or those of a couple whose children have already departed. Moreover, the alliances which provide support for family members shift during the life cycle. Children who require support at an early age are able to provide support for other family members as they grow older.

An additional factor which the clinician must take into consideration is the varied meanings which terminal illness has to individuals at different personal and familial developmental stages. Family members will conceptualize death with varied levels of sophistication depending on their emotional and developmental level of functioning. It is also important to note whether the terminally ill member is an older individual who has lived a full and productive life, or whether he or she is a younger person for whom the family has held many hopes and expectations. The latter case is especially traumatic and the therapist should expect the family to utilize more denial and to be more emotionally reactive to the reality-oriented issues surrounding the illness.

FAMILY COPING TASKS

The stress induced by a terminal illness can result in multiple levels of possible dysfunction within any family. The quality and extent of dysfunction experienced will vary according to the family system's historical capacity to adapt to stressful situations. An accurate picture of the problems of a particular family can only be achieved if the clinician obtains a clear understanding of the family's history, structural organization, valued reinforcers, and general behavioral styles. This includes knowledge of the functional role played by the ill member, the imposed changes in role behavior, the family's conceptualization of the sick role, the impact of previous deaths on family life, the degree of denial being employed, attitudes toward the health care system, resources for support available outside the family, and past patterns of communication, coping, and adaptation. The aim of assessment is to enable the therapist to design interventions that will aid the family in restoring a sense of stability so that it might cope more adequately with the demands of the present crisis and the impending crisis of bereavement. The ultimate goal of the behavioral family therapist is to enable the family to return to a healthy rather than pathological state of equilibrium.

Although each family unit brings to the crisis of terminal illness its own unique framework, there are identifiable coping tasks—inherent in the death crisis itself—that all families must negotiate. The family clinician might be asked to intervene when breakdown has occurred or at an earlier stage when signals of distress in the family system first become apparent. In either case, the therapist uses an understanding of the family to facilitate and bolster adaptive strategies for dealing with the progressive demands of the living–dying process. The remainder of this chapter focuses on the variety of coping tasks that a family must face in resolving the crisis of terminal illness. Three case examples are provided to illustrate the use of behavioral family systems techniques in modifying a family's maladaptive attempts to cope with the stress of losing one of its members.

Denial Versus Acceptance of the Illness

The period following the diagnosis of a terminal illness is a particularly stressful one for the family. Reactions are potentially so intense with so much information to digest that some denial of the reality of the diagnosis is necessary for the continued effective functioning of the family. By denial we do not mean a total distortion or reversal of reality, but rather an adaptive strategy whereby the family seeks to avoid extreme disequilibrium, attempting to accommodate to the news at a more tolerable pace. Weisman (1972) identifies three orders of denial and acceptance. In first-order denial, the facts about the illness are denied, including the diagnosis. Less extreme is the second form where implications or inferences to be drawn from the illness or its signs are denied. Third-order denial is characterized by an acknowledgment of the illness and its progression, a realization of the limited effects of treatment, but a denial of death as the ultimate outcome. Like the individual, the family system responds to terminal illness with a balance between denial and acceptance. A healthy balance between these strategies will enable the family unit to continue functioning with a sense of purpose and meaning while making necessary changes and accommodations to meet the needs of the dying member.

Denial in families takes many forms, but almost always involves a breakdown in the family's communications network. Examples of denial include a reluctance on the part of family members to inform the patient about the true nature of the illness; denial of the illness by the dying member which is reinforced by the family's reluctance to confront the subject; or the inability of family members to discuss the meaning and impact of the diagnosis on their daily lives.

Failure to resolve these difficulties will interfere with the family's ability to develop adaptive coping skills as the illness progresses. Prolonged inability to communicate openly about the nature of the illness is problematic since it both isolates the dying patient and places stress on the rest of the family unit. The family, by not acknowledging the truth, denies the dying patient the important opportunity to talk about feelings, fears, wishes, and concerns during the course of the illness. The rest of the family also suffers during this stage as behavioral patterns develop which drain off some, but not all, of the tension. In fact, these patterns often manifest themselves to therapists as presenting problems. The symptoms which may emerge as a result of the family's difficulty in accepting a terminal illness will depend on the unique history and structure of the particular family, but such symptoms may include marital discord or psychosomatic complaints.

Interventions at this stage in the family's adjustment process can be critical for alleviating maladaptive behaviors and for establishing behavioral alternatives that may result in more effective coping for the dying person and the family. The following case example illustrates how early denial of a terminal illness can express itself in family dysfunction. Based on a thorough evaluation of family interaction, behavioral family systems interventions were implemented in order to alter maladaptive alliances and sequences of behavior.

Case 1

Mr. and Mrs. S. sought help because of difficulties they were experiencing with their 14-year-old son, Mark. Mark had been picked up repeatedly for car theft and had been reported to the authorities for chronic truancy in school. While this was given as the presenting problem, three additional factors became apparent during the first interview: Mrs. S. had been recently informed that she was suffering from terminal cancer, a fact that both Mr. and Mrs. S. were reluctant to discuss; their eldest child, Jay, now 17, had manifested similar delinquent behavior three years earlier when Mr. S. was hospitalized for severe heart problems (which were treated with successful bypass surgery); and both Mr. and Mrs. S. were more withdrawn and depressed than was normal for them. In fact, the S.'s were so depressed that they had virtually abdicated many of their parental tasks (e.g., cleaning house, fixing meals).

Another important factor was the manner in which the illness was denied. Although the diagnosis of cancer was openly acknowledged in the family, discussion of the implications of the disease was avoided. The children's questions about Mrs. S.'s illness were met by quick reassurances and a change of subject. Occasional mention of the disease was followed by vehement arguments between Mr. S. and Mark.

The most glaring bit of information gleaned in this interview was that the S.'s refused to discuss their serious illnesses, past and present, and the effect that such silence had on their children. During both the illness of father, and now mother, this refusal to discuss things increased the tension to such a degree that someone was needed to help the family escape from the aversive situation. First Jay, and now Mark, was selected for that role. Specifically, by getting into trouble and setting himself up as a scapegoat, Mark's behavior over the previous six months offered the family the distraction they needed to avoid their depression about the reality of Mrs. S.'s impending death. One of the systemic dysfunctions which helped to encourage this behavior was Mr. and Mrs. S.'s mutual depression and withdrawal which further limited the effectiveness of an already weak parental alliance. This breakdown in the parent subsystem led to inconsistent messages about Mark's behavior. For example, although his parents would threaten to punish Mark for his misbehavior (i.e., forbid him to leave the house, withhold privileges in the house) Mr. S. often sabotaged the punishments by confiding in Mark that he understood how Mark's mind worked because he too used to get in the same sort of trouble when he was a boy.

From the therapist's perspective, Mark's misbehavior was reinforcing to the family for two reasons. It enabled all family members to fend off the grief from which there was no escape, and it helped Mark to get some of the attention that he was denied due to his parents' withdrawal and depression. Nonetheless, the family was not aware of these factors and felt very distressed by the entire situation. By the time the S.'s got to the therapist's office they were desperate, telling Mark, "you're going to kill your mother if you don't start acting better."

A number of steps were taken to remove Mark's distraction or scapegoating behavior from the center of the family stage and replace it with the denied reality of Mrs. S's impending death. The first was to note with empathy how difficult it was for the family to face the mother's cancer and to relabel Mark's behavior as an attempt to lift the spirits of the family. Further, it was noted that while Mark meant well, it seemed that the family was now telling him that they didn't want him to act this way anymore. Although there was some resistance to the notion that Mark was well-meaning rather than bad, this relabeling was important as it caused Mr. and Mrs. S. to re-examine their view of him as malicious. This intervention effectively raised their sense of hope and helped them to feel more motivated toward working together in their parental alliance in order to bring their son into line. Hence, much of the first phase of therapy was aimed at helping the parents to create order in their home. Problems were raised regarding Mark's behavior, and solutions were sought with the whole family present.

As behavior therapists have noted, positive rewards must be provided for all people involved in a family if change is to occur. An attempt was made to do just that. One of Mark's difficulties was conceptualized as his sense of loneliness resulting from his parents' depression and withdrawal. Therefore he was encouraged to replace what had become a very problematic relationship with his parents with a closer tie to his brother, i.e., structurally shifting his alliance to the sibling subsystem. Although this strategy (attempted in separate sessions with the brothers) did not directly address the family's need to grieve, it did provide Mark with a relationship in which he could vent some of his feelings without getting into arguments. It also gave him a role model with whom he could identify since Jay had experienced similar problems in the past and had succeeded in improving his behavior significantly. Thus Jay was encouraged to take Mark under his wing to help him to do the same thing.

At the same time, Mark's parents were encouraged to reward themselves for their improved cooperation in disciplining Mark, by going out on movie dates (the only place where "we can forget everything"). Finally, everyone was instructed to congratulate Mark as his behavior, particularly around school attendance, began to improve.

In the second phase of the treatment the therapist confronted the issue of terminal illness with the family. As there was still an enormous resistance to the topic at this point, the issue was attacked by discussing first with Mr. S. and later with the rest of the family their reactions, feelings, attitudes, and fears about his heart condition which was now well under medical control. It was clear that Mr. S. functioned as the family censor and therefore any change of the family pattern involving a discussion of previously taboo subjects would require his approval. The therapists's intention was to shape, slowly, the family's ability to tolerate stressful topics through successive approximation. Therefore, after Mr. S. allowed the therapist to talk with him about his illness in the past tense, other family members were encouraged to discuss their reactions to it as well. This discussion prompted both Mr. and Mrs. S. to recall the painful loss of significant others early in their lives which neither of them had fully resolved. Talking about these deaths in the present helped them to restructure their cognitions about death. They realized that despite their earlier fears that these losses would destroy them, they had managed to survive quite well. Although talking about death was painful, they came to see that it was not devastating. With the therapist's support, the S.'s moved through discussions of previous losses and life-threatening illnesses to broaching the topic of Mrs. S.'s terminal disease.

Once the denial began to lift, everyone began to grieve openly and appeared more depressed. Although Mark tried to distract people early in this process by getting into a fight at school for which he was suspended, the tactic did not work; the family responded differently this time by setting limits without overreacting. The rest of therapy was spent supporting the family in their grief work, helping them to get things in order for Mrs. S.'s impending death, and trying to help Mrs. S. feel as comfortable as possible through the painful chemotherapy process. Three months prior to Mrs. S.'s death the S. family stopped therapy because Mrs. S. became very weak. However, they returned for four sessions after Mrs. S.'s death and indicated that although Mark was still not achieving up to expectations, he had not stolen a car or been involved in any serious trouble for eight months. The modified family rule remained intact as the family continued to grieve and attempted to re-orient their lives without Mrs. S.

Establishing a Relationship with Health Caretakers

An important set of skills that a family must learn in order to cope effectively with a terminally ill member, is how to interact with and respond to the physician and other health caretakers. Adaptive coping requires that family members procure an appropriate amount of information from the health-care team to guide actions and expectations at each phase of the illness. Although the family should encourage the patient to take an active role in the planning and implementation of his or her own treatment, it is frequently necessary for family members to make arrangements on behalf of the patient. Family members also have to learn assertive skills and even how to express constructive anger toward health caretakers in such a way that relationships with health personnel are not jeopardized.

Several maladaptive responses are possible. A family's sense of helplessness in the face of terminal illness often turns to anger and frustration which may then be directed at health caretakers. Such hostility may be expressed in direct confrontation with medical staff or, more passively, through noncompliance with medical advice. In the extreme, a family's anger and frustration can lead to a "shopping around" phenomenon in which the family continues to seek disconfirmation of the diagnosis or a miracle cure. These reactions are attempts at adaptation by the family. The anger and the cognitions supporting this affect often fend off feelings of depression and powerlessness, and thus provides family members with some sense of control in this painful, uncertain process.

An information-sharing conference which includes the family, the health-care team, and the family therapist consultant has proven helpful in alleviating a family's anxiety and cognitive distortions of the illness. Second, it reduces distrust of medical staff, thereby promoting more open communication between family and staff (Binger et al. 1969).

Meeting the Needs of the Dying Person

In time, most families are able to resolve the initial denial and confusion characteristic of the diagnostic phase and move on to some
degree of acceptance. This period is marked by an active desire on
the part of family members to meet the special needs of the dying
individual. The family as a whole develops strategies to accommodate
to the changing needs of the dying person. Effecting a balance between the patient's increased dependency and continued need for
autonomy is particularly important. If the dying person is an adult,
this means making some concrete accommodations to maximize
capacities for continued involvement in family affairs without over-
taxing capabilities. It may be quite difficult for the family to tolerate
increased dependency and regression in a formerly capable and responsible adult member. There is always the risk that the family system will not be able to relinquish its dependency on the dying adult,
and thus persist in holding unrealistic expectations of the patient's
capacity to function.

On the other hand, the family might react by assuming too many
of the patient's former responsibilities, thereby excluding the patient
more than is necessary from family affairs. When the dying member
is a child, the anguish involved in witnessing suffering and deterioration causes many parents to respond in an overprotective and over-
indulgent manner. Such parents unwittingly fail to encourage growth-
oriented activities and thus compromise the child's continued development. Children might be kept out of school or might be forbidden
to participate in peer activities despite their physical capability to
manage these situations.

The family must create a safe atmosphere in which the dying person is free to make needs and wants known, without fear of incurring
the resentment or disapproval of family members. Optimally, the patient should feel confident that physical as well as emotional needs
will be tended to within the context of the family. Healthy adaptation to a dying person requires an open communication system so
that the dying person can share his painful anxieties and concerns
with his or her loved ones. All too often, when dying people try to
express their concerns to family members they are met with quick
reassurances that "all will be well" or that there is no need to discuss
unpleasant topics. From a behavioral perspective, these responses

aversively condition the patient to avoid the subject and leave him or her emotionally isolated from most significant relationships. This constitutes a form of abandonment of the dying person, on the part of the family, and a failure to support and reinforce the patient at a critical time.

Finally, the family system must remain flexible enough to recognize when additional care is needed and to seek out such support in the social environment. There are times when the patient may want an outsider to talk to so that certain very private and personal feelings can be expressed away from the family. Sometimes the patient's physical limitations become a source of embarrassment to family members. In these circumstances, it may alleviate the patient's sense of shame to have someone outside the family, such as a nurse or hospice aide, attend personal hygiene needs. Again, communication and negotiation are vital dimensions of behavioral intervention.

The following case example illustrates the difficulties encountered by a couple in accommodating the needs of a patient in the final stages of multiple sclerosis. A behavioral family systems intervention is applied in promoting adaptive solutions to these difficulties.

Case 2

Mr. and Mrs. C. sought help for marital difficulties stemming from the management of Mr. C.'s multiple sclerosis. Mr. C. was a 48-year-old man who at the time of the initial interview was paralyzed from the neck down. Mrs. C. was a 35-year-old woman who had married her husband fifteen years earlier despite her knowledge that he had a progressive illness which would eventually cripple and kill him.

A history revealed that the marital discord was directly related to the disease, since the first prolonged conflicts emerged at approximately the same time that Mr. C. became confined to a wheelchair. The frequency of such conflicts increased with each successive exacerbation of the illness. The trauma of confinement to a wheelchair was heightened for Mr. C., for concurrent with this event Mrs. C. took over responsibility for the real estate business which he prided himself on having established and built. This transfer of power upset Mr. C. on different levels, but the complaint that he articulated was his concern that his wife was working too hard, leaving him alone at home, feeling lonely and useless. This was a sore point for the C.'s and Mr. C.'s efforts to convince Mrs. C. to spend more time at home were to no avail. As a result, Mr. C. felt rejected and responded as he had in other similar situations in his past: he became combative and verbally abusive. Obviously, this was also difficult for Mrs. C. since she was struggling to do a good job at a business she knew little about and was unable to elicit much help or support from her husband. Not only did he get angry at her when she put in long hours, but he also refused to consult with her about business matters. When asked about this behavior, Mr. C. stated that withholding his assistance was the only way he knew to get back at his wife for what he perceived as her neglect of him. Nonetheless, Mrs. C. responded by deciding to continue working long hours and struggling through the problems alone.

The underlying issue in most of the C.'s fights was Mr. C.'s sense of rejection. Thus the fact that Mrs. C. unintentionally manifested rejecting behavior around some of the more personal tasks which Mr. C. requested of her was particularly relevant. Specifically, although she continued to change the urine bag, help Mr. C. wash in the morning before the day nurse arrived, periodically reposition him in the bed to avoid bed sores, and attempt to satisfy him sexually, she communicated her disdain for these tasks nonverbally. Mrs. C. felt she could not verbalize her negative feelings both because she felt guilty about them and because Mr. C. managed to block her attempts to discuss these issues.

A typical fight for the C.'s would start in the morning and unfold in the following manner. Mrs. C. would awaken and almost immediately become irritable at the thought of changing Mr. C.'s urine bag. Mr. C. would sense this and respond with some form of verbal provocation, by reviving an argument from the previous evening, by criticizing the way in which Mrs. C. was currently ministering to him, or by attacking her for going into work so early. Despite these provocations, Mrs. C. would continue to do her job, but would become so rattled that she would make a mistake, i.e., spill some urine, causing an escalation of the process. Eventually Mrs. C. would leave for work feeling so angry that she would hardly say goodbye, thus "proving" to her husband that she was growing tired of him and their life together, and causing him to ruminate all day about the deterioration of their relationship. Finally, when Mrs. C. returned from work later than she had intended, partially because of business and partially because the situation at home was so ungratifying, Mr. C. would yell at her, beginning yet another cycle of conflict-producing behaviors.

The first set of problems broached in the therapy was the interactions focused around Mr. C.'s regressed physical condition. This was accomplished by asking each spouse what could be done to make things better at home. Although reluctant to respond at first because she feared getting into a fight, Mrs. C. eventually stated that she would like to be relieved of the responsibility of ministering to Mr. C.'s physical needs in the morning. Further, she said that it would help if she could figure out a way to do both a good job at the family business and to spend as much time with her husband as he wanted. Mr. C. stated that things would be better if his wife spent more time at home. Therefore, the first approach was to establish a new marital contract that allowed Mrs. C. more independence from tasks she did not like and also gave Mr. C. more time with his wife. One intervention that helped to put this contract into operation was the suggestion that the C.'s have conferences one day each week to discuss matters related to the family business. Although Mr. C. objected to this plan, he was encouraged to go along with it for the following reasons: he was an expert whose consultation would help Mrs. C. become more efficient at work and thus have more time available to spend with him, and these meetings would allow him to feel needed by his wife rather than rejected by her. The ultimate aim of these meetings was to make it possible for both Mr. and Mrs. C. to run the business together out of their home. As it was acknowledged that the first meeting would be difficult, the therapist agreed to attend the session. This task not only offered Mrs. C. expert help, but it also allowed Mr. C. to feel more useful as well as to spend more time with his wife.

Since this proposal did not directly address any of Mrs. C.'s primary requests, the contract was expanded so that the day nurse's responsibilities would now include helping Mr. C. with his morning routines. Once the contract was implemented, some of the fighting subsided, but Mr. C.'s continued provocation of fights in the morning suggested that he was somewhat uncomfortable with the new arrangement. This led to a second phase of contracting which was marked by Mr. C.'s admission that he was frightened that he would become an invalid and that he would eventually be sent to a nursing home to die. He felt that having his morning hygiene attended to by a nurse rather than by his wife fed into this fear since he perceived it as one short step away from a home. Mrs. C. responded to Mr. C.'s admission by assuring him that she had no intention of sending him away from her and expressed her wish to make him feel less vulnerable. Their contract was modified so that Mrs. C. agreed to stay in the room with Mr. C. to offer him support while the nurse tended to his morning routine. Much of the tension in the marriage was dissipated as a result of the couple's increased communication and modified behavior contracts.

Although Mr. C. died six months later due to unexpected complications related to his disease, the couple managed to effect a much better relationship toward the end of their lives together.

Maintaining a Functional Equilibrium

Despite the changes and confusion generated by the crisis of terminal illness, the family unit must continue to develop strategies for maintaining emotional and interpersonal equilibrium. The tasks during this phase center on preserving a sense of normalcy and routine while simultaneously making necessary role shifts and balancing the special needs of the dying member with the needs of other family members.

The decreased capacities and increased dependency of the ill member exert a stress on each family member. This requires not only a redistribution of responsibilities and functions, but also a major diversion of emotional support toward the dying member, often at the expense of other members in the family. The ordinary structural boundaries which have regulated family homeostasis in the past break down, and must be reconstructed if the family is to maintain a sense of continuity and integrity. For example, if the illness affects the member of the family who is responsible for the economic support of the family, this responsibility must be assumed by another able member. Such role shifts are very stressful for the family and may bring additional hardships to bear on those who are already emotionally vulnerable. Moreover, the redistribution of responsibilities must occur in such a way that the family manages to perform the patient's former functions while not shutting him or her out of family life.

Often the family system's homeostatic maneuvers to preserve the status quo will undermine the smooth transition of intrafamilial roles and functions. A formerly able husband who prided himself on his ability to provide for his family may resent his wife's mobility and independence and thus find himself engaged in competitive struggles with her. Another example can be found in the reactions of the siblings of a dying child. Increased demands for attention, regressive behavior, somatic complaints or other symptoms in siblings are reflective of an attempt to return to an earlier homeostatic pattern where parental attention had been more evenly distributed.

Attending to the growth-oriented needs of all family members is a formidable task in the face of impending loss. The needs of each member depend on the nature of the specific developmental tasks faced at a given time. The disruption in family life created by a life-threatening illness can interfere with important developmental tasks for children, such as school achievement, peer relationships, the establishment of age-appropriate heterosexual relations, and separation from the family. Siblings of a dying child may experience jealousy and guilt, become preoccupied with fears of separation or their own death, or may regress and withdraw from age-appropriate tasks. The concrete caretaking needs required by the dying patient, or the re-alignment of family tasks and responsibilities, may overburden young adult family members and interfere with their attempts to separate from the family and establish autonomous lifestyles. The family system must be flexible enough to recognize symptoms of distress in its members and to make appropriate adjustments to alleviate the stress on a particular member.

The case of the D. family provides a good example of the difficulties a family may encounter in trying to balance the needs of the dying member with those of other family members. In this case, the family's customary methods for coping with stress became dysfunctional for several members. Interventions were geared toward helping the parental subsystem generate alternative coping strategies.

Case 3

The D. family was referred to the clinic by an oncologist who was working with Emily D., an 8-year-old whose disease was currently in remission. Dr. A. was concerned both because Emily had become increasingly depressed over the past six months, and because word had reached him from the pediatrician in the same health clinic that John, Emily's 6-year-old brother, had become school phobic in the fall. Also, Dr. A. noticed that Mr. and Mrs. D. spent a good deal of their time in his office fighting with one another and when they were not fighting they seemed highly anxious.

An initial attempt to formulate an operational definition of what was happening at home revealed that both Emily's depression and John's school phobia were related to the D.'s reaction to the diagnosis of Emily's leukemia. Particularly relevant to the genesis of these problems was the D.'s frequent quarreling behavior which began almost from the day of diagnosis (approximately six months earlier). Instead of using each other as resources during the trying period and helping their children adjust to the new situation, the couple reverted to a familiar pattern of bickering under stress. The fights usually involved some aspect of Emily's care (e.g., whether she should attend school or play with friends) and almost always had the same outcome: Mr. D. would respond by either psychologically withdrawing or by exploding and then storming out of the house. Mrs. D. responded to these behaviors by taking her children over to her mother's house where she would vent her anger about Mr. D. At the time of the first interview this pattern was occurring approximately one to two times per week.

John's refusal to attend school was related to this pattern. Although he stated that he stayed away from school because he did not like it there, other behavior-maintaining factors became apparent. First, his symptom returned to him some of the attention he had recently lost as a result of his parents' concern about Emily. Also, Mrs. D.'s decision (over Mr. D. and Emily's objections) to remove Emily from school amplified John's fears about Emily's sickness and motivated him to stay closer to his sister. Finally, it was found that Mrs. D. unwittingly rewarded John when he stayed home by serving him and Emily breakfast in bed. She would then sit with them and watch daytime television for much of the afternoon.

Emily's depression was also connected to her parents' struggle. They were so busy fighting about what they thought was the right thing to do that they lost sight of her own wishes and needs. Specifically, she missed both going to school and playing with her friends after classes, and she was frightened by all the restrictions which had been placed on her. She was also upset by the fighting she witnessed between her parents and worried that it was her fault.

Because the initial evaluation sessions with the family suggested that the primary problem was the ineffectiveness of the D.'s spouse and parental subsystems, sessions were held with the couple alone, as well as with the entire family. It was hoped that shoring up spouse and parental boundaries in separate sessions would enable the family to deal more effectively with John's school phobia, Emily's depression, and Emily's terminal illness.

The first task in the couples' phase of therapy was clarifying with Mr. and Mrs. D. why they thought they were fighting. Mr. D. spoke first, stating that he was upset with Mrs. D. because he thought she was overprotective toward their daughter, she tended to ignore his opinion, and she acted without his approval on important parental decisions. Mrs. D. countered by complaining that her husband neither showed good sense when it came to disciplining the kids, nor stayed around to resolve disagreements regarding those decisions. One item which was strikingly absent from this discussion was the possibility that the fighting was related to the news of Emily's terminal illness. The closest they came to such a reference was a vague allusion by Mr. D. to the fact that Mrs. D. blamed him and his family for Emily's illness because one of his sisters had died at age ten from the same disease.

Following this discussion, the cognitive factors maintaining the above-mentioned provocative behaviors were examined. Of primary importance was the undiscussed fact that Mr. and Mrs. D. both believed that Mr. D.'s genetic endowment was responsible for Emily's disease. Since this conceptualization of leukemia as an hereditary disease which could be passed directly from one parent to an offspring was a medical issue that warranted medical clarification, the referring oncologist was asked to attend a couples' meeting. In this meeting, Dr. A. clarified that although there might be a genetic factor related to leukemia, the research was inconclusive and his experience suggested there was no such relationship. In any case, his recommendation that no blame be assigned was helpful as it enabled the D.'s to move past the isolation caused by Mrs. D.'s anger and Mr. D.'s depression and, for the first time since the diagnosis, to experience, together, the full impact of their impending loss. As painful as this was, it was a positive experience which marked the beginning of the reconstruction of their marital system.

Also related to the D.'s fighting behavior was the fact that Mr. D. had a history of losing his temper as an adolescent and therefore learned very early to control himself by escaping provocative situations. Clearly, the cognitive schema developed in his adolescence was not helpful in his present relationship with

Mrs. D. In contrast, Mrs. D. as a child had had a nonnurturant relationship with both of her parents. As a result, she learned to respond to the perceived withdrawal of support with fierce independence. This early experience also led her to vow that her children would never feel neglected.

Recommendations were made to extinguish these conflict-producing conditioned responses of both Mr. and Mrs. D. First, Mr. D. was instructed to substitute his psychological and physical withdrawal behavior during arguments about the children with time-out periods in the cellar (working out on a punching bag or having a quiet beer alone). In return, Mrs. D. was advised to stop reacting to fights about the children by acting unilaterally, but rather to wait until Mr. D. had returned from the cellar to finish their discussions. Although this was difficult for the couple at first, it eventually proved helpful in eliminating some of the quarreling, enabling them to resolve, jointly, several critical areas of conflict.

Regulation of Affect

The equilibrium of the family is also strained by the intense levels of emotion which the knowledge of death engenders. While patterns of emotional expression within a family persist in a style similar to that which preceded the illness, the regulation of affect is an important family task during the living–dying interval. We spoke above about the importance of permission to grieve within the family. The permission to share painful affects is crucial to maintaining flexible lines of communication within the family, but adaptive coping also requires a conscious regulation of feelings and behaviors in accordance with the family's *appraisal* of the life situation confronting them. Futterman and Hoffman (1972) found that the timing of parental grieving was coordinated with other adaptive tasks, and that feelings, in general, were monitored or modified in the service of maintaining equilibrium. Obviously, remissions and exacerbations of an illness bring about a shifting in the range and intensity of emotions that a family must tolerate. Exacerbations are associated with a reactivation of the grieving process, while remissions allow some relief from these intense emotions. A major cognitive and affective task for the family system is the regulation of hopefulness in the face of uncertainty. Family members, as well as the patient, need to balance the optimism resulting from a temporary remission against the inevitability of further episodes of the illness (Mailick 1979).

The management of positive and negative affect among family members is complicated by the presence of a dying member. Normal patterns of emotional interchange become distorted as the family attempts to deal with the dying process. The expression of negative feelings may be suppressed or prohibited in order not to add to an already stressful situation. Resentments and animosities may build up between family members and eventually undermine cooperation. Hostilities may flare up during a relatively stable period in the illness, further disrupting the system's equilibrium. We have found that working with families to establish flexible communicational boundaries is the best safeguard against the dysfunctional behavior resulting from the inhibition of emotional expression under stress. This means predicting and anticipating with the family the emotional reactions they might experience, bringing out into the open any fears regarding consequences of affective expression, and helping each member to express feelings in an appropriate manner.

Negotiating Extrafamilial Relationships

The family's usual pattern of interaction with the social environment is disrupted when someone in the family faces a terminal illness. First, there is the issue of how much information the family wishes to share with people peripherally involved with themselves or the dying person. The less permeable the family boundary is with the outside world, the more secretive and isolated the family is likely to be. Second, the intense disruption and depletion of emotional resources which a terminal illness creates within the family limits family members' abilities to maintain an active interchange with the social environment. As families experience depression and helplessness, they become more withdrawn from relationships in the social sphere. On the other hand, friends and relatives often do not know how to react to the family during the living–dying interval. This confusion frequently causes even concerned persons to distance themselves from the painful situation. The tendency of people to maintain a certain social distance from the dying leaves the family without needed social support during this critical phase.

Maintaining friendships during the terminal phase can be a complicated task for the family. Resentment toward friends for their good fortune can sometimes undermine previously sound relationships. Family members often feel alone in their plight and thus have trouble responding to empathic overtures by friends and relatives. There may also be pressure from within the family system itself for members to relinquish their social relationships in favor of focusing energy on the heightened needs of the family.

In a study of parents of leukemic children, Binger et al. (1969) found that families used a number of simultaneous outside supports during the living–dying interval. The clergy was found to be an important source of support to families where a meaningful relationship with clergy preceded the illness; however, *de novo* introduction of religious figures was of little help. The primary physician, nursing staff, and social service personnel were specified as major supports to the family during the crisis of illness. Parents of other leukemic children often formed mutually supportive relationships that endured even after the death of the children. Support groups for parents facing the loss of a child have been found helpful in a variety of settings (Borstein and Klein 1974; and Gilder et al. 1978). We believe that multiple family groups, as conceptualized by Laqueur (1976), have potential to provide support in resolving the difficulties unique in dealing with terminal illness.

Coping with the Post–Death Phase

The actual death of a terminally ill family member brings to a climax the painful reality for which the family has been preparing. Ideally, the process of anticipatory grief will have both buffered the intensity of the loss and enabled the family to have begun a resolution of the coping tasks by the time the death occurs. Still, the ultimate loss of hope and removal of the dying person from the family brings into focus the final stage of family griefwork. The family must accept the finality of the loss, relinquish its attachment to the loved one, and ensure the survival of the modified family unit. Bowen (1976) suggests that the failure to resolve the death of a family member fully can result in an "emotional shock wave," that is, "a network of underground 'after shocks' of serious life events that can occur anywhere in the extended family system in the months or years following serious emotional events in the family" (1976: 339). Shock wave symptoms can include physical, emotional, or social dysfunctions.

To prevent such dysfunctional reactions from occurring, Bowen advocates an active approach in which the therapist coaches the family on how to handle events surrounding the death of a loved one. The function of funerals is deemed crucial in helping families to resolve a loss. In Bowen's approach, families are encouraged to confront rather than shrink from the intense emotions surrounding death. The goal of involvement in the death process is to help the family to realize the death and to experience their grief in a supportive network of friends and family so that they can move on to a healthy resolution of the normal grieving process. This approach favors the involvement of children and the largest possible extended family and friendship system, an open casket, prompt obituary notices, a public funeral with the body present, and a funeral service which is as personal as possible.

Avoidance of situations that evoke the memory of the deceased and thus reactivate grief has been found to play an important role in unresolved grief reactions (Ramsay 1977). In fact, Ramsay (1976) has had success in using prolonged exposure through *in vivo* flooding techniques when treating pathological grief reactions. The rationale underlying both Ramsay's individual behavioral approach and Bowen's family approach is that a grief reaction will become pathological only if no confrontation with the intense emotions surrounding a loss occurs and the emotional reactions have no time to extinguish themselves.

This perspective underscores the importance of extending the therapeutic relationship to include the period surrounding the death and, optimally, the first several months subsequent to the death. Coaching the family at the time of death provides a source of support to family members in their efforts to make decisions and to solve problems during a period of intense distress. Families often need help and encouragement to perform many of the functions that are difficult in the short run but beneficial in the long run. For example, families may require encouragement to let children be involved in the funeral process, or to allow a more complete expression of affect by all members than would otherwise be allowed.

Once the funeral process is over, the family faces the larger task of establishing a new equilibrium that integrates the many changes in the intra- as well as extrafamilial environment that were initiated in the living–dying phase. The grieving process must occur simultaneously with the re-equilibration process. While initially the deceased member will continue to be a vital force in family life, this role must be relinquished so that the deceased becomes a cherished memory rather than a silent participant in directing family activities. The realignment of family roles must be solidified following the death of a family member. This usually involves a redistribution of instrumental and socioemotional functions within the family.

Relationships with persons and institutions in the social environment will also need to be realigned. Some relationships will need to be terminated, others resumed, others altered, and finally new ones cultivated in accord with the family's new status and the modified needs of family members. Often it is necessary and adaptive to seek persons in the environment who can replace some of the functions previously provided by the deceased and irreplaceable by the surviving nuclear family. An example might be the employment of an uncle or grandparent to buttress the parental subsystem following the death of one spouse.

The family therapist can continue to be of assistance to the family during the post–death phase. Helping the family to anticipate their needs and reactions, facilitating communication to make explicit the nature of the changes the family is undergoing and how such changes affect each member, and supporting the family's attempts to renegotiate relationships with the outside world are crucial areas of behavioral systems intervention in the post–death phase. While the ability of a family unit to re-equilibrate in a healthy manner is affected by numerous factors, active behavioral family systems-oriented interventions can be effective in preventing pathological grief reactions that compromise both an individual and a family's potential for continued growth following the loss of a loved one.

CONCLUSIONS AND SUMMARY

This chapter examined behavioral family systems approaches to helping families cope with terminal illness. The discussion was oriented around specific coping tasks that therapists must help families confront during the living–dying process. We emphasized the importance of making a thorough assessment of the family to gauge and guide planned interventions. Structural, problem-solving, and behavioral concepts were incorporated to assist the therapist in making such evaluations. Then, the coping tasks of denial versus acceptance of the illness, establishing a relationship with health caretakers, meeting the needs of the dying person, maintaining a functional equilibrium, regulation of affect, negotiating extrafamilial relationships, and adjusting to the post-death phase were delineated and, with the use of three case studies, therapeutic strategies were proposed. These factors together comprise an integrated family model in behavioral thanatology.

REFERENCES

Berkowitz, B.P., and Graziano, A.M. Training parents as behavior therapists: A review. *Behaviour Research and Therapy*, 1972, *10*, 297-317.

Binger, C.M., Ablin, A.R., Feuerstein, R.C., Kushner, J.H., Zoger, S., and Mikkelsen, C. Childhood leukemia: Emotional impact on patient and family. *The New England Journal of Medicine*, 1969, *280*, 414-418.

Borstein, I.J., and Klein, A. Parents of fatally ill children in a parents' group. In B. Schoenberg, A. Carr, A. Kutscher, D. Peretz, and I. Goldberg (Eds.), *Anticipatory grief*. New York: Columbia University Press, 1974.

Bowen, M. Family reaction to death. In P.J. Guerin (Ed.), *Family therapy: Theory and practice*. New York: Gardner Press, 1976.

Christensen, A., Johnson, S.M., Phillips, S., and Glasgow, R.E. Cost effectiveness in behavioral family therapy. *Behavior Therapy*, 1980, *11*, 208-226.

Cohen, M.M., and Wellisch, D.K. Living in limbo: Psychosocial intervention in families with a cancer patient. *American Journal of Psychotherapy*, 1978, *32*, 561-571.

Futterman, E.H., and Hoffman, I. Crisis and adaptation in the families of fatally ill children. In E.J. Anthony and C. Koupernik (Eds.), *The child in his family: The impact of disease and death* (Vol. 2). New York: Wiley and Sons, 1973.

Gilder, R., Buschman, P.R., Sitarz, A.L., and Wolfe, J.A. Group therapy with parents of children with leukemia. *American Journal of Psychotherapy*, 1978, *22*, 276-285.

Haley, J. *Problem-solving therapy*. San Francisco: Jossey-Bass, 1976.

Jackson, D.D. Family interaction, family homeostasis, and some implications for conjoint family psychotherapy. In J. Masserman (Ed.), *Individual and family dynamics*. New York: Grune and Stratton, 1959.

Johnson, C.A., and Katz, R.C. Using parents as change agents for their children: A review. *Journal of Child Psychology and Psychiatry*, 1973, *14*, 181-200.

Laqueur, H.P. Multiple family therapy. In P.J. Guerin (Ed.), *Family therapy: Theory and practice*. New York: Gardner Press, 1976.

Lieberman, R. Behavioral approaches to family and couple therapy. In G.D. Erickson and T.P. Hogan (Eds.), *Family therapy: An introduction to theory and technique*. New York: Jason Aronson, 1976.

Mailick, M. The impact of severe illness on the individual and family: An overview. *Social Work in Health Care*, 1979, *5*, 117–128.

Minuchin, S. *Families and family therapy*. Cambridge, Mass.: Harvard University Press, 1974.

Patterson, G.R., Reid, J.B., Jones, R.R., and Conger, R.E. *A social learning approach to family intervention*. Eugene, Oregon: Castalia, 1975.

Ramsay, R.W. A case study in bereavement therapy. In H.J. Eysenck (Ed.), *Case studies in behavior therapy*. London: Routledge and Kegan Paul, 1976.

Ramsay, R.W. Behavioural approaches to bereavement. *Behavior Research and Therapy*, 1977, *15*, 131–135.

Raphael, B. Preventive intervention with the recently bereaved. *Archives of General Psychiatry*, 1977, *34*, 1450–1454.

Sobel, H.J. Projective cognitive assessment. In T. Merluzzi, C. Glass and M. Genest (Eds.), *Handbook of cognitive assessment*. New York: Guilford Press, 1981.

Von Bertalanffy, L. General system theory. *General Systems*, 1956, *1*, 1–10.

Watzlawick, P., Beavin, J.H., and Jackson, D.D. *Pragmatics of human communication: A study of interactional patterns, pathologies, and paradoxes*. New York: W.W. Norton and Company, 1967.

Weakland, J.H., Fisch, R., Watzlawick, P., and Bodin, A.M. Brief therapy: Focused problem resolution. *Family Process*, 1974, *13*, 141–167.

Weisman, A.D. *On dying and denying*. New York: Behavioral Publications, 1972.

8 IMAGERY AND TERMINAL CARE
The Therapist as Shaman

Jeanne Achterberg and
G. Frank Lawlis

In the Western world of the 20th century the care of the dying, or even of the patient whose disease threatens a lifestyle, has been largely a technological process of attempts to keep failing hearts beating and tissues, organs, or cells nourished and alive. How ironic that when the fact of mortality is confronted, when the uniquely human need to review life and the afterlife is manifest, and when relationships enter a new and sensitive era, so much assistance is offered to counteract the inevitable demise of the soma, and yet so little guidance is offered for a bewildered psyche.

At earlier stages in the evolutionary development of humankind, the recognition of dying as a metamorphosis or a period of reckoning was not overshadowed by the need to produce one more life-signalling blip on an oscilloscope. Rituals were developed that gave structure and status to the event. Myths that predicated these rituals or rites of passage granted maps to live by and mental images with which to resolve some of the frightening uncertainty. It is safe to speculate that, as a whole, our culture is currently mid-myth when it comes to the process of dying. Even the trusted tenets of contemporary religions have lost foothold, as attempts to integrate literal interpretation of the sacred books with science throw belief systems into a shifting paradigm of confusion (Campbell 1972).

Some structure for death ritual does exist, but the dictates primarily concern the final disposition of those already dead and the mourning process for those who remain to experience the loss. The emphasis on ritual for the living instead of the dying is not unique to our culture. The Bororo Indians of Brazil, for example, made death the central focus for ceremonies and social life, recognizing that death is the single greatest crisis not only for the individual but for society (Levak 1980). Here, in this nearly extinct tribe, a "mother" is assigned to the deathbed, where she gives symbolic birth to a child spirit. The spirit of the deceased assumes physical embodiment in a selected person who then is accepted by the "mother by death." She is given the full duties and responsibilities as if directed to a natural child. The procedures for mourning the deceased are thereby integrated into community life. The intensive and prescribed bedside vigil and the images of a promised incarnation no doubt offer comfort to the dying person, the passive recipient of the mother's ministrations.

In Western religion, simple perfunctory deathbed rituals—the sacraments, confessions, the making of a final peace—are incorporated into religious practice, offering comfort as well as signalling that a religious figure has given permission for the life bonds to dissolve. On a far larger scale, and with much greater detail, ceremonies are planned for the bereaved. The wakes, food, song, familiar chants, and special eulogies ostensibly are designed to honor the dead. But perhaps of more import, they are used to give structure to the grieving and the catharsis.

When no religious tradition for mourning exists—and this is quite common—the funeral directors reign as mythmakers, as designers of bereavement paths, honor, and preparation of the deceased. The issues involved in allowing a group outside a spiritual tradition, and inside a monetary venture, to determine death rituals have been well articulated in recent years (see Mitford 1963) and will not be debated here. Suffice it to say that unless strong traditions are developed for dying that take into consideration the idiosyncratic lifestyles of each individual, and in which some control and self-responsibility can be exercised, then the base interests of a professional group will be served.

In a similar vein, the loss of self-responsibility and the subservience to the medical system that a dying patient often experiences in a hospital geared toward curative interventions are described thoughtfully by many (Kubler–Ross 1969, 1975; and Ramsey 1974). The sentiments have spawned a rehumanization of the dying process through movements emphasizing dying at home, the hospice concept of special care, Shanti (Garfield 1978), and Shanti-like projects whose concern it is to counsel the dying.

As mental health specialists, we are beginning to have a sense of the contribution that our discipline and related fields of practice might make to the study and counsel of the dying patient. It is already an integral, albeit often unrecognized, aspect of our work as scientists of human behavior. As stated by Dag Hammarskjold:

> No choice is uninfluenced by the way in which the personality regards its destiny, and the body its death. In the last analysis, it is our conception of death which decides our answers to all the questions that life puts to us. . . . Hence too, the necessity for preparing for it (Osis and Haraldsson 1977:1).

If we do not include spiritual and cognitive conceptualizations into our outcome-predicting equation for behavior, then potent variables are omitted. In our own work with patients suffering from chronic or acute physical disease, we have found that belief systems are powerful predictors not only of how dying occurs, but also of a patient's response to treatment (Achterberg and Lawlis 1978, 1980a; Achterberg et al. 1980; and Gibbs and Achterberg 1978). If a patient believes that God is just, that terminal pain is to be expected and perhaps even deserved, and that when the time comes one should be grateful for the proximity of heaven, then we can anticipate a passive and accepting response to treatment, to the diagnosis itself, to hospitalization, and to our services.

On the other hand, a patient may wish to believe in an afterlife, but is confused by spiritual teachings. This patient may harbor self-punitive notions of having allowed illness to occur since certain schools of thought believe that you have total control over your destiny, including disease. Combine this with childhood religious residuals of predestination (i.e., when your time comes, it comes), throw in archetypal hints of reincarnation, and you have the contemporary man or woman; one who is likely to seek and receive psychological aid upon hearing a life-threatening diagnosis. This response is also contingent upon a belief system. The primary difference is that the religious system has prescribed routes and images for the course of dying, while the other lacks a path encompassing the complex, often conflicting set of understandings.

The purpose of this chapter is to describe an interdisciplinary use of imagery in terminal care. We intend to show how the clinical applications of imagery techniques can serve as one link in the integration of seemingly diverse thanatological paradigms. Traditional existential methods of care, cognitive-behavioral perspectives, and spiritual dimensions of the dying process merge as a patient's imagery is focused upon. In all three cases, a patient's responsibility is underscored, self-control is valued, and the therapist assumes the role of collaborator, guide, teacher, and shaman. The overall goal is to maintain a truly humanistic frame of reference in patient care.

PERSONAL RESPONSIBILITY IN DEATH

Our intention in all of our work with life-threatening disease is to understand *lifestyle*, particularly as it is redirected away from health. We herald the day in our evolution when death can be a conscious decision, a recognition that life has been well-lived and yet is at its zenith, when the ravages of disease are no longer necessary to shut down vital organs. As a willful species, we may well be approaching the point where we can listen sensitively to our own accomplishments, our cognitions, our environment, our spiritual attunement, and determine lifespan. Certainly, we are seizing responsibility in other previously sacred sectors of existence: in health care, in the birthing process, in marital vows. In a sense, we are gradually backing off from ill-fitting cultural mandates and embracing unique individual concerns.

Taking personal responsibility in the dying process is exceedingly rare, although we all can recite family or case histories of wonderful older people who quietly and carefully got their affairs in order, and after having lived good, full lives, died peacefully in their sleep with no apparent disease. As mentioned earlier, the rites of dying are essentially passive in design. They are paternal. The poor victim lies there, the authority figure does something, IV's are changed, blood is drawn, the sign of the cross is made over a heaving chest, hands are patted, and relatives, friends, or health professionals often talk baby-like language to perfectly sane, conscious adults—the epitome of paternalism.

In reviewing the literature, we are able to find only a few scattered reports of cultures that view dying as an active process during which both patient participation and self-respect are recognized. One such culture is the Alaskan Indians who exhibit a "willfulness about their death, their participation in its planning, and the time of its occurrence that showed a remarkable power of personal choice" (Trelease 1975:33). The author contrasts his observations with those of the traditional belief that "death comes like a thief in the night, unexpected and unprepared for" (1975:36). He also suggests that human volition plays a determining factor in dying, just as it does in every other aspect of life.

The Advocate-Shaman-Therapist

If participation and self-responsibility for the dying process are desirable psychobiosocial goals, then the health professional or therapist must vacate the traditional paternalistic role that fosters patient dependency. Gadow (1980), for example, discusses the position of a patient advocate. Advocacy, she states:

> . . . is based on the principle that self-determination is the most fundamental and valuable human right and therefore a greater good than any health care can provide. The professional, while obligated to act in the patient's interest, is not permitted to define that interest in any way contrary to the patient's definition (390).

Advocacy expresses the ideal that individuals should be positively assisted in exercising their freedom of self-determination and self-control.

We might add to Gadow's discussion that the notion of advocating for a patient's best interests, as he or she defines them, has some built-in failure. Regardless of good intentions to assist a patient in living out a desired goal, whether it be to go home and die in a familiar bed or cease debilitating chemotherapies, bucking the system often takes incredible amounts of energy. Supporting a patient in these decisions may result in a subsequent restriction of the advocate's activities by hospital medical personnel. It is nevertheless a desirable approach which is growing in popularity and is consonant with the goals of self-responsibility, self-control, and determination. All three goals are part of a humanistic behavioral medicine.

The therapeutic approach, with advocacy in mind, should (1) take into consideration the patient's value system, (2) attempt to clarify that cognitive system for both the patient and the therapist, and (3) work creatively with those elements that appear to serve the patient's best interests. Not only is it important to foster a patient's comfort (usually the central focus of counseling with the dying), but we must also use aspects of the patient's belief system to aid in conflict resolution. The therapist, therefore, serves as a guide and collaborator, hoping to remove some uncertainty from the path and to insure that all possible richness can emanate from the event. Our aim is to have each sense heightened to the experience, and every memory passing in the life review, savored and resolved.

Who has the infinite wisdom to serve in this capacity? Who can combine metaphor with the concrete; spiritual quest with the preparation of a last will and testament; the need to reach out with the need to introspect? Clearly, as therapists we stand in awe of the requisites for the task, yet the need for interdisciplinary trans-spiritual therapists exists. Rarely have we been challenged to mix, so uniquely, our science with our art. Not only are we proposing that the wisdom of scientific and behavioral observation enter into the so-called sacred ground of the dying, but we are also describing therapy as a shamanistic function.

Therapist-as-shaman is not an unusual concept in view of our past history. Shamen have always been the psychological guides and healers. One of the key differences between the shaman's role and the therapist's is one of emotional, mental, and psychological involvement with the patient. It is integral to the shaman's art, but antithetical to the ingrained concept of objectivity that permeates the usual training and practice of health care. One must question how useful and sensitive a therapist can be in working with dying patients when responsibility for emotional, subjective involvement with the patient is not taken. Also, the shaman creates myths and upholds their substance, while the traditional therapist confronts myths so that they often lose their power over behavior. We believe that myths for dying need to be examined, even taught and perhaps created, because a modern-day wasteland exists in this area.

IMAGERY: A THERAPEUTIC TECHNIQUE

What techniques would be most valuable for this advocate-shaman-therapist to use in counseling and studying the dying? Certainly, any application should allow the patient to remain responsible, active, and self-respecting throughout the process of decisionmaking. A technique we have termed "imagery" has proven to be the most useful in our hypothesis testing and therapeutic interventions. Imagery itself refers to the products of the imagination, or the images, that appear to be the precursors of verbal behavior both in ontogeny and phylogeny. We have traced the neurological development and pathways elsewhere and will not detail them here (Achterberg and Lawlis 1980a). Because images are a more basic function than language, because the network is intricately involved with the emotional circuits of the nervous system, and also because very vivid images are correlated with physiological change, they serve as a bridge between mental and physical function.

Imagery, as we conceive it, is a cognitive representation of any sensory function without the external stimulus that normally triggers the sensory pathways. Visual pictures that occur during dream and fantasy are images. We also include in our definition other senses such as audition, olfaction, and even the kinesthetic phenomena that occur when imagining the familiar muscular activity of walking. Imagery blends art and science, satisfying the scientist as well as the practitioner within us. It has a 3,000 year history in medicine (Samuels and Samuels 1975), extending from the Greeks in the tradition of Cos, through virtually every folk ritual, to present day medicine, behavior therapy, and psychology.

It is imagery that often constitutes the dying patient's reality in all cultures, all religious groups. In the altered state of consciousness reached while dying, language loses priority in favor of a more primitive response (and remember, primitive means "first" or "primary," not necessarily "less well developed"). This internal expression appears rich in symbol and was described in some detail by Carl Jung (1965) following a near-death experience of his own. The images are common to Christian mystics, to Tibetans, to Hindus, to psychics, and apparently to Americans with little or no esoteric information (Hine 1978, Moody 1976; and Osis and Haraldsson 1977).

A final reason why we decided to take a closer look at the imagery process was that we had attempted to predict response to treatment based on cancer patients' psychological profiles as well as their blood analyses (Achterberg and Lawlis 1977, 1979). Consistently, the patients' images of their disease, their treatment, and their immunological system—scored and objectively measured using a projective

instrument called the IMAGE–Ca (Achterberg and Lawlis 1978)—
were the most powerful predictors of follow-up physical status. The
blood analyses, on the other hand, offered only a current, unpredictable picture of the patient's condition. It appeared that the images
patients hold, often unconsciously, indicate future directions in
disease.

We can categorize imagery applications to the dying patient or the
patient with life-threatening disease within four basic, but overlapping functions. These applications are: (1) to clarify the disease and
the treatment process itself under the rubric of patient education or
image programming; (2) to develop coping mechanisms to counter
fear and pain; (3) to enable material stored at preconscious or unconscious levels to emerge as clarifications of value systems and to assist
in the resolution of past issues or future planning; and (4) to react
and interact sensitively with a patient's own dying images.

Imagery as Patient Education

Perceptions of disease, including the mechanism of action of any
medical interventions, vary tremendously but they are inevitably involved in well-being. When people perceive themselves as healthy,
they act in healthy ways. When they believe themselves to be sick,
behavior is typically passive.

An example proffered by Dr. Irving Oyle (original source unknown) is of a gentleman who underwent surgery, was observed to
have widely metastasized cancer, had the incision closed, and was
sent home. Apparently the man and his family interpreted this as
meaning that he could go home in good health. Several years later,
this same man suffered a heart attack. Recognizing him as the individual who had, years earlier, been diagnosed with terminal cancer,
the physician ordered an autopsy only to discover that there was no
evidence of any of the cancer. On the other hand we remember the
tragic instance of a woman who died the same day she was given a
diagnosis of breast cancer. The pronouncement of her malignancy
was made after the biopsy and she was informed that a mastectomy
was planned within days. She immediately began to recall with much
emotion her mother's identical diagnosis and the events of her pain-
filled, difficult dying. She declared, "I will not die like she did." The

strength of her determination led to a death within hours from cardiac arrest.

Both patients formed powerful images of their internal condition — one of health and the other of inevitable and rapid death. Neither could have been predicted using statistical indices. Images of disease often determine behavior in less dramatic ways, even for people who are adequately educated regarding their diagnosis and prognosis. One patient was diagnosed with lung cancer at age 50. He was a well-educated banker and we assumed he would be reasonably informed about his condition. Nevertheless, he perceived his tumors as tiny bugs, crawling through his lungs, chewing at the tissues. He felt that as long as he smoked cigarettes and kept smoke in his lungs, the bugs would die from lack of air. Even when it became necessary to use oxygen periodically to breathe, he continued to smoke. The bugs, he believed, thrived on oxygen, and therefore it was more necessary than ever to continue blocking their passage with smoke.

Education that provides accurate and positive mental images consonant with medical findings is a challenge to all phases of health care, but particularly when the diagnosis is terminal. It requires an expression of hope and faith from the therapist, and a willingness to pursue life as long as the patient actively expresses that goal. We know, however, from other sources (see particularly, Johnson et al. 1978) that when patients are well-informed, the hospital days are decreased, sensations of pain are diminished, and healing time is shortened. The information is particularly effective when it includes how a patient might expect to feel. Health professionals often believe that information of value to us is the crucial information for the patient. This is not always the case. When confronted with illness and hospitalization, the need to understand the sensations of treatment, the disease, the experience of being in a surgical unit, the smell of the hospital, and the sounds of forboding machines, usually override the technical and medical details of the condition and information on survival statistics.

The specific nature of the education or image-programming is naturally dependent upon the diagnosis and prognosis. We have developed a battery of audiovisual materials for image-programming (Achterberg and Lawlis 1980b). Patients are asked to listen to audiotapes which describe their disease and healing process in language that is designed for comprehension by those who have had at least a seventh-grade education, but does not insult the intelligence of those who have tried to educate themselves about their conditions. The patients are then shown pictures from health publications. (Nilsson's *Behold Man* 1973 and several atlases of anatomy have been invaluable.) We have also developed a series of symbolic, cartoon drawings with the assistance of an artist, and have compiled drawings by patients to depict the disease, the treatment, and the healing process.

Creative and useful information has come from the patients as they have attempted to communicate with us in words, in pictures, sometimes even in sculpture or dance, how it feels to be a heart or cancer patient. Important, too, is how they conceptualize effective treatment. The drawings completed by a 28-year-old male diagnosed with malignant melanoma, together with a 2-hour taped monologue, depict positive imagery of powerful chemotherapy, complete with an elementary but scientifically correct version of its cytotoxic mode of action. The activity of an immunotherapy that he was receiving was also accurately drawn and described. This constitutes patient understanding at its finest—accurate, simple, and positive, even in the face of tremendous biomedical side-effects.

Our image-programming focuses on healing or mechanisms of stabilization rather than on deterioration. Patients tend to create sufficient images of deterioration with the available education materials. One brought us a pamphlet she had received following the diagnosis of a disease that was in its early stages and for which a 75 percent chance of complete and total remission existed. The pamphlet began, "So, you've been diagnosed with _____." Then followed explanations on what is known about the condition, but why there is still no cure. The final discussion covered wheelchair care and care of the bedridden.

Thus many patients are negatively programmed from the beginning. Although we are obligated as patient educators to explain the disease itself, we do not have to dwell on the destructive aspects. Well-meaning friends and relatives usually have plenty to say about other people they have known who had similar conditions. These descriptions are usually replete with the horrors of treatment or the death itself. Furthermore, patients must, by law, be given full information on each conceivable negative outcome of treatment. We wonder whether equal time is ever given to describe, in simple terminology, how the treatment works to quell the disease.

Much of the information, both positive and negative, is provided when patients are in a state of near shock, immediately following diagnosis. Retention is likely to be nil. We have found that when relaxation instructions are given prior to the education session, not only is the information retained, but desensitization occurs. The relaxation instructions are formalized on audiotape (or given personally, time permitting) and include information on deep breathing and on relaxing all major muscle groups (Achterberg and Lawlis 1980b). The experience of Johnson and her colleagues (1978) is similar to ours: sensory education or information is more effective when preceded by relaxation instructions.

The educational aspect of imagery, then, begins with relaxation and is followed by information on the disease, on treatment, and on healing mechanisms, using as much media as possible; it stays consonant with available information on the disease, yet focuses less on images of deterioration than on stabilization or healing. Behavioral and cognitive components are integrated into a strategic patient-centered intervention.

Imagery as a Coping Tool

Desensitization involves the presentation of noxious stimulus while the individual is in a relaxed state. The notion is that the new physical responses are conditioned to previously aversive stimuli (i.e., responses of lowered sympathetic nervous system arousal level) since it is not possible to be physiologically relaxed and fearful (or anxious) at the same time.

For many people who have been diagnosed with a life-threatening disease, the fear of the disease is more of a detriment to a healthy lifestyle than are the symptoms themselves, at least early in the course of the illness. They may become phobic, reacting with uncomfortable and negative responses each time they think of their health. As one woman recently exclaimed, "My disease is such an obsession— I can't get it out of my mind day or night." Patients may become hypersensitive to all physical signs, to every ache and palpitation, and to each innuendo suggestive of impending demise. The spiral of misery is compounded by loss of sleep and by muscle tension. Lack of sleep is well-accepted as a potent aspect in the lowering of pain thresholds and muscle tension produces and exacerbates the painful state. Hence, a patient may suffer not only from the consequences of a disease, but may also unconsciously create much of the existing pain.

The repeated presentation of audiovisual information regarding disease, while patients are in a relaxed state, defuses unpleasant thoughts of the disease. Healing images consistently offered give the individual substitute mental pictures. Instead of visualizing tumors growing without control, patients can develop substitute images of chemotherapy or white blood cells destroying tumors. When people are receptive to medication, and anticipate effectiveness, it is likely to have a more pronounced consequence. The images formed by the expectancies that one has regarding the effectiveness of medication (inert or not) are, after all, the basis for the so-called placebo effects.

Another approach for pain relief using imagery is a form of self-hypnosis. Patients often develop this technique themselves, out of frustration with pain medication. One man with a head and neck cancer that seemed to enlarge daily told us that he had long ago learned to control his pain. As far as he was concerned, he was pain-free despite obvious large, open lesions. His method was to relax deeply and imagine a bulldog whenever he felt a twinge of discomfort. This bulldog was his imagined "pain eater," and for him it worked therapeutically.

Less exotic but nevertheless a very real tool for pain intervention is relaxation itself. Relaxation, with or without accompanying images, decreases muscle tension, a major contributor to almost all pain states. The natural tendency of the body when damaged is to support itself using the surrounding musculature. While this is adaptive for some conditions, eventually the splinting or the dysponesis (chronic muscle tension) produces pain and encourages inactivity, which in turn creates more discomfort. (See Chapter 4.)

We assure our patients that we believe their pain is real, but we also try to convince them of the power of their own minds with drawings of endorphins (the body's own narcotics) in action. The drawings depict "Mr. Pain" traveling down a neuron and jumping the synaptic cleft. The endorphins (as well as other narcotics) are shown blocking the pain at the presynaptic membrane. We explain that endorphins may be responsible for the "spookier" things like the placebo effect, hypnosis, and even the relief they feel when totally relaxed (Levine 1978).

One of the greatest phobias is the fear of dying. The fear generally appears to be of dying, not death, and familiarity robs it of fearful mystery. In two studies (Carey 1974; and Gibbs and Achterberg 1978), terminal patients were found to have lower death anxiety if they had dealt with the death of someone close. The death phobia can be dealt with in the same way as the disease phobia; by deeply relaxing the patients and then creating with them, in their value system, mental images of dying peacefully, in circumstances they find most comforting. This guided imagery trip will be discussed in more detail later, since it serves as a device both for planning and for developing personal myths.

For the health care professional the imagery exercise is also invaluable. Our first experience was with Virginia Hine, author of *Last Letter to the Pebble People* (1979), as guide. Her infinite wisdom on such things, we predict, will soon be legendary. She guided us and our students through our own aging process. We mentally imaged the visage we desired for ourselves, our activities, our cumulation of wordly and spiritual possessions. We then saw ourselves dying a death by design, visualized the aftermath, the place and manner of burial. We wrote our own eulogies, and in doing so, went through a subtle but rapid self-examination. After all, if one wants to achieve certain goals, have special influences on the world after death, then behavior must be consciously examined to determine whether indeed it is in line with the objectives. Far from being a morbid exercise, the guided imagery is perhaps one of the most effective ways to begin viewing dying as a willful act, certain features of which are retained within our own realm of control.

On a hypothetical level, repeated imagery expeditions that sample the depth of experience and emotion might be an effective way for the novice therapist to begin counseling with the terminally ill patient. But perhaps it is of more direct benefit to the therapist during that inevitable time when one's own mortality is confronted. We remember sitting stunned, for hours, over Kubler–Ross's writings as the reality of our own death was exposed like a nerve, of hiding from patients who were very sick because their youth, or their speech, or their history reminded us of ours. We recall reading fervently from sources which seemed to provide evidence of an afterlife so that mortality could prove to be a lie, or convincing ourselves that people did not die who really wanted to live (and we would not die until good and ready). All of that served a purpose, but the deliberate planning and depth of sensory experience is lacking when compared to that which accompanies imaging oneself living through a desirable life, and dying what we personally consider a good death.

Imagery as Clarification and Resolution

We use imagery to tap material from unconscious levels when it appears to be valuable for the patient in either the resolution of an issue or in values clarification. One of the core issues in working with very ill patients comes forth in this context. That is, when does the therapist cease doing life counseling and begin death counseling? How long and under what circumstances do you advocate the continued struggle for health? What do you do about the denial of death?

Sometimes the patient readily admits that to continue living is not worth the effort. Often, however, a patient will give the socially acceptable response ("I'm going to lick this yet" or "Don't worry, I'll be home by Thanksgiving"), to protect family and loved ones from his or her true feelings. The patient may be ambivalent.

As William James noted in many of his writings, the will and the imagination are often in conflict. He also maintained that in such cases the imagination, not the will, predominated. The imagination then, is a source of material for our own therapeutic decisionmaking. Because drawing or painting involves the more intuitive, creative right hemisphere of the brain, we often rely on pictures to give us information from the imagination. Words reflect information available at the conscious level.

We recently collected drawings by a 73-year-old patient who had been involved in a week-long psychotherapy session geared to life change, overcoming disease, and painful self-inspection. Daily, the potential he had within his own body for overcoming disease was discussed. At the end of the week he was asked to draw his disease and his immunological system or white blood cells. In his first drawing, his white blood cells appeared as useless as snowflakes, melting on the growing tumors. Sensing our keen dismay, he redrew the picture on a napkin and with pride, presented it after lunch. The sole difference was the presence of arms. His life had been rich from his perspective, his children were happily married, and he had done what he set out to do. Yet, his verbalization affirmed his desire to conquer the illness. He died within weeks of our meeting. We now see how brazen we often were in insisting, or assuming, that living is always the desirable alternative.

We have also used other-guided imagery trips to assist patients in planning or contemplating complex questions. It has often been said that prayer is asking questions, and meditation is listening for answers. The answers to perplexing issues seem to emerge more readily in a state of reverie. The patients are guided through deep relaxation and suggestions are given for exploring some of the issues. Decisions cannot be forced; the patients are allowed to symbolize them as they wish. The decisions may not appear until after the unconscious resolves them, balances them with an emotional state, and then permits them to emerge into consciousness.

The case of Walter G. illustrates this type of imagery. Walter was a retired palm reader and trusted reveries since he had used them for years to gain access to intuitions. After his hospitalization he was forced to dispose of a few prized possessions. He had two cars, a gold watch, and a small piece of land. He also had two sons for whom he had little affection. Walter asked for someone to lead him into what he called a "garden of calm" and then to merely listen to him say what came into his mind. In the garden, he imagined many flowers and old friends, saw the cars rusting, and saw the watch being given away. When he returned to our mutual reality he interpreted the images to mean that he should sell the cars to pay for his funeral expenses and taxes, the watch should be given to an old girlfriend, and the land should be given to his sons. We were unable to follow the logic of his decisionmaking, but could see that he felt good about his plan.

The imagery procedure for resolution or clarification allows the individual to bring forth thoughts from the unconscious, to interpret them, and to mesh that information into awareness as a cognitive and behavioral determinant.

Imagery as Reality for the Dying

The final application of imagery with the terminally ill patient is the most intriguing, the most important, and the most difficult to discuss and understand in the conventional behavioristic framework. The therapist will have a personal decision to make: to interact, as a worldly counsel and shaman, with the imagery that occurs naturally as death approaches, or to encourage the patient to return to our reality by means of traditional psychotherapeutic intervention. In other words, the therapist decides what is real and what is not real.

Euphemistically speaking, dying imagery seems to be like a pilot's communication as the plane approaches a landing. It is a dialogue with an unknown entity, and we occasionally are privileged to be eavesdroppers on one side of the interchange. Our first experience with the images of dying was during a study of terminal cancer patients in a county hospital (Gibbs and Achterberg 1978). During interviews and testing designed to measure death anxiety as a function of pain and religiosity, approximately half our patients spontaneously offered us their visions. All seemed serene and comforted by the apparitions of their religious figures or of a deceased loved one. We found that the same patients who reported wonderful visions tended to have lower scores on Templer's Death Anxiety Scale (Templer 1972) and higher "Intrinsically Religious" scores on Allport's (Allport and Ross 1967) Intrinsic versus Extrinsic measure of religiosity.

The latter finding indicated that these individuals were more likely to have integrated their religion into a lifestyle, according to Allport's and Ross's interpretation. The visions seemed functional and were reported to precede the final calm that we see so often just prior to death. Some simply saw a shining light or a beautiful garden that comforted and beckoned. Others reported conversations with Jesus. In one case, Jesus was said to have appeared at the foot of the bed and described new tumors in a woman's brain. She eventually encouraged her reluctant young physician to do a brain scan and the first indications of brain metastases were observed.

These images or visions are quite different from psychotic hallucinations that are typically nonintegrated and often only auditory (Siegel and West 1975). According to the Osis and Haraldsson (1977) study, in most cases these visions could not be related to drugs or to the products of disease. Whatever their cause, they exist as a reality for the patient and are extremely therapeutic in that an elation of mood typically follows. They also seem to give permission to relinquish a tenuous hold on life, promising entry into a far more desirable state.

It is vital for the therapist to be cognizant of a 1968 Gallup poll. According to this survey, at least 75 percent of all Americans believe in some sort of life after death. (It would be most interesting to discover how that percentage shifts in the face of an actual threat to life.) The visions that are reported may serve as a preview of this stage. At first the image may be held at bay, but eventually it gives insight into an idiosyncratic promised land. The Osis and Haraldsson collection of experiences is highly recommended for identifying these images and their frequency of occurrence, as well as for the comparison between an American sample and an Indian group.

We frequently marvel at how patients cling to life, even after extensive organ and tissue damage. The struggle, as patients emerge into lucidity and lapse again into netherland, is a decisionmaking time. Conflicts are brought to the fore, often debated with an entity *in absentia*. A typical image reported by the articulate patient is a symbol of a barrier: a river to be crossed or a doorknob that needs turning. Even with all organs near failure, the psyche enters into a final arbitration. The images are vividly manifest to the dying person.

One of us had the extraordinary privilege of being the student of Ginny and Aldie Hine as Aldie started to describe the images he experienced well in advance of his death. We say "student" rather than "researcher" because it was with Aldie and Ginny that our previous understanding of death and cancer began to look shallow. The tools originally chosen to study the group to which this couple belonged were put aside in favor of rapt attention. Aldie had started a life–death struggle the last time we saw him. He was receiving radiation therapy as a palliative procedure in order to buy a little more time and to shrink painful tumors to a tolerable size. Prior to his radiation therapy each day, he would premeditate on the healing process and then go into a deeper meditation during the radiation treatments. Both Ginny and Aldie were trained as scientists, and that scholarly bent, plus the keen desire to record sensitive impressions, led them to report those images which had special meaning.

One day during the premeditative state, Aldie began to see himself in the future, very ill and in pain. He saw himself awakening, then reported his vision:

> I called to Ginny, rather loudly I thought. I asked her to make ready a tape recorder for, as I told her, the moment of choice had come. . . . As the struggle between life and death began, I kept trying to talk to her and, at times, to

answer questions she asked. . . . I could tell, and I think Ginny could tell, which side of the choice I was on because as I undulated upside down for the death state and right side up for the living state, the language I had available to me changed. It was normal English in the living state, but I don't know what language it was for the other. It was very apparent to me that the cards were stacked against living. When I rolled into the living position (face up), the pain returned twofold. In the death position there was no pain at all. One interesting thing was that death presented me with a re-experience of things in childhood. The life side apparently offered equal inducements but in a different realm. I didn't even know what they were then. . . . I don't know as the basis for the choice was ever clearly stated but I chose for life, ending a two-hour struggle. I returned to my body and the pain returned to me (Hine 1979: 61–62).

Months later, during the last few days of Aldie's life, the images returned. Ginny reports:

His eyes, distant and gray-filmed, yet somehow full of purpose, were searching the ceiling over my head as I stood at the foot of his bed. They were not sweeping aimlessly back and forth. He would focus now here, now there, on what appeared to us to be empty space. Sometimes it was as if he were talking to someone who was pacing back and forth. There were statements and questions, affirmations, and head-shakings. Some of what he said was understandable if your ear was sharp. . . . He was engaged in exchange that seemed to have the urgency of decision about it (131).

Later, when asked by a son whether someone was in the room with them, Aldie replied, "Death," and said that it was benevolent. In another instance, when a daughter was with him, he reported two presences to whom he was alternately talking and listening. He identified these as Love and Death. Ginny reported that there was a sense of argument during the dialogue, sometimes the energy of a crucial struggle. Once she observed him grab the triangle bar over his head, turn it upright like a club, and then shake it slowly at an unseen presence.

The dialogue with the unseen images ended about two hours before Aldie died. On the morning of his death, the family heard him say several times, "Yes, I'm ready. . . . Okay. . . . Yes." Or, as Ginny reports, " 'I'm so glad. . . . I'm ready.' He was addressing the presences he had called Death and Love, confirming and acknowledging as if an agreement had been reached" (Hine 1979 137). It was very clear to the eighteen family and near-family members who were present in the Hine home during Aldie's dying that death, for him, was a decision, an active self-controlled process. Ginny stated: "In a life and death struggle we always assume that the struggle is for life against death. . . . There comes a time in each human life when life itself becomes the lesser state and the victorious must struggle for death" (135).

CONCLUSIONS AND SUMMARY

All study that attempts to provide a universally understood data base must move from the single case study to categorizations of many similar experiences. Death and dying imagery are no exceptions. Guidance for understanding this topic is provided by the sensitive theorizing of Klass and Gordon (1978-1979). These investigators attempt to identify how people transform their world when death is encountered. They use the concept of transcendence: "a transformation of the perception; the problems that the prospect of death presents—meaninglessness, fear of nonbeing, separation anxiety are overcome" (20).

Their study involved videotaped interviews with dying people. About one-third of their population did not appear to transcend. But of those for whom death precipitated a transformation, four concepts were devised to describe the experiences. The first set is *ordinary* versus *nonordinary reality*, borrowed from Carlos Castaneda's study of shamanism (1968). For Castaneda, ordinary reality is that which is acceptable in one's culture; nonordinary is not. Death imagery, visualizations, or hallucinations are currently nonordinary realities and cognitions in Western culture. This is so even though Klass and Gordon, as well as Greeley (1976), report that about half of their cases experienced a reality that was not socially acceptable. This agrees with the findings we reported earlier in the chapter.

The second concept is the *mythic mode* versus the *interpretive mode*. The mythic mode lives out an archetypal pattern, with transcedence achieved by overcoming the human condition and integrating death with other aspects of life experience. Klass and Gordon cite Carl Jung's (1953) idea that personal transformation is done in the sequence of fantasy, with intellectual understanding occuring later if it is needed. The interpretive mode is a more active intellectual process where death is not an integral part of a meaning system. The process of transcendence is to integrate death into that system. Both

Christianity and the humanist psychology used by one of their interviewees were classified as instances of the mythic mode. In their sample, however, the interpretive mode was more common.

The four variations of transcendence in an encounter with death are: (1) ordinary–mythic; (2) ordinary–interpretive; (3) nonordinary–mythic; and (4) nonordinary–interpretive. In latter instances we would anticipate death imagery. Regarding the nonordinary–interpretive, the researchers stated: "Our experience is that people monitor themselves carefully in reporting these experiences, picking up very slight clues about how the researcher regards such experience" (34). In this instance, the images would be intellectualized until they fit into an existing belief system, or that system would be modified to account for the images. In the mythic mode, however, the images are often familiar to the psyche and thus require little intellectualization to make sense.

In our earlier example, Aldie's transformation or transcendence images could best be described in the nonordinary–mythic mode; certainly they were understood by him and his family within the tradition of a lifelong pattern. Nevertheless, the mode does not necessarily prescribe immediate acceptance of death, even though the images themselves are well accepted and integrated. The utility of the Klass and Gordon classification is to understand the process, the kinds of imagery one might experience, and whether those images are likely to be accepted, integrated, or perhaps even rejected by the individual. It is a necessary, even exciting beginning to describe and categorize these death images, particularly when combined with the near-death experience work of Moody (1976) and others.

Psychology and its allied professions face the possibility of becoming a major component in the process of dying. At times when a religious figure cannot be clearly identified or when no one accepts the role of counselor or guide, the therapist may well become the shaman, the myth-bearer or creator, who helps the individual translate meaningfulness from life to death. Moreover, the role becomes one of personal commitment to allow transference and countertransference, in a classical analytic perspective, while perhaps endangering one's own emotional safeguards.

On a more traditional level, we perceive our roles as counselors for the dying and for the survivors. Counseling necessitates strategies and skills to clarify, and perhaps to confront, the needs of the patients. These skills may include relaxation approaches, psychotherapy, or just listening, all of which we have described in an imagery framework.

We also envision the role of psychologist, social worker, nurse, or psychiatrist as a health-care educator and consultant: explaining and communicating through the senses and the intellect what conditions of life exist and the intentions of the health-care program. The greater concern the caretaker has for the quality of this process, the more he or she comforts and advocates for the patient. This is the essence of a humanistic model. Introducing nontraditional techniques need not preclude patient-centered perspectives.

Finally, the health caretaker is a scientist. He or she remains aware of the need for methodical observation, even if it only involves standard note-taking. Developed instruments or questionnaires should be used to enrich the ultimate challenge for the behavioral sciences: understanding the dying.

REFERENCES

Achterberg, J. and Lawlis, G.F. Psychological factors and blood chemistries as disease outcome predictors for cancer patients. *Multivariate Experimental Clinical Research*, 1977, *3*, 107–122.

Achterberg, J. and Lawlis, G.F. *Imagery of cancer: A diagnostic tool for the process of disease.* Champaign, Ill.: Institute for Personality and Ability Testing, 1978.

Achterberg, J. and Lawlis, G.F. A canonical analysis of blood chemistry variables related to psychological measures of cancer patients. *Multivariate Experimental Clinical Research*, 1974, *4*, 1–10.

Achterberg, J. and Lawlis, G.F. *Bridges of the bodymind: Behavioral approaches for health care.* Champaign, Ill.: Intitute for Personality and Ability Testing, 1980a.

Achterberg, J. and Lawlis, G.F. The bodymind audio tape program. Dallas: Medisette, Inc., 1980b.

Achterberg, J., Peyton, S., Helm, P., and Lawlis, G.F. Burn injury: Psychosocial aspects. *Archives of Physical Medicine*, October, 1980.

Allport, G.W. and Ross, J.M. Personal religious orientation and prejudice. *Journal of Personality and Social Psychology*, 1967, *5*, 432–443.

Campbell, J. *Myths to live by.* Viking Press, 1972.

Cary, R.G. Emotional adjustment in terminal patients: A quantitative approach. *Journal of Counseling Psychology*, 1974, *21*, 433–439.

Castaneda, C. *A separate reality*. New York: Simon and Schuster, 1968.

Gadow, S. Caring for the dying: Advocacy or paternalism. *Death Education*, 1980, *3*, 387–398.

Garfield, C. (Ed.). *Psychosocial care of the dying patient*. New York: McGraw-Hill, 1978.

Gibbs, H.W. and Achterberg–Lawlis, J. Spiritual values and death anxiety: Implications for counseling with terminal cancer patients. *Journal of Counseling Psychology*, 1978, *25*, 563–569.

Greely, A. *Death and beyond*. Chicago: Thomas More Press, 1976.

Hine, V.H. Altered states of consciousness: A form of death education? *Death Education*, 1978, *1*, 377–396.

Hine, V.H. *Last letter to the pebble people*. Santa Cruz: Unity Press, 1979.

Johnson, J.E., Rice, V.H., Fuller, S.S., and Endress, M.P. Sensory information, instruction in a coping strategy, and recovery from surgery. *Research in Nursing and Health*, 1978, *1*, 4–17.

Jung, C. *Two essays in analytic psychology*, trans. by R.F.C. Hall. New York: Meridien Books, 1953.

Jung, C. *Memories, dreams, reflections*. New York: Vintage, 1965.

Klass, D. and Gordon, A. Varieties of transcending experience at death: A video-tape based study. *Omega*, 1978–1979, *9*, 19–36.

Kubler–Ross, E. *On death and dying*. New York: MacMillan Company, 1969.

Kubler–Ross, E. *Death: The final stage of growth*. Englewood Cliffs, N.J.: Prentice–Hall, 1975.

Levak, M.M. Motherhood by death among the Bororo Indians of Brazil. *Omega*, 1979–1980, *4*, 323–334.

Levine, J., Gordon, N. and Fields, N. Hormones and behavior. *The Lancet*, 1978, *11*, 654.

Mitford, J. *The American way of death*. New York: Simon and Schuster, 1963.

Moody, R.A. *Life after life*. New York: Bantam, 1976.

Nilsson, L. *Behold man*. Boston: Little, Brown and Company, 1973.

Osis, K. and Haraldsson, E. *At the hour of death*. New York: Avon, 1977.

Ramsey, D. The indignity of "death with dignity." *Hastings Center Studies*, 1974, *2*, 51.

Samuels, M. and Samuels, N. *Seeing with the mind's eye*. New York: Random House, 1975.

Siegel, R.K. and West, L.J. (Eds.). *Hallucinations: Behavior, experience and theory*. New York: John Wiley and Sons, 1975.

Templer, D.L. Death anxiety in religiously very involved persons. *Psychological Reports*, 1972, *31*, 361–362.

Trelease, M.L. Dying among Alaskan Indians: A matter of choice. In E. Kubler–Ross (Ed.). *Death: The final stage of growth*. Englewood Cliffs, N.J.: Prentice–Hall, N.J., 1975.

SPECIAL TOPICS IN BEHAVIORAL MEDICINE

9 PREVENTING BURN-OUT AND REDUCING STRESS IN TERMINAL CARE
The Role of Assertive Training

Richard A. Kolotkin

Death is an inevitable consequence of life, an integral part of human existence, yet few topics arouse as much personal discomfort as that of dying. Prior to 1959, the study of death was virtually an unknown discipline within general psychology (Pearlman, Stotsky, and Dominick 1969). Recently, however, we have witnessed a dramatic increase of interest in death and dying. Contemporary discussions of death now address themselves to the psychological demands of terminal illness. With the growth of this new orientation has developed a concern for the needs of both patient and health professional as they attempt to cope with the emotional demands of life-threatening illness (Garfield 1979; Vachon, Lyall, and Freeman 1978; and Weisman and Sobel 1979).

Sophisticated inquiry has been slow to develop. Adequate empirical studies of the psychosocial impact of terminal illness on both caretakers and survivors remain scarce and those which do exist tend to be of questionable validity (Monat and Lazarus 1977; and Shady 1976). Anecdotal evidence, however, suggests that terminal care does exact an emotional toll on the caretaker; professionals who care for the terminally ill experience strong affective reactions as a consequence of their employment (Hay and Oken 1979; Klagsbrun 1979; and Vreeland and Ellis 1969). The literature indicates that constant confrontation with death can produce both affective and physiological reactions that may interfere with patient care, professional satisfaction, and the personal well-being of the provider. The care of the dying is quite stressful, and the responses of the professional to the stressors of terminal care may or may not be adaptive for the dying patient and the entire health care system.

Maladaptive reactions to the experience of stress are widely documented. Numerous studies investigating human response to stressful vocational circumstances underscore the fact that exposure to high levels of job-related stress, such as that reported by most terminal-care practitioners (Hay and Oken 1979; Maslach 1979; Pearlman et al. 1969; and Weisman 1970), results in lowered job performance and reduced personal satisfaction (Cobb and Rose 1973; Howard 1976; and Nelson and Smith 1970). The term "burn-out" is often used to refer to the many adverse physical, emotional, and behavioral consequences of prolonged exposure to stressful circumstances (Cherniss 1980; Freudenberger 1974, 1977; Maslach 1979; Maslach and Pines 1977; and Mattingly 1977).

In terminal care, both stress and burn-out can have numerous adverse effects on caretakers, patients, and survivors. Maslach (1979) cites burn-out as a primary cause of poor delivery of health and social services, and as a major etiological factor in staff absenteeism, professional apathy, cynicism, increased job turnover, and lowered staff morale. Vachon (1979) cites unmanageable stress as being significantly related to interpersonal conflicts among caretakers, poor patient care, reduced self-esteem, and decreased job satisfaction. These and other authors (Freudenberger 1974, 1977; Hay and Oken 1979; Klagsburn 1979; Maslach and Pines 1977; Mattingly 1977; and Vachon et al. 1978) feel that providing caretakers with training in social skills, self-expression, and interpersonal communication would reduce practitioners' vulnerability to burn-out.

In behavior therapy, the term "assertive training" is typically used to refer to those behavioral interventions that are designed to enhance social skills and to facilitate interpersonal functioning. In this chapter I will discuss the potential contribution of assertive training to the prevention of burn-out in terminal care. The goal of assertive training in this context is to provide those responsible for the dying with a repertoire of coping and stress-management skills that will facilitate adaptation to terminal-care stressors. I will first present a case example of burn-out and then relate burn-out symptomatology to the stress and stressors of terminal care. I will then discuss the research that supports the use of assertive training to reduce vulnerability to burn-out. Finally, I will present a list of the procedures that I use in my clinical assertive training–stress management workshops.

CASE EXAMPLE: NURSE R

Nurse R was exhausted. Each morning she woke up for work feeling tired and angry. She could not seem to get out of bed. The head nurse on the terminal-care ward where she worked was beginning to comment on Ms. R's growing tendency to arrive late. Because of this, she was anxious about being criticized on the job and depressed about her deteriorating job situation. Today she was feeling hungover. Last night she had had an argument with her sister. Afterward she could not fall asleep despite her exhaustion. Drinking seemed to help, but she always suffered the consequences the next day. The liquor was also causing her already nervous stomach to feel even worse. Now she was getting headaches. Nurse R. found that nightmares also interrupted her sleep. She had even been gaining weight.

As Ms. R. started to get out of bed, she laughed to herself about the patients she would see. They were such a demanding lot, she thought to herself, always asking questions about cancer and death. Their families were even worse. On the other hand, she had found that if she looked busy, smiled, and kept moving, they would usually leave her alone. Why bother her anyway? Wasn't it the doctor's job to talk to them? Maybe Mrs. M. would die today and then her family would stop pestering them all. Even insulting Mr. M. had not gotten them off their back. Maybe today she could find a place to hide for awhile and be alone. That could help, but she sometimes felt so guilty. Her mood, in fact, was terrible. Up and down all of the time. Perhaps she should just get out of nursing. Anything seemed better than that job. Just thinking about the hospital seemed to cause her anxiety, anger, and disgust.

While drinking her morning coffee, Nurse R. found herself thinking about how she had changed. She was not the same highly competent and motivated nurse who had wanted a transfer from orthopedics about a year ago. She knew that she had little experience with dying cancer patients, but the routine of orthopedics had often felt meaningless and boring. At the time that she requested the transfer Nurse R. had been toying with the idea of going back to school and getting a degree in counseling. She was thirty-one and a change to psychiatric nursing had sounded interesting. But she received her transfer and it had all been so interesting at first. Now she could not believe how involved and concerned she had been with her patients. She had made it a point to spend a little extra time with each one of them. She had tried to get to know their families and friends. She had even volunteered for some evening shifts and weekends. Her colleagues had noticed, commenting how she spent more time with her patients than with them. They had also complained that she was territorial and was making it difficult for them to see these patients. She could not understand the complaints. She just wanted to do a good job. She just really cared.

Things started changing after the first few patients died. Nurse R. felt terrible and wished she could have done more. She had found it extremely difficult to talk to the families. No one seemed to care and it did not seem okay to feel that way. Besides, no one else seemed to feel upset by the death of patients, so why should she? No, something was wrong with her. She had wanted to talk to others but was afraid of being criticized or laughed at. So she decied to avoid her colleagues. In staff meetings she felt anxious and did not want to talk about patients. A few times she had been criticized for changing the topic in meetings and for laughing inappropriately. No one seemed to care, they just criticized. There was just nowhere to turn.

UNDERSTANDING STRESS AND BURN-OUT

The concept of stress is widely misunderstood. Part of the misconception stems from its inconsistent usage in our everyday language. The term is commonly used in reference both to circumstances we find anxiety-producing and to the emotional reactions to these demanding circumstances. A more precise definition requires that we use the term only when speaking of those physiological and emotional responses that accompany exposure to threatening life experiences. The term stressor should be used to denote those environmental circumstances in which stress is elicited (Spielberger 1979).

Despite the generally accepted belief that stress has only negative physiological and emotional effects, the organism's stress response serves an important adaptive and protective function. In the face of real or imagined threat the body responds with a series of hormonal changes that increase our adaptive capabilities and chances for survival. Thus stress is actually essential to life because it is associated with greater levels of resistance and increased adaptive capacity in the face of challenging life events.

Initial formulations of stress assumed that only physical events or chemical agents could elicit the stress response. More recent research, however, clearly shows that stress can occur even in the absence of objective or physical threat. These studies show that a person's subjective appraisals and expectations will also produce stress. Thus, if we define a situation as difficult or aversive (Dobson and Neufield 1979), feel uncertain about or unable to predict a situation's out-

come (Averill 1973), anticipate a negative result (Lazarus and Averill 1972), perceive ourselves as being unable to cope (Lazarus and
Alfert 1964; and Neufield 1976), or define an event as ego-threat-
ening (Lazarus 1967) we will experience stress. The term "effective
stressor" is often used to refer to situations that elicit stress in the
absence of serious objective danger.

The General Adaptation Syndrome

Research investigating human response to effective stressors suggests
that similar physiological responses are elicited by a wide variety
of threatening thoughts or events. According to Selye (1956), the
human organism responds in a predictable and stereotypic fashion
when confronted with any of a variety of stressors. Selye refers to
the entire sequence of physiological responses that follow exposure
to a stressor as the General Adaptation Syndrome (GAS).

In the first stage of the GAS an "alarm reaction," stimulated by
a stressor, mobilizes the defensive and protective resources of the
organism. Continued exposure to the stressor causes the organism to
enter the "stage of resistance." During this stage the body uses its
resources to maintain homeostatic balance in the face of continued
threat. When resistive resources are depleted, the organism enters
into the final GAS stage, the "stage of exhaustion." Here the organism's ability to cope with the continued experience of stress is dras-
tically reduced. We succumb to the threat which initially precipitated
the GAS. In extreme cases, irreversible damage or even death may
occur during exhaustion.

The predictable nature of human reaction to stressful circumstances has important implications for understanding burn-out in
terminal care. As a syndrome, most writers (Cherniss 1980; Freudenberger 1974; and Maslach 1979) agree that burn-out results from
continued exposure to job-related stressors with which the individual
has been unable to cope. The fact that burn-out is characterized by
physical and emotional exhaustion, fatigue, increased physical discomfort, apathy, withdrawal, and interpersonal sensitivity implies
that those exhibiting burn-out symptomatology have exhausted their
capacities to cope. They have succumbed to the stressors of terminal
care. If viewed as representing the final stage of the GAS, burn-out
indicates that they are not equipped to deal with the stressful psy-

chosocial and affective realities of their employment. To avoid the disruptive consequences and decrements in job performance associated with continued exposure to vocational stress, skills other than those provided by medical training are necessary in terminal care.

Analysis of the GAS shows, however, that burn-out need not be a frequent occurrence in terminal care. The prevention of burn-out could be accomplished by implementing an intervention designed to (1) help providers alter stressful circumstances that signal GAS onset, or (2) increase the caretaker's ability to deal effectively with threatening situations before the stage of exhaustion is reached. Given the unavoidable nature of stress and its potential enhancement of adaptive capabilities (Tache and Selye 1978), any intervention should be directed at the management, rather than the elimination, of stresses associated with terminal care.

STRESS IN TERMINAL CARE

Those involved in terminal care are confronted daily with that which most people in our society want to deny: the reality of death. In terminal care, particularly, the health-care professional's antipathy toward death exaggerates the human and unpleasant emotional reactions to the end of life that are so commonly observed in our society. For the medical provider who has invested much time and energy in learning how to prolong life, caring for the dying will stimulate disquieting anxieties and strong fears. For those who care for the terminally ill, stress reactions will occur in response to situations personally or professionally threatening.

The clinical literature indicates that professionals involved in terminal care must confront their own feelings toward death before they can effectively care for those whose death is imminent (Shady 1976). A number of studies note that physicans, nurses, and medical students perceive terminal illness as extremely threatening and that they typically prefer to avoid death-related thoughts and feelings (Feifel, Hanson, Jones, and Edwards 1967; Pearlman et al. 1969; and Saul and Kass 1969).

There is an unfortunate paradox here. On the one hand, the data show that affective arousal is a prevalent reaction among those involved in terminal care. On the other hand, the behavioral and emotional prescriptions for the so-called competent professional often require the caretaker to remain objective and to deny or isolate emotions. As a result, although painful emotions are likely to be aroused in terminal care, they are frequently seen as an abnormal or inappropriate response to the death of a patient. Thus, emotion in terminal care is often associated with a sense of professional inadequacy, self-doubt, guilt, frustration, anger, failure, and helplessness. (Bugen 1978; Maslach 1979; Shady 1976; and Weisman 1970). In the face of such ego-threat, stress is likely to be high.

Other contradictory prescriptions concerning emotions and objectivity contribute to the stresses of terminal care. Cultural expectations require extensive affective expression from those who interact with the dying. Yet identification with the dying patient can dramatically increase the emotional discomfort associated with object loss, and the caretaker may objectify the patient to increase distance and decrease personal vulnerability (Hay and Oken 1979). Though society asks the provider to be human and emotional, the requirements of terminal care foster a need for objectivity. Despite the overtly functional nature of this objectivity, it may cause caretakers to question their basic self-worth and humanistic attitudes. These threatening cognitions and conflicts, as well as the realistic anticipation of negative outcomes (i.e., death), are very likely to be a source of stress for health care professionals.

Professional Training and Stress

Cultural and professional anxieties over death are not the only sources of stress for those involved in terminal care. Professional training itself may contribute to the discomfort of working with the dying patient.

Health professionals, including those responsible for the dying, are taught that the goal of medical care is the continuation of life. Since medical training involves learning skills for saving lives, repeated confrontations with the dying may signal a sense of failure in the minds of those who can no longer effectively apply their medical expertise (Hay and Oken 1979; and Schulz and Aderman 1976). Because professional medical training fosters the belief that scientific expertise and intensive medical knowledge are adequate preparation for all aspects of medical care (Weisman 1970), the interpersonal and emotional requirements of terminal care are often unexpected. Providers are likely to experience stress when they learn that their extensive repertoire of medical skill is inadequate when they are confronted with the psychosocial and affective demands of terminal care.

Despite the fact that those involved in terminal care are often unprepared to meet the nonmedical demands of terminal illness, these caretakers expect to maintain consistently high levels of professionalism and competence in all medical situations. Because the discrepancy between these idealistic expectations and the harsh realities of terminal care will be threatening to the professional's self-esteem and sense of self-efficacy (Bandura 1977), stress is bound to be quite high.

Additional sources of threat and stress are inherent in the care of the dying. Terminal or intensive care often requires quick and decisive life-saving action by nurses and doctors. The urgency of these medical decisions does not allow caretakers sufficient time to confirm their accuracy. As a result, responsibility and high levels of uncertainty are commonly found in terminal-care settings. Adequate feedback concerning the appropriateness of these crucial decisions is, in fact, usually not immediately available unless the patient dies. Since situational difficulty, uncertainty, ego-threat, and reductions in informational feedback (Averill 1973; and Cassell 1979) all contribute to stress, these factors are likely to produce emotional unrest.

Professional Responses to the Stresses of Terminal Care

Vulnerable to burn-out because of their training and idealism, health caretakers typically rely on their own resources and spontaneous coping strategies. Yet the prevalaence of burn-out implies that the professional's usual coping responses fail to reduce job-related stress adequately. Because of the serious consequences of burn-out, this is a significant clinical and professional problem.

Clinical reports of burn-out collected from various disciplines show that there are similar responses which mark professionals' attempts to adapt to vocational stress (Cherniss 1980; Daley 1979; Freudenberger 1974, 1977; Maslach 1976, 1979; Maslach and Pines 1977; and Mattingly 1977). In most reports the following characteristic responses of burn-out are cited: physical and emotional exhaustion, increased somatic disturbance, free-floating anxiety, cynicism, client dehumanization, personal dehumanization, limited frustration tolerance, interpersonal sensitivity, rigidity, negativism, decrements in social functioning, absenteeism, increased chemical dependency, familial upset, increased self-doubt, decreased empathic ability, and loss of professional identity. In terminal care, which requires extensive personal responsibility, professional vigilance, human sensitivity, and high levels of physical and emotional energy, such responses to unremitting stress detract from the quality of patient care. Patients may find themselves alone and abandoned as they confront their own imminent death. This abandonment may heighten a patient's emotionality (Weisman 1970) and perhaps even increase the probability of premature death from various life-threatening illnesses (Hackett, Cassem, and Wishnie 1979; and Weisman and Sobel 1979).

Patient dehumanization also has an extremely negative impact on terminal care. Although often used as a coping strategy by health caretakers, dehumanization is more likely to augment than to reduce the effects of the stressors of terminal care. It may reinforce the professional's feelings of inhumanity, self-doubt, inadequacy, hopelessness, and guilt. Rather than serving to protect the professional from vocational stress and the process of burn-out, dehumanization may actually accelerate the onset of stress-related symptomatology by creating additional sources of threat for providers.

Although inconclusive, the research investigating professional responses to the dying underscores that clinicians also tend to protect themselves from the stresses of impending patient death through both verbal and physical avoidance (Schultz and Aderman 1976). Kastenbaum (1967), for example, found that 82 percent of the nurses he studied responded with some form of verbal avoidance to patients' statements concerning death. Oken (1961) found a similar tendency among doctors responsible for cancer patients. Weisman (1970) has also suggested that professional staff may hide behind verbal formalities and socially acceptable platitudes in an attempt to cope with their own emotional arousal.

A number of authors observe that caretakers increasingly avoid dying patients as death becomes imminent (Kastenbaum and Aisenberg 1972; and Livingston and Zimot 1965). Behavioral avoidance of the dying not only detracts from the quality of patient care, but also ultimately exacerbates a professional's level of distress. This avoidance can accentuate existing feelings of self-doubt, guilt, and personal or professional inadequacy. Like dehumanization, avoidance provides little real relief from the anxieties of terminal care. Further-more, it may actually contribute to burn-out.

Since a provider's response to vocational stress detracts from per-sonal satisfaction and patient care, clinical and medical needs under-score the importance of preventing burn-out. Research in this area, although sparse and largely uncontrolled, notes that programs that teach social skills, encourage affective expression, increase self-aware-ness, and build social support systems can prevent the onset of burn-out (Bugen 1979; Klagsburn 1979; Maslach 1979; Maslach 1979; Maslach and Pines 1977; Mattingly 1977; and Vachon, Lyall, and Freeman 1978). Because assertive training is specifically designed to achieve these goals, it is a viable humanistic strategy to use in the prevention of burn-out. Both logical and empirical considerations support the preventative applicability of this behavioral intervention.

ASSERTIVE TRAINING FOR STRESS MANAGEMENT IN TERMINAL CARE

A detailed account of assertive training procedures and skills is be-yond the scope of this chapter. For practitioners interested in a more complete treatment of the conceptual and research issues involved in assertive training, I recommend Rimm and Master's (1979) behavior therapy text, or Whiteley and Flowers's (1978) recent book, as intro-ductory readings. I would also recommend Lange and Jakubowski's (1976) comprehensive guide to assertive training for appropriately trained professionals who are interested in leading an assertive train-ing group. In addition, a number of self-help guides (Adler 1977; Alberti and Emmons 1974; Chenevert 1978; and Jakubowski and Lange 1978) are available for those who would like to learn assertive skills, but cannot find an appropriate group to attend. As a strategy for the prevention of burn-out, however, assertive training is likely to be more effective in those settings where institutionalized assertive training programs have been effectively integrated into the fabric of the hospital system (Hackett and Weisman 1977; Klagsburn 1979; Maslach and Pines 1977; and Wodinsky 1964).

Definition of Assertion

For behavior therapists assertive training is a multifaceted behavioral intervention designed to teach social skills, encourage appropriate affective and self-expression, increase personal awareness of maladaptive cognitions, and reduce anxiety in interpersonal situations. In this context, assertion encompasses any socially acceptable expression of thought or affect, as well as verbal statements consistent with a defense of personal dignity and individual rights (Wolpe 1958, 1969; and Wolpe and Lazarus 1966). A factor-analytic study of assertive behavior suggests that it includes behaviors that express either positive or negative feelings, are in defense of personal rights, express opinions, ask for favors, take initiative with others, and refuse unreasonable requests (Gay, Hollandsworth, and Galassi 1978).

Initial theoretical formulations of the relationship of anxiety to assertion clearly support using assertive behavior as a means to reduce anxiety. Wolpe (1958) viewed assertion, like relaxation, as essentially incompatible with anxiety. While psychophysiological evidence affirming this contention is tentative at best (Rimm and Masters 1979), clients who have participated in assertive training groups typically report feeling less anxious (Kazdin 1974; Kolotkin 1979b; McFall and Marston 1970; and Nietzel, Martorano, and Melnick 1977), calmer (Rimm et al. 1976), and less angry or tense (Rimm et al. 1974) in stressful interpersonal situations.

Since interpersonal interactions with patients or survivors in terminal care can elicit much tension and anxiety for the caretaker, these data indicate that assertive training can be effectively used to combat uncomfortable feelings. Because reductions in interpersonal anxiety should cause the practitioner to redefine nonmedical interactions as less difficult, aversive, or threatening, assertive training should also change many of the subjective appraisals that produce stress. Assertive training can therefore reduce a practitioner's vulnerability to burn-out by increasing resistance to the discomforts of stress and by altering the frequency and intensity of the stress response.

Assertion and Coping

Other data indicate that assertive training could have a substantial impact in reducing experiences of stress elicited by the ego-threats of terminal care. Working from a behavioral model, but not in a terminal care setting, Kazdin (1979) demonstrated that participants in assertive training classes could increase their sense of self-efficacy. In a recent study I also found (Kolotkin 1979b) that assertive training will result in an increased sense of self-efficacy as well as in an improved sense of social potency and self-control, whether or not participants actually apply their new assertive skills to behavior. Furthermore, other studies note that assertive training can improve self-concept and augment performance self-esteem (Mayo and Pearlman 1977; Percell, Berwick, and Deigel 1974; and Stake and Pearlman 1980). Since an improved self-concept is likely to alter many of the stress-producing cognitions that mark practitioners' appraisals of the degree of threat, difficulty, and aversiveness involved in terminal care, stress reduction is likely to follow assertive training.

Improved self-concept and self-efficacy can also directly augment a practitioner's coping activities. According to Bandura (1977), efficacy expectations influence the effort an individual expends when confronted by a stressor, and how long he or she will try to cope with aversive circumstances. As caretakers develop a belief in their personal effectiveness, they are likely to redefine a stressful terminal-care situation as manageable, and then to initiate and persist with effective coping behavior. They may later learn more generalized coping activities since effective behaviors will be reinforced by the absence of stress.

Because assertive training can augment feelings of personal competence, it can also facilitate a caretaker's introspective efforts to confront and cope with the feelings of inadequacy and helplessness stimulated by terminal care. The need to deny, avoid, and dehumanize may then be reduced. By learning to discuss feelings and fears associated with their employment, providers can discover personal affective reactions to death and the reactions of others. This increased awareness should also lower reliance on maladaptive defensive strategies and, as a result, contribute to improved patient care.

Assertion and Cognitions

Data that indicate that assertive individuals produce fewer self-defeating and irrational cognitions than nonassertive individuals also reinforces the viability of assertive training as a stress management strategy. Schwartz and Gottman (1976), for example, demonstrate that minimally assertive people tend to have a greater number of negative thoughts about themselves than do highly assertive individuals. The data also indicate that nonassertive people may have unrealistic standards of perfection and an unrealistic concern for the feelings of others (Alden and Safran 1978). Moreover, highly assertive individuals expect more favorable consequences from others for their assertive expression than do their nonassertive counterparts (Eisler, Frederiksen, and Petersen 1978).

Because cognitive factors are a major stimulus for the activation of the GAS, these data underscore the hypothesis that increased assertion among caretakers could reduce GAS onset and thus subsequently prevent burn-out. Modifying expectations of negative outcomes, situational difficulty, and aversiveness should reduce stress among practitioners. Since caretaker idealism seems to be a major etiological factor in burn-out, altering both standards of perfection and irrational fears of offending others should also lower practitioner vulnerability to burn-out.

Behavioral Skills and Assertion

In addition to providing direct relief from anxiety and tension and affecting alterations in stress-related cognitions, assertive training programs teach concrete behavioral skills that have clear applicability for stress management in terminal care. The ability to take the initiative with others, express opinions, define one's legitimate rights, refuse unreasonable requests, or ask for favors can directly enhance a provider's job satisfaction by facilitating a change in stressful circumstances or by providing an adaptive exit from situations in which the GAS has been activated. Because assertive training involves learning specific behavioral skills to avoid interpersonal conflict while fostering self-expression and social exchange, providers who practice assertive behavior are able to find direct relief from the pressure cooker of pent-up feelings. By relieving affective pressure appropriately, the clinician will increase resistance to burn-out. The availability of better resources will facilitate other coping behaviors and further fortify resistance to exhaustion.

Assertive training skills are applicable across a wide range of potentially stressful terminal-care situations. For example, asking for clarification, feedback, or information (three basic assertive skills) can decrease stress by providing clinicians with accurate information about the consequences of their professional choices. Because stress is reduced by both feedback (Averill 1973) and information (Cassel 1979), assertive training should have a major impact on stress in settings, such as terminal care, where information and feedback are often not readily available.

Self-assertion and effective communication skills are also valuable to providers when interacting with dying patients, their families, other members of the health-care team, or other hospital personnel. Situations in which it is necessary to talk with a patient about his or her medical condition or to ask colleagues for help and support represent two of the many stressful terminal-care situations in which effective interpersonal skills are needed. The effective management of stress through direct assertive action will reduce the caretaker's need to resort to passive, defensive maneuvers that interfere with patient care. By modeling effective communication styles as they interact with families of the dying, clinicians will also indirectly teach family members and patients the benefits of open communication. The satisfaction achieved from this strategy will have a major impact on reducing the sense of inadequacy and the associated stress that contribute to the onset of burn-out.

For those professionals who repeatedly fail to assert themselves in employment settings, the risk of burn-out remains high. While short-term defensive strategies often provide temporary reductions in anxiety, they also increase vulnerability to burn-out by fostering future avoidance, feelings of inadequacy and impotence, and a sense of self-doubt. Failing to manage stress in a direct, assertive manner, caretakers may ruminate about particular vocational situations and decisions. Such ruminations perpetuate the stress response, increase its intensity, and accelerate exhaustion. The strain of passive rumination is evident in increased muscular tension, psychosomatic pain, and heightened blood pressure as the body's resistive resources are depleted. In such cases failure to reduce stress will induce high levels of painful or damaging affective and autonomic arousal, ultimately resulting in exhaustion and burn-out.

OBSTACLES TO ASSERTION IN TERMINAL CARE

Many obstacles to effective assertion in terminal care exist. Individuals will not risk self-expression because they question their ability to produce an effective assertion or they fear offending others or embarrassing themselves. Lack of social-skill knowledge and feelings of anxiety may, therefore, prevent expressions of thoughts, feelings, and preferences that are crucial for managing vocational stress and developing or maintaining a sense of personal competence. Fear of the doctor, for example, may inhibit a particular nurse from asking for needed assistance. Not knowing what to say may preclude an open discussion of death with the terminally ill. The provider may hesitate talking about the personal discomforts of terminal care because of fears of embarrassment or ridicule. The family of the dying may be avoided because of personal discomfort and fears of interpersonal inadequacy. These failures to communicate, motivated by both personal and professional anxieties, do little to reduce the stress associated with these inevitable occupational circumstances. The tendency to avoid or to withdraw from these situations actually increases vulnerability to burn-out by fostering self-doubt.

Nonassertive behavior is also subtly irrational. In terminal care, for example, the failure to express feelings or to ask for help or feedback is often fueled by the fear of being seen as nonobjective and nonprofessional. In the long-run, however, it is this lack of assertion that causes the result it is designed to avoid. Because nonassertion will increase vulnerability to professional burn-out, and because burn-out leads to decrements in job performance, continued nonassertion can eventually cause professional dysfunction. When burned-out, the caretaker will inevitably exhibit incompetent behaviors, and be evaluated by peers as inept. Thus, in those situations in which expressive avoidance occurs, the lack of assertion and the desire for self-protection can actually produce exactly that which was feared in the beginning. Nonassertion, while overtly functional, indeed represents an irrational option for those involved in caring for the dying (Ellis and Grieger 1977).

Fears of peer evaluation are not the only motivation for nonassertion in terminal care. Fear of upsetting the dying and their families also motivates interpersonal avoidance. The fear of not knowing what to say to the terminally ill patient, for example, causes the caretaker to avoid interactions with patients or to say nothing. Since professional wisdom encourages those responsible for the terminally ill to discuss their patient's impending death (Schulz and Alderman 1976), the failure to communicate may stimulate latent fears of professional inadequacy. Again, rather than actually reducing stress, avoidance through nonassertion may nurture a sense of self-doubt and exacerbate the stresses of terminal care.

Although feelings of anxiety concerning self-assertion in terminal care settings may be irrational, the lack of social-skill knowledge is often real. I believe that this is so because most people never have the opportunity to learn effective social and interpersonal skills. Typically, educational settings—including those devoted to medical training—assume the existence of such skills and do little to insure their development. Although numerous courses provide the complex medical skills required for patient care, few educational institutions offer courses that specifically teach social skills. The prevalence of burn-out and the heavy interpersonal demands of the medical setting suggest that this practice is ill-advised. Specific training in social, expressive, and interpersonal skills is, in fact, likely to help providers meet the psychosocial needs of patients, reduce their own vulnerability to burn-out, and eventually improve patient care.

Professional education not only provides few opportunities for the acquisition of social-skills knowledge, but it also inadvertently contributes to provider nonassertion. In the professional socialization process, most health-care professionals learn behavioral passivity rather than assertion. For many caretakers, the seemingly adaptive compliance with the implicit rules of their employment prevents self-expression and subsequently limits opportunities to acquire effective assertive skills. Those who are assertive in such an environment are often punished. Moreover, relatively few assertive role models are likely to exist in the hospital setting because of professional socialization.

Due to the lack of role models, the professional prescriptions against assertion, and the failure of most medical training institutions to offer social skills training programs, most practitioners are not equipped with adequate social-skill knowledge. This increases the risk of burn-out for providers. The serious personal and institutional consequences of burn-out underscore the necessity of implementing institutionalized social-skills training programs to reduce the risk of this disorder. Institutionalization of these programs is crucial to encourage increased provider participation and to help clinicians overcome the systemic obstacles to self-assertion existing in most hospital settings. As with other skills, assertion requires a learning period. During and after this learning period the support of the institution is necessary to insure that assertive efforts are not punished. Providing an environment in which self-expression is accepted is a necessary step if we are to reinforce caretakers to practice their new social skills.

COMPONENTS OF ASSERTIVE TRAINING

Although behavior therapists offer no standard program for social-skills interventions, the important components of assertive training can be abstracted from the literature. Over the last few years I have developed a program which has met with considerable participant satisfaction. More importantly, my research indicates that this intervention exerts major impact on social skills, participant anxiety, feelings of self-efficacy, social potency, and self-control (Kolotkin 1979a, 1979b). The components of this program are:

1. *Educational Mini-Lectures*: This phase of the assertive training program is conceptually consistent with the approach recommended by Meichenbaum (1977) for stress-inoculation training. It is designed to provide participants with a basic conceptual framework for understanding decrements in assertive behavior and to solicit their views regarding nonassertion. Included are brief discussions of the contributions of education and socialization (e.g., sex or role stereotypes) to nonassertion; the importance of defining assertion as a skill; a conceptual approach to understanding the differences among nonassertion, assertion, and aggression; and an overview of the workshop. The situational nature of nonassertion is emphasized, as is the transfer of current skills to chronically difficult situations.

2. *Discrimination of Assertion, Nonassertion, and Aggression*: Because many people fail to express themselves for fear of offending others, assertion is often facilitated by teaching participants to distinguish among assertive, aggressive, and nonassertive behaviors. Didactic lectures and discussion, modeling, role-playing, and homework assignments achieve this goal. After establishing behavioral guidelines for each response mode, I usually solicit difficult interpersonal situations from participants and model an assertive, aggressive, and nonassertive response. Between modeling trials I ask group members to categorize each response and to discuss those nonverbal and verbal behaviors that caused them to label the response as they did. Participants are encouraged to role-play assertive, aggressive or nonassertive responses to additional sample situations that they provide. I believe that it is essential to use sample situations generated by participants in order to maintain interest and flexibility in the workshop. Participants in terminal-care settings, for example, use this as an opportu-

nity to define difficult interactions and to understand that other providers also find aspects of their employment to be stressful.

Homework requires group members to rate a series of standard situations and responses by response type and to focus on the images that they develop as they make these ratings. They are also asked to imagine themselves being assertive in each situation and to employ an image of coping models receiving positive consequences from their assertions. These imagery instructions are based upon literature that indicates these factors facilitate the acquisition and generalization of assertive behavior (Kazdin 1974, 1975).

3. *Skills Training*: Here participants develop concrete behavioral skills required for effective assertion. This phase of training focuses on specific discussions of nonverbal and verbal contributions to communication and emphasizes the importance of viewing assertion as an honest information exchange rather than a manipulative tactic. Training focuses on using various "I" statements in a problem-solving format that enables participants to develop their own assertive style. During group meetings participants are again encouraged to work on personally relevant situations. I complete some modeling and role-playing, although I have found imagery techniques to be extremely useful in skills training. Homework is designed to reinforce practice and to insure positive consequences for assertion by using imagery and graduated *in vivo* practice. The actual application of assertive skills in a variety of increasingly stressful circumstances is consistent with the application phase of stress-inoculation procedures.

4. *Cognitive Restructuring*: This component asks group members to become more aware of irrational thoughts that inhibit assertion, produce maladaptive emotional arousal, or elicit unnecessary stress (Kolotkin in press). My approach is to use reading assignments, didactic mini-lectures, and structured homework practice assignments to teach participants rational thinking. These assignments are based upon rational-emotive therapy (Ellis and Grieger 1977) techniques. (See Chapter 6.) Participants learn a problem-solving strategy that is used to alter irrational obstacles to assertion, reduce cognitive-behavioral rigidity, and decrease stress. Rational thinking is presented to group members as a skill and *in vivo* application to difficult or stressful interpersonal situations is encouraged.

5. *Deep Muscle Relaxation*: Because anxiety can inhibit assertion and interfere with rational problem-solving, I include instruction

in deep muscle relaxation. I use a variation of Lazarus's (1971) procedure. Relaxation is presented as a skill, augmented by practice, that can be used to counteract anxiety and the experience of stress. I also include a stress-inoculation phase in which participants are asked to imagine stressful interpersonal or vocational situations and then to reduce situational anxiety by applying any of the behavioral techniques (including relaxation) that have been included in the workshop.

6. *Practice*: This behavioral component is also consistent with stress-inoculation training procedures and with the literature indicating that practice contributes to the acquisition and generalization of assertive behavior. Practice procedures include imagery, covert modeling, behavioral rehearsal, self-monitoring, and self-reward strategies. These procedures are based upon an extensive review of the literature (Kolotkin 1978) and include specific components designed to enhance learning and transfer.

CONCLUSIONS AND SUMMARY

Terminal care requires that clinicians learn multifaceted skills to help them cope with the many stressors inherent in their employment. The increasing incidence of burn-out among providers suggests that the stress-management strategies typically employed by those responsible for the dying are inadequate. While the literature underscores the need for interpersonal skills in terminal care, the lack of social-skill knowledge and irrational fears concerning self-expression insure that providers will rely on destructive defensive strategies to cope with vocational stress. Since medical training institutions typically fail to include courses in social skills, many caretakers are unprepared for the realities of their employment. This lack of preparation, combined with provider idealism, is likely to result in high levels of vocational stress and increased vulnerability to burn-out. The consequences of burn-out for provider and patient require that effective preventative programs be incorporated into medical training and terminal-care settings.

As a primary or secondary preventative strategy, assertive training represents an extremely viable and humanistic intervention program with significant stress-management applications for terminal care. The institutionalization of assertive-training programs in medical settings should result in reduced risk of provider burn-out, enhanced job performance, increased vocational satisfaction, and improved care for the dying. Because modeling of appropriate social skills by medical staff should also encourage self-expression for patients, their families, and survivors, assertive training can also have a generalized impact on patient and survivor satisfaction in terminal-care settings.

REFERENCES

Adler, R.B. *Confidence in communication: A guide to assertive and social skills.* New York: Holt, Rinehart & Winston, 1977.

Albert, R.E., and Emmons, M.L. *Your perfect right: A guide to assertive behavior* (2nd edition). San Luis Obispo, California: Impact Press, 1974.

Alden, L., and Safran, J. Irrational beliefs and nonassertive behavior. *Cognitive Therapy and Research*, 1978, *2*, 357–364.

Averill, J.R. Personal control over aversive stimuli and its relationship to stress. *Psychological Bulletin*, 1973, *80*, 286–303.

Bandura, A. Self-efficacy: Toward a unifying theory of behavioral change. *Psychological Review*, 1977, *84*, 191–215.

Bugen, L.A. Emotions: Their presence and impact upon the helping role. In C. Garfield (Ed.), *Stress and survival: The emotional realities of life-threatening illness.* St. Louis: C.V. Mosby Company, 1979.

Cassel, J. Psychosocial processes and "stress": Theoretical formulations. In C. Garfield (Ed.), *Stress and survival: The emotional realities of life-threatening illness.* St. Louis: C.V. Mosby Company, 1979.

Chenevert, M. *Special techniques in assertiveness training for women in the health professions.* St. Louis: C.V. Mosby Company, 1978.

Cherniss, C. *Professional burn-out in human service organizations.* New York: Praeger Publishers, 1980.

Cobb, S., and Ross, R.M. Hypertension, peptic ulcer and diabetes in air traffic controllers. *Journal of the American Medical Association*, 1973, *224*, 489–492.

Daley, M.R. Burnout: Smoldering problem in protective services. *Social Work*, 1979, *24*, 375–379.

Dobson, K.S., and Neufeld, R.W.J. Stress-related appraisals: A regression analysis. *Canadian Journal of Behavioral Science*, 1979, *11*, 274–285.

Eisler, R.M., Frederiksen, L.W., and Peterson, G.L. The relationship of cognitive variables to the expression of assertiveness. *Behavior Therapy*, 1978, *9*, 419–427.

Ellis, A., and Grieger, R. *Handbook of rational-emotive therapy.* New York: Springer Publishing Company, 1977.

Feifel, H., Hanson, S., Jones, R., and Edwards, L. Physicians consider death. *Proceedings of the 75th Annual Convention of the American Psychological Association*, 1967, *2*, 201–202.

Freudenberger, H.J. Staff burn-out. *Journal of Social Issues*, 1974, *30*, 159–165.

Freudenberger, H.J. Burn-out: Occupational hazard of the child case worker. *Child Care Quarterly*, 1977, *6*, 90–99.

Garfield, C. (Ed.). *Stress and survival: The emotional realities of life-threatening illness*. St. Louis: C.V. Mosby Company, 1979.

Gay, M., Hollandsworth, J., and Galassi, J. An assertiveness inventory for adults. *Journal of Counseling Psychology*, 1975, *22*, 340–344.

Hackett, T.P., Cassem, N., and Wishie, H. The coronary-care unit: An appraisal of its psychological hazards. In C. Garfield (Ed.), *Stress and survival: The emotional realities of life-threatening illness*. St. Louis: C.V. Mosby Company, 1979.

Hackett, T.P., and Weisman, A.D. Reactions to the imminence of death. In A. Monat and R. Lazarus (Eds.), *Stress and coping: An anthology*. New York: Columbia University Press, 1977.

Hay, D., and Oken, D. The psychological stresses of intensive care unit nursing. In C. Garfield (Ed.), *Stress and survival: The emotional realities of life-threatening illness*. St. Louis: C.V. Mosby Company, 1979.

Howard, J.H. Management productivity: Rusting out or burning out? *The Business Quarterly*, 1975, *40*, 44–49.

Jakubowski, P., and Lange, A.J. *The assertive option: Your rights and responsibilities*. Champaign, Ill.: Research Press, 1978.

Kastenbaum, R. Multiple perspectives on a geriatric "death valley." *Community Mental Health Journal*, 1967, *3*, 21–29.

Kastenbaum, R., and Aisenberg, R. *The psychology of death*. New York: Springer, 1972.

Kazdin, A.E. Effects of covert modeling and modeling reinforcement on assertive behavior. *Journal of Abnormal Psychology*, 1974, *83*, 240–252.

Kazdin, A.E. Covert modeling, imagery assessment, and assertive behavior. *Journal of Consulting and Clinical Psychology*, 1975, *43*, 716–724.

Klagsbrun, S. Cancer, emotions, and nurses. In C. Garfield (Ed.), *Stress and survival: The emotional realities of life-threatening illness*. St. Louis: C.V. Mosby Company, 1979.

Kolotkin, R.A. *An experimental investigation of the efficacy of programmed generalization in a structured intervention for increasing assertiveness*. Unpublished Ph.D. dissertation, University of Minnesota, 1978.

Kolotkin, R.A. Response generalization following assertive training: Yes the response does generalize. Paper presented at the 87th Annual Convention of the American Psychological Association, New York, 1979a.

Kolotkin, R.A. Behavioral and personality changes subsequent to assertive training. Paper presented at the 13th Annual Convention of the Association for
Advancement of Behavior Therapy, San Francisco, 1979b.

Kolotkin, R.A. *Coping with stress.* Sherman Oaks, California: Alfred Publishing Company, in press.

Lange, A.J., and Jakubowski, P. *Responsible assertive behavior: Cognitive/
behavioral procedures for trainers.* Champaign, Ill.: Research Press, 1976.

Lazarus, A.A. *Behavior therapy and beyond.* New York: McGraw-Hill Book
Company, 1971.

Lazarus, R.S. Cognitive and personality factors underlying threat and coping.
In M.H. Appley and R. Trumbull (Eds.), *Psychological stress.* New York:
Appleton-Century-Crofts, 1967.

Lazarus, R.S., and Alfert, E. The short-circuiting of threat by experimentally
altered cognitive appraisal. *Journal of Abnormal and Social Psychology,*
1964, *69*, 195-205.

Lazarus, R.S., and Averill, J.R. Emotion and cognition: With special reference
to anxiety. In C.D. Spielberger (Ed.), *Anxiety: Current trends in theory and
research,* Vol. 2. New York: Academic Press, 1972.

Livingston, P.B., and Zimet, C.N. Death anxiety, authoritarianism, and choice
of specialty in medical students. *Journal of Nervous and Mental Disease,*
1965, *140*, 222-230.

Maslach, C. Burn-out. *Human Behavior,* 1976, *5*, 16-22.

Maslach, C. The burn-out syndrome and patient care. In C. Garfield (Ed.),
Stress and survival: The emotional realities of life-threatening illness. St.
Louis: C.V. Mosby Company, 1979.

Maslach, C., and Pines, A. The burn-out syndrome in the day care setting. *Child
Care Quarterly,* 1977, *6*, 100-113.

Mattingly, M.A. Sources of stress and burn-out in professional child care work.
Child Care Quarterly, 1977, *6*, 127-137.

Mayo, M., and Pearlman, J. Assertive training for women: A follow-up. *Journal
of the National Association for Women Deans, Administrators, and Counselors,* 1977, *40*, 49-52.

McFall, R.M., and Marston, A.R. An experimental investigation of behavior
rehearsal in assertive training. *Journal of Abnormal Psychology,* 1970, *76*,
295-303.

Meichenbaum, D. *Cognitive-behavior modification: An integrative approach.*
New York: Plenum Press, 1977.

Monat, A., and Lazarus, R. (Eds.). *Stress and coping: An anthology.* New York:
Columbia University Press, 1977.

Nelson, Z.P., and Smith, W.E. The law enforcement profession: An incident of
high suicide. *Omega,* 1970, *1*, 243-244.

Nietzel, M., Marturano, R., and Melnick, J. The effects of covert modeling with
and without reply training on the development and generalization of assertive
responses. *Behavior Therapy,* 1977, *8*, 183-192.

Neufeld, R.W.J. Evidence of stress as a function of experimentally altered appraisal of stimulus aversiveness and coping adequacy. *Journal of Personality and Social Psychology*, 1976, *33*, 632–646.

Oken, D. The physician, the patient, and cancer. *Illinois Medical Journal*, 1961, *120*, 333–334.

Pearlman, J., Stotsky, B., and Dominick, J. Attitudes toward death among nursing home personnel. *The Journal of Genetic Psychology*, 1969, *114*, 63–75.

Percell, L.P., and Berwick, P.T. The effects of assertive training on self-concept and anxiety. *Archives of General Psychiatry*, 1974, *31*, 502–504.

Rimm, D.C., Hill, G.A., Brown, N.N., and Stuart, J.E. Group-assertive training in the treatment of expression of inappropriate anger. *Psychological Reports*, 1974, *34*, 791–798.

Rimm, D.C., and Masters, J.C. *Behavior Therapy* (2nd edition). New York: Academic Press, 1979.

Rimm, D.C., Snyder, J., Depue, R., Haanstad, M., and Armstrong, D. Assertive training versus rehearsal and the importance of making an assertive response. *Behavior Research and Therapy*, 1976, *14*, 463–469.

Saul, E.V., and Kass, J.S. Study of anticipated anxiety in a medical school setting. *Journal of Medical Education*, 1969, *44*, 526–532.

Schulz, R., and Aderman, D. How the medical staff copes with dying patients: A critical review. *Omega*, 1976, *7*, 11–21.

Schwartz, R.M., and Gottman, J.M. Toward a task analysis of assertive behavior. *Journal of Consulting and Clinical Psychology*, 1976, *44*, 910–920.

Selye, H. *The stress of life* (revised edition). New York: McGraw–Hill, 1956.

Shady, G. Death anxiety and care of the terminally-ill: A review of the clinical literature. *Canadian Psychological Review*, 1976, *17*, 137–142.

Spielberger, C. *Understanding stress and anxiety*. New York: Harper and Row Publishers, 1979.

Stake, J.E., and Pearlman, J. Assertiveness training as an intervention technique for low performance self-esteem women. *Journal of Counseling Psychology*, 1980, *27*, 276–281.

Tache, J., and Selye, H. On stress and coping mechanisms. In C.D. Spielberger and I.G. Sarason (Eds.), *Stress and anxiety*, Vol. 5. New York: John Wiley & Sons, 1978.

Vachon, M.L. Staff stress in care of the terminally ill. *Quality Review Bulletin*, 1979, *May*, 13–17.

Vachon, M.L., Lyall, W., and Freeman, S. Measurement and management of stress in health professionals working with advanced cancer patients. *Death Education*, 1978, *1*, 365–375.

Vreeland, R., and Ellis, G. Stresses on the nurse in an intensive care unit. *Journal of the American Medical Association*, 1969, *208*, 332–334.

Weisman, A. Misgivings and misconceptions in the psychiatric care of terminal patients. *Psychiatry*, 1970, *33*, 67–81.

Weisman, A., and Sobel, H. Coping with cancer through self-instruction: A hypothesis. *Journal of Human Stress*, 1979, 5, 3–8.

Whiteley, J.M., and Flowers, J.V. *Approaches to assertion training*. Monterey, California: Brooks/Cole Publishing Company, 1978.

Wodinsky, A. Psychiatric consultation with nurses on a leukemia service. *Mental Hygiene*, 1964, 48, 282–287.

Wolpe, J. *Psychotherapy by reciprocal inhibition*. Stanford, California: Stanford University Press, 1958.

Wolpe, J. *The practice of behavior therapy*. Oxford: Pergamon, 1969.

Wolpe, J., and Lazarus, A.A. *Behavior therapy techniques: A guide to the treatment of neurosis*. Oxford: Pergamon, 1966.

10 BEHAVIOR THERAPY IN CORONARY HEART DISEASE
Lifestyle Modification

Michael J. Follick, Bruce S. Gottlieb, and Joanne L. Fowler

Coronary heart disease (CHD) is currently the foremost cause of death in the United States. This disease accounts for more deaths nationally (51 percent) than all other causes combined, resulting in nearly 700,000 deaths each year. The American Heart Association estimates that, at any time, over 4 million Americans are disabled either by recurrent chest pain or by reduced cardiac function due to CHD. Each year an additional 2 million individuals develop clinical manifestations of CHD, resulting in disability or death. The annual cost of diseases of the heart and blood vessels is about $20 billion and approximately 228 million work hours per year are lost due to CHD (Leon 1976).

Coronary heart disease is a condition in which the heart's blood supply is restricted due to narrowing of the coronary arteries. This is a result of advanced atherosclerosis, which consists of fatty deposits, scarring and often calcification in the innermost layers of arteries. Artherosclerosis is a chronic, progressive disease, beginning in childhood and progressing throughout an individual's lifetime. This narrowing of the coronary arteries can ultimately result in a reduced blood flow to the heart. If the muscles of the heart do not receive an adequate supply of blood, angina pectoris occurs and is experienced as transient chest pain (Friedberg 1966). Angina occurs primarily during physical exertion when demands on the heart are increased. An increasingly important perspective on coronary disease is that coronary tone may vary, probably as a consequence of autonomic nervous tone, transiently aggravating the areas of arterial narrowing. In more severe cases, the blood supply may be blocked off completely, resulting in a myocardial infarction (MI). A myocardial infarction is commonly referred to as a heart attack and consists of necrosis (i.e., death) of some portion of the heart muscle. In still other cases, the deficiency in oxygen supply may kill a person suddenly, without warning, by disrupting the electrical impulses that control the heartbeat (Jones 1979). Thus, regarding its clinical aspects, the process of CHD is best viewed as a continuum from the asymptomatic state to symptoms of angina pectoris or myocardial infarction and ultimately death (Daniel 1979).

We review here the behavioral and psychological factors related to the development of CHD and the management of the patient following myocardial infarction. We discuss how behavior patterns are related to the pathogenesis of CHD and how the course of the illness can be influenced by lifestyle modification. Common psychological reactions to different stages of the patient's illness are identified and their relationships to survival and recovery are discussed. We devote specific attention to behavior therapy techniques and their relevance to the management of the patient with CHD. While the CHD patient is similar in many respects to other terminally ill patients, we argue that the use of behavior therapy procedures with these patients represents a highly effective and humanistic approach to influencing both the quality and quantity of life.

ETIOLOGY

Although the relationship between atherosclerosis and CHD is well understood, the atherosclerotic process is not; the mechanisms relating the major risk factors to atherosclerosis have not yet been determined. Research indicates that numerous psychological and behavioral—as well as physiological—factors contribute to the atherosclerotic process and the risk of heart disease (Jenkins 1976). Those variables or behaviors that increase the likelihood that a person will develop CHD are called risk factors. In order for a physiological variable and the behavior that influences it to be considered a true risk factor, it must be shown that individuals with that behavior have a higher incidence of CHD than those without it, and that this relationship holds independently of other characteristics (Jones 1979). Variables identified as major CHD risk factors include cigarette smoking, obesity, hypertension, high levels of serum cholesterol, excessive dietary fats, and low exercise levels. There are also a number of fixed risk factors, such as sex and diabetes mellitus. In addition, psychological and social factors can influence standard risk factors through overt behavioral practices and internal psychophysiological mechanisms (Jenkins 1976). One such factor is psychological stress, occurring when an individual anticipates either physical or psychological harm. Another stress related risk factor is the Type A coronary-prone behavior pattern. Individuals with this behavior pattern have a marked sense of time urgency, an exaggerated sense of task involvement, and are hostile, competitive, and hard driving. The number and severity of these risk factors are directly related to the incidence of CHD.

The major risk factors all involve behavior on the individual's part: smoking cigarettes, overeating, consuming a high saturated fat and high cholesterol diet, leading a sedentary lifestyle, dealing poorly with stress, and engaging in behavior patterns that engender stress. Most of these behaviors are modifiable by behavior therapy techniques. Modifying the afflicted person's risk-related behaviors is believed to influence the course of CHD and ultimately to reduce morbidity and mortality (Meyer et al. 1980; and Stamler 1979). While the presence of risk factors is related to the risk of heart disease, and risk factor reduction influences the disease process, the precise mechanism that mediates this relationship has not yet been determined.

Cigarette smoking produces a substantial increase in the risk of MI. One 10-year-study of 6,975 white men found that the incidence of a major coronary event was two times higher for those smoking a pack or more of cigarettes a day than for nonsmokers (McIntosh, Stamler, and Jackson 1978). Tar, nicotine, and noxious gases are the three principal agents found in cigarette smoke. Tar is apparently unrelated to atherosclerosis because it is not carried in the blood stream. Nicotine is actually a stimulant that increases autonomic activity and thereby may potentially increase the strain on the heart. In addition, nicotine is believed to be atherogenic. Carbon monoxide accelerates the rate at which atherosclerosis is developed in rabbits. While it is uncertain how this chemical accelerates the atherosclerotic process in man, it is clearly related to CHD. In observing humans exposed to high levels of carbon monoxide, a higher incidence of CHD has been found (McIntosh, Entman, Evans, Martin, and Jackson 1978).

Another major risk factor is essential hypertension, defined as a sustained elevation in blood pressure of unknown origin. For individuals whose diastolic blood pressure is 85 to 94 mg. Hg., the mortality rate due to heart disease is 60 percent higher than that associated with blood pressure below 85 mm. (McIntosh, Eknoyan, and Jackson 1978). A linear relationship exists between elevations in blood pressure and the incidence of cardiovascular disease and, without therapy, about 50 percent of hypertensives die of CHD. High blood pressure results in a strain on the heart and damage to the arteries and is believed to accelerate the atherosclerotic process (Kaplan 1980). Essential hypertension is influenced by a number of psychological and behavioral variables, including some of the same factors that influence CHD incidence (e.g., obesity, stress). The interaction among these variables, hypertension, and CHD must be unravelled before the relationship between hypertension and heart disease is completely understood.

There is an exponential relationship between cholesterol levels and CHD beginning at a serum level of 220 mg. (McIntosh et al. 1978). A 22-year-study of men aged 30 to 39 found that when the serum cholesterol level is more than 250 mg./dl., the individual is three times more likely to develop CHD than if his cholesterol level is less than 200 mg./dl. (Kannel 1978). Hypercholesteremia (i.e., elevated cholesterol levels) appears to be the primary cause of atherosclerosis. However, elevated serum cholesterol level is not the only factor, and researchers are now focusing on the ratios of the two primary lipoproteins that transport cholesterol in plasma, low-density lipoproteins (LDL) and high-density lipoproteins (HDL). High levels of LDL-cholesterol increase the risk of CHD, whereas high levels of HDL-cholesterol are associated with a decreased rate of CHD (Castelli et al. 1977). Despite considerable controversy, most researchers and clinicians believe that serum cholesterol levels are influenced by dietary intake of saturated fats and cholesterol and that HDL-cholesterol is influenced by exercise patterns (Stamler 1979). Cholesterol and plasma lipoproteins are also influenced by cigarette consumption, obesity, and psychological stress.

Overweight people have a distinctly increased incidence of cardiovascular disease and death that is dependent upon the extent of their obesity. In general, obese individuals have double the incidence of stroke and congestive heart failure and a 50 percent greater risk of CHD. There appears to be no direct relationship between excessive adipose tissue and CHD, and Gordon and Kannel (1976) speculate that obesity increases the risk of heart disease through its influence on blood lipids, blood pressure, and carbohydrate intolerance. Hypertension is more common among obese individuals. As a result of their extensive work in the area, Kannel and Gordon (1979) conclude that: "... because it reversibly promotes atherogenic traits like hypertension, diabetes, and hyperlipidemia, reduction of overweight is probably the most important hygienic measure (aside from the avoidance of cigarettes) available for the control of cardiovascular disease" (p. 256).

Stress can also play a significant role in the development of CHD. For example, the stress of work perceived to be beyond one's capabilities is significantly correlated with CHD (Theorell and Rahe 1971). Researchers also report a marked increase in the number of life changes in the six months prior to an MI compared with the same period one year earlier (Rahe and Lind 1971). Another stress-related risk factor is the Type A coronary prone behavior pattern. One study reports the incidence of CHD in individuals with Type A pattern to be between 1.7 and 6 times greater than individuals without this pattern four-and-a-half years after being judged healthy (Rosenman et al. 1970). Glass (1977) contends that the intensity of the Type A individual's response to uncontrollable life stresses is greater than for other individuals, resulting in excessive elevations in catecholamines. Peripheral catecholamines that are released under stress are believed to play a role in producing arterial injury and are thus implicated in plaque formation and CHD. Catecholamines also raise blood pressure by leading to a narrowing of the systemic arterioles. Hypertension may eventually lead to further arterial damage or myocardial infarction. Thus, it appears that it is the interaction between the Type A behavior pattern and stress that relates to the pathogenesis of CHD.

COURSE

Over the past several decades, the evidence relating risk factors to the onset of CHD has resulted in the development of numerous programs designed to influence risk-related behaviors in an attempt to reduce the incidence of CHD. This approach is referred to as primary prevention and is perhaps best typified by the Stanford Heart Disease Prevention Program (e.g., Meyer et al. 1980). This major clinical intervention trial attempts to reduce the incidence of heart disease by increasing people's knowledge of risk factors and modifying their diet, smoking, and exercise patterns. While numerous programs with a similar focus are currently under way (e.g., Pawtucket Heart Health, Minnesota Community Prevention Program for Cardiovascular Disease), the ultimate impact of primary prevention efforts on the incidence of CHD is not yet known. However, the major concern of this chapter is what is referred to as secondary prevention: risk-factor modification in individuals who have already manifested symptoms of CHD such as angina pectoris or MI. In the symptomatic patient, these behavioral changes are an integral part of medical care and ultimately are important in influencing the course of the illness; in particular, the likelihood of reinfarction or death. In addition to these lifestyle modifications, there are several other factors that must be addressed once an individual has manifested coronary heart disease.

Phases of Recovery

Individuals who survive the onset of an MI are generally hospitalized for several weeks before returning home and to the community. At different periods during the individual's recovery, a number of possibly maladaptive responses may be engaged in that might mitigate the recovery process and influence subsequent morbidity and mortality. Three phases of recovery can be delineated; at each phase, the manner in which the individual responds can influence the course of recovery. Phase 1, Acute Onset, begins at the time of the MI and includes the person's initial emotional and behavioral reactions to the onset of the illness. Phase 2, Coping with Treatment and Initial Adaptation, includes those events occurring in the hospital setting and the development of plans to return to the community. Phase 3, Lifestyle Modification and Risk Factor Reduction, is a continuous phase beginning with discharge from the hospital and extending through the remainder of the individual's life. Modifying the individual's behavior patterns can maximize the likelihood of a complete recovery from an MI and a return to a productive and satisfying way of life. While the behavioral approach is not the only intervention procedure appropriate to these factors, numerous behavior change strategies are applicable to the problems associated with this terminal disease.

CHD and Terminal Illness

It is the potential to influence the course of the disease through behavior change strategies that differentiates CHD from other terminal illnesses. All terminal illnesses involve not only organic changes — the course of the illness — but also the psychosocial stages related to the illness (Weisman 1972). While organic pathology leads to many personal and social changes in the lifestyle of an affected individual, psychosocial stages follow a sequence that is not wholly determined by physical factors. Despite a partial or complete return to function, the individual always faces a threat of further relapse, disability, and symptoms. While the final decline may be years away, terminally ill individuals are often acutely aware of the inevitability of death. This can result in distinctive social and emotional problems at different phases of each and every terminal illness. Appropriate resolution of these psychosocial problems may be necessary at every stage to insure an acceptance of the outcome (Weisman 1972).

Coronary heart disease patients, like other terminally ill patients, are afflicted with a condition that involves a component of helplessness and a threat of death. However, the manner in which the CHD patient adjusts to the condition can have a marked impact on function and survival. The individual must assume personal responsibility in treatment to prolong life and reduce distress. Patients with CHD may have to adapt their lifestyle to their physical limitations, while learning to accept changes in functioning. CHD patients are distinguished from other terminally ill patients by the fact that they can engage in lifestyle modifications that may influence the course of the disease and ultimately reduce subsequent morbidity and mortality.

PSYCHOLOGICAL FACTORS IN RECOVERY FROM MYOCARDIAL INFARCTION

Probably as many as 50 percent of those individuals who experience an MI die before they reach the hospital. Those who survive the immediate onset are faced with a multitude of medical and psychosocial factors that need to be considered as the individual adjusts to an altered physical status. A number of common emotional reactions manifested by these patients during the adjustment to the onset of the MI and the coronary care unit are potentially life-threatening, and can influence the person's survival and future functional capacities. In the following section, we will review the three major phases of recovery and discuss the common emotional reactions and adaptive demands associated with each phase.

Phase 1: Acute Onset

Coronary heart disease is often associated with a sudden onset, posing a major life crisis to unsuspecting individuals. Without warning, an individual's functional capacity can be radically altered. Confronted with a potentially lethal disease, the individual's mobility is restricted, he or she is unable to fulfill family and vocational roles, and he or she may feel a loss of control over personal functioning and the environment. Scalzi (1973) describes the typical patient's initial reaction to an MI as shock and disbelief. This phase is generally short-lived (usually from 24 to 72 hours) and is characterized primarily by anxiety and denial. Occasionally, aggressive sexual behavior will occur. Each of these reactions has behavior response patterns associated with it and can be treated with behavior therapy procedures.

Anxiety. Anxiety is essentially a fear response that is manifest when an individual perceives a situation as threatening or harmful. Behaviorally, the patient may have an increased verbalization rate, be unable to concentrate or retain information, and evidence insomnia. The individual may also experience muscle tension, palmar sweating, tremulousness, or tachycardia. These symptoms are the result of autonomic arousal associated with anxiety. It is the autonomic arousal and the concomitant strain on the cardiovascular system that increases the patient's risk for extending the original damage or reinfarction during this phase. Thus, it is necessary to maintain the patient in as relaxed and calm a state as possible.

In the MI patient, anxiety is often caused by fear of death or chronic disability. The environment and procedures of a coronary care unit can also be anxiety provoking. For many, that setting is a strange, incomprehensible place, which can further engender anxiety. Developing complications or observing them in others might also make the threat of death more salient and thereby generate greater fear. Similarly, the individual can misinterpret information or experiences. For example, the patient may misperceive general weakness as permanent physical disability or pain in the arm as the onset of a paralysis. Interestingly, patients have been observed to manifest anxiety in response to medical team rounds, and Jarvinen (1955) reports that more patients died in conjunction with ward rounds conducted by the chief surgeon than at all other times.

Since anxiety is often the result of exaggerated fears and misconceptions, it can often be reduced by providing the patient with more complete and accurate information. The patient should be educated regarding staff routines, the use and purpose of surrounding equipment, and the various procedures that will be employed. In addition, the patient should be told what information regarding his or her condition is significant and to whom such information should be reported. Patients should also be encouraged to ask questions and to seek clarification whenever there is ambiguity. For example, one patient was observed to be crying and very emotionally distressed. When the staff questioned the patient, they learned that he believed that he was about to die because they had removed his cardiac monitor electrodes. The patient had misunderstood the nurses' explanation and misperceived the removal of his cardiac monitor electrodes to mean that he was hopeless and about to die. In reality, the patient was becoming stable, and was doing so well that it was felt he no longer needed to be continuously monitored. Thus, it is important for the staff to ensure that patients clearly understand what they have been told. It is critical to note that not all patients respond to detailed information in a uniform fashion. Some patients are extremely sensitized, and detailed information can actually increase their emotional distress. The staff must be sensitive to individual variability, basing information given to the patient on the patient's needs and ability to handle the information.

While information and patient education is important and can be a sufficient intervention with many patients, there are instances when a more direct intervention is required. A relaxation training procedure (e.g., Bernstein and Borkovec 1973) can be an effective adjunct to antianxiety medication or an alternative when such medications are contraindicated. This procedure involves progressive muscle relaxation with deep breathing exercises and is designed to produce a state of relaxation that is incompatible with anxiety and emotional arousal. This procedure can also distract the patient from his or her preoccupation with the condition and provide a sense of control over behaviors and emotions. However, it must be employed with caution in the early phases because of potential contraindications. If a patient has an unstable cardiac function, it is best not to employ a tension release protocol, but rather to use a procedure that relies more on imaginal techniques (Horan 1973). If the patient is able to employ imagery and to visualize relaxing and calming scenes, he or she can use this self-control procedure to induce a state of relaxation and thereby reduce anxiety and autonomic arousal.

Perhaps the most cost-effective way of reducing a patient's anxiety is through the support and reassurance of the staff. Once the staff has identified specific behaviors or thoughts that appear to increase a patient's anxiety, they can selectively reinforce alternative or incompatible behaviors. This helps the patient learn self-control strategies that will reduce emotional arousal. It also gives the patient a sense of control that further reduces distress. It is also important for the staff to involve the patient's family members since different family members can have a selective influence on the patient's emotional state. The staff can work with the family to increase the amount of time the patient is in contact with those who engender a sense of comfort and reduce anxiety, while decreasing the patient's contact with those who increase emotional arousal.

Denial.   Denial is nearly always observed to some extent during this phase and can often extend into later phases. It consists of behaviors that indicate a failure to accept either obvious facts or the significance of the situation. Some patients simply refuse to believe that a problem exists and often contend that there has been a misdiagnosis. Denial is most commonly manifest by the individual avoiding discussion of the MI. There may be cheerful discussions of other issues while the severity of the condition is minimized. Even while in the coronary care unit, the individual may disregard activity, diet, or smoking restrictions as if to show that the condition is not serious. Patients often try to confirm their denial by asking different staff members the same questions, soliciting answers that best suit their personal beliefs.

Denial is a normal defense mechanism used to alleviate anxiety by altering the perception of the threat. A person who is suddenly confronted with an acute MI has had no time to prepare for the experience of being a patient or the implications of the disease. During the period of shock and disbelief, denial is common. At this point, denying one's illness or its life-threatening aspects may be an effective means of coping with this major threat. The patient's denial reduces anxiety and concomitant autonomic arousal, and thereby decreases the patient's risk of reinfarction during this critical period of cardiac instability. Hackett, Cassem, and Wishnie (1968) report that those patients who evidence denial during this acute phase have the best survival record in the coronary care unit. Therefore, it may not be appropriate to intervene during this acute phase.

Denial requires intervention only when it disrupts the patient's treatment or leads to behavior that is detrimental to physical welfare. Confrontation or threats of the potentially fatal consequences are not usually appropriate tactics for dealing with denial and often engender conflict between the patient and the staff. During the first few days of hospitalization, the impact of the event must be slowly integrated into the patient's beliefs. It is necessary that the staff be understanding and supportive while reinforcing specific sick-role behaviors. Staff attention and reassurance are perhaps the most important reinforcers during this phase.

It has been found that unresolved emotional upsets during the acute phase of the MI can result in a greater risk of mortality within six months following discharge. Garrity and Klein (1975) report that 41 percent of the nonadjusters die within six months of discharge, compared to 8 percent of those patients considered to have adjusted well. The authors speculate that members of the well-adjusted group continue to manage health threats and losses in ways that minimize emotional distress and thereby reduce concomitant physiological arousal. Chronic psychophysiological arousal, especially in subjects with impaired hearts, is believed to mediate the relationship between emotional adjustment and the incidence of reinfarction and death six months post–MI.

Epinephrine (i.e., adrenalin) and norepinephrine have been implicated in mediating adjustment and reinfarction, although other mediators probably all play a role. An increase in these neurotransmitters is observed in plasma and urine in response to a variety of situational stressors and can have a taxing effect on the cardiovascular system. Researchers find increases in catecholamine excretion to be linked to psychological arousal and to the onset of postinfarct complications (Garrity and Klein 1975). These findings suggest that helping individuals manage their emotional responses during the acute onset phase can reduce morbidity and mortality in both the short- and long-term. It is important then not only to be concerned about the patient's physical status and needs, but also to identify maladaptive coping patterns so that appropriate interventions can be selected. The health-care team must help the patient through the acute phase both medically and psychologically, and identify those chronic maladjusters who will require further therapy when their medical condition is stabilized.

Phase 2: Coping with Treatment and Initial Adaptation

Once the patient passes the acute crisis phase—the first 48 to 72 hours—the physiologic condition usually begins to stabilize and the intensive fear of death begins to diminish. However, an additional 15 to 20 percent of heart attack victims will not survive the next several weeks. The risk of morbidity and mortality is increased for those individuals with a poor psychological adjustment or who have difficulty coping with the stress of medical procedures.

Depression. While anxiety is usually most pronounced in the first and second days following admission, depression often appears on the third and fourth days as the patient begins to realize the possible impact of the heart attack on work and family responsibilities (Cassem and Hackett 1973). At this point, patients' thoughts often center on activities that they assume will have to change. Depression typically results from feelings of helplessness, the perception of being unable to engage in previously enjoyed activities, and fears of impending death. Thus, there is usually an expected loss or an anticipation of a non-reinforcing state of affairs, in other words, not being able to do what one would like. These clinical observations of patients in the coronary care unit are consistent with the cognitive and behavioral models of depression proposed by Seligman (1975) and Lewinsohn (1975).

Behaviorally, the depressed patient looks sad and listless, has little appetite, and frequently has crying spells. Movements and speech might be slowed and the content of speech may reveal feelings of hopelessness and helplessness. The patient may have misperceptions of the extent of the MI and the impact that it will have on future functioning. Often, patients feel that all previously enjoyed activities will no longer be possible and perceive themselves as permanently disabled. While a serious depression is often treated effectively with antidepressant medication, this approach is contraindicated in the patient with a cardiac condition because of the rhythm-disrupting effects of the antidepressant medication.

The behavioral models of depression have clear implications for intervention with depressed MI patients. The Learned Helplessness model (Seligman 1975) posits that depression is the result of the patient's exposure to uncontrollable stressors, leading to the expectation of uncontrollability and a state of helplessness. Consequently, the patient believes that nothing he or she does will have any impact on the situation. The implication of this model is that the health-care team can help restore the patient's sense of control or mastery. The health-care team should assist the patient in restructuring cognitions to evaluate the situation more objectively and engage in goal-directed behavior. The majority of patients who reach a hospital with a good coronary care unit can be expected to survive the MI and return to society. The patient must realize that there is hope for the future and that he or she has a role in determining the outcome of the situation. A patient may be correct in assuming that most previous activities are now precluded. However, an individual may fail to consider that it might be possible to engage in a modified aspect of a previously enjoyed activity (e.g., coaching instead of playing the sport). The patient can begin working toward future goals during this phase and should be involved in the process of deciding how to modify activities and set realistic goals. Engaging in lifestyle modification decisions should help to re-establish the patient's sense of control and reduce feelings of helplessness.

In reducing emotional distress, it is helpful to encourage the patient to talk about feelings. This allows patients to express their most prominent concerns, which can then be addressed by the treatment team. For example, often patients have mistaken beliefs (e.g., "I will never be able to have sex again") that can be readily corrected with appropriate information and counseling. In addition, the patient should be told that depression is a common response to an MI and that attitudes and behaviors are critical in overcoming this problem.

A major contributor to depression is the individual's physical condition at this phase. In one study, weakness was the most distressing symptom reported and inactivity was the most frustrating state complained of by the patients (Cassem and Hackett 1973). This is being countered in many hospitals by the early mobilization of CHD patients with uncomplicated MIs. McNeer et al. (1978) report that patients discharged from the hospital within two weeks after their MI suffered no greater morbidity and mortality than those who stayed in the hospital longer. Programs with an emphasis on activity have led to an improvement in nearly all manifestations of depression, including improved sleep, better eating habits and digestion, and an improved sense of well-being (Cassem and Hackett 1973).

In addition to the physiological effects of conditioning, physical activity involves goal-directed behavior that may help re-establish the patient's sense of control and combat fears of invalidism. This approach also provides specific behavioral activities for patients, as opposed to the many activities they are denied (e.g., do not smoke, do not overeat, do not eat high cholesterol foods). One helpful procedure is to have the patient engage in a regularly scheduled and incremental exercise program. Charts and graphs are particularly useful because they offer objective evidence that progress is being made. In addition, these graphs regulate the patient's activity level and protect against over-zealous or over-cautious behavior. Many patients are unable to engage in a systematic exercise program on advice alone and need the structure provided by charts and graphs or by organized group programs.

CHD patients are also exposed to highly stressful diagnostic and surgical procedures. Cardiac catheterization is perhaps the most stressful diagnostic procedure and is targeted by behaviorists who wish to assess the efficacy of cognitive-behavioral interventions.

Cardiac Catheterization.   Cardiac catheterization is an invasive medical procedure in which a catheter is inserted to the heart through the femoral or brachial artery. Angiographic study of the coronary arteries is conducted to determine the extent of obstruction. Similar to all invasive medical procedures, cardiac catheterization can be conceptualized as a crisis, often resulting in an inordinate amount of stress.

Acute elevations of anxiety can lead to pre- and postprocedural complications. Kendal and his colleagues (1979) compared the effects of a cognitive-behavioral and a patient education intervention to both an attention placebo control and a current hospital procedures control group. The results indicate that the cognitive-behavioral and patient education procedures were significantly more effective than the controls and that the cognitive-behavioral intervention produced the greatest reduction in self-reported anxiety prior to, during, and following cardiac catheterization. The cognitive-behavioral intervention, applied in three sessions during the two days prior to catheterization, involved: (1) the labeling of stress; (2) identifying stress-related cues (e.g., increased heart rate); (3) discussing cognitive coping strategies; (4) reinforcing individual coping styles; and (5) modeling and rehearsing cognitive coping skills.

The results of this study support the utility of cognitive-behavioral interventions in reducing a patient's anxiety regarding cardiac catheterization procedures.

Coronary Artery Bypass.   Coronary artery bypass surgery is another highly invasive medical intervention conceptualized as a crisis, often generating exceptionally high levels of anxiety and distress. Bypass surgery is a procedure whereby the obstructed or occluded portions of the affected coronary arteries are bypassed or replaced with healthy vessels removed from other areas of the patient's body. This is a delicate and complicated surgical procedure with the potential for numerous medical and psychological complications.

When a patient is first told of the need for bypass surgery, he or she may initially respond with a state of shock or disbelief and later evidence feelings of helplessness and fear of impairment as surgery draws near (Rakoczy 1977). Patients facing dangerous medical procedures often become disproportionately anxious (Janis 1958). High levels of anxiety associated with coronary artery bypass surgery can lead to an avoidance of the procedure, may interfere with the actual procedure, and in fact increase postoperative complications (e.g., delayed recovery). Numerous psychological reactions to surgical procedures are reported in the literature, the severity of the reaction often reflecting the severity of the procedure (Weiss 1966).

Some researchers have speculated that the course of recovery is not only dependent on physical factors, but is also influenced by psychological variables. This has led to an increased emphasis on preoperative interventions, specifically emphasizing preoperative information and education. For example, Johnson (1972) reports that anticipatory distress concerning pain and discomfort is lessened if accurate information about the physical sensations experienced postoperatively are given to the patient preoperatively. In addition, numerous postoperative factors such as length of stay, complaints of pain, and requests for medications seem to be influenced by preoperative educational interventions. Thus, it is important to ensure that the patient receives adequate preoperative education and, with patients evidencing extreme anticipatory anxiety or distress, a structured cognitive-behavioral intervention may be necessary (c.f. Case Example 1, p. 287).

Coronary artery bypass surgery not only has preoperative complications, but also can produce some unique postoperative complications. Blacher (1975) describes a postoperative traumatic neurotic reaction to bypass surgery, characterized by repetitive nightmares and marked anxiety. Some patients report awakening during the surgical procedure, unable to move or inform anyone of their state of consciousness because they are paralyzed by a neuromuscular blocking agent (viz. curare). While this experience can be extremely traumatic for the patient and can produce lasting psychological difficulties, it is often resolved by a discussion with the patient focusing on an explanation of their experience. When the patient receives information from members of the health-care team acknowledging the occurrence of the experience and explaining that it is due to the intricacies of balanced anesthesia, their symptoms usually subside within a few weeks. However, the experience for some patients is so traumatic that a more lasting emotional reaction may result, posing serious complications to future medical intervention. In one case, a woman was so frightened by her experience that she refused any follow-up medical care and would not even watch television programs related to medicine. When this patient was transported to the emergency room due to recurring cardiac difficulties, her conditioned emotional reaction of extreme anxiety caused her to refuse treatment. A systematic desensitization procedure was employed whereby the patient gradually progressed through a hierarchical presentation of anxiety-provoking stimuli until she was able to watch medically related shows on television. Eventually, she was even able to watch an audiovisual tape of open heart surgery. The patient's severe anxiety was alleviated and she consented to further surgical intervention.

Psychological Barriers to Rehabilitation. The continuation of maladaptive levels of anxiety and depression during this phase can influence the patient's ultimate adjustment and pose serious limitations to rehabilitation. Living with impending death and with the fear of sudden death is central to this phase of heart disease. Even if the patient can accept the possible imminence of death, he or she must still cope with the fear of other losses due to physical limitations. These fears may persist throughout the recuperation period and, if prolonged or intense, interfere with satisfactory progress (Schwabb 1970).

Continuation of the patient's denial through this phase is a major obstacle to adjustment and should be the target of intervention by the health-care team. Croog et al. (1971) report that, in a study of 345 men suffering from their first MI, 20 percent denied that they had had a heart attack three weeks after admission to the hospital. The patient may persist in engaging in a variety of counterphobic activities. Patients often attempt to prove to themselves and others that medical restrictions, especially those pertaining to diet, sex, and cigarette consumption, do not pertain to them. These self-destructive behaviors are often an attempt to avoid the anxiety of the situation. Denial can also lead to a serious disregard of significant symptoms, a refusal to accept medical care or recommendations, and postponement of care, and may influence the level of cooperation with therapeutic interventions. As a result of denial then, the patient is more likely to complicate the course of the illness and increase the risk of death.

Denial is also found in a "giving up" syndrome in which the patient is convinced that another, perhaps fatal, heart attack will occur regardless of lifestyle modifications (Granger 1974). These patients refuse to lose weight, stop smoking, or reduce tension because they are sure that it will not do any good. For example, a patient who was referred by his physician for a behavioral smoking cessation intervention argued that attempts to quit smoking would precipitate a heart attack. He felt that since stress increases the risk of heart attack, and since attempting to stop smoking generates significant stress, it would be better for him to continue smoking. Intervention is difficult with these patients because, without direct questioning, they appear overtly compliant and cooperative to rehabilitation recommendations, but never, in fact, make any progress.

It is also important for the health-care staff to begin to prepare the patient during this phase for a return to vocational and marital roles and responsibilities. This can reassure the patient with an uncomplicated MI that he or she is not expected to become a cardiac cripple and that a return to prior levels of functioning is likely. Since many patients have a pronounced fear of invalidism, intervention at this phase can reassure the patient that a return to work and enjoyable activities is possible. In their review of the literature, Croog et al. (1968) conclude that return to work is related to the severity of the heart attack and the number of heart attack episodes experienced by the patient. However, approximately 20 percent of all postcoronary patients with uncomplicated MIs do not return to work despite the fact that they are physiologically capable of doing so. Psychological factors have been implicated in mediating the patient's failure to return to work (Nagle et al. 1971). Sanne (1973) concludes that patients limit their physical exertion because they fear deleterious consequences, rather than because of physical limitations.

Emotional support, encouragement, and education are necessary during this phase to counteract the patient's fears and instill the motivation to develop a plan and maintain involvement in treatment. The numerous cardiac teaching programs employed in the past several years represent such attempts to assist the patient. They provide the patient with information regarding the illness, its ramifications, and what should reduce the probability of recurrence. Knowledge of symptoms to anticipate when discharged from the hospital can reduce the patient's fears and lead to appropriate responses by the patient. However, it is important to include the family in this educational process, because their reactions to the patient's illness can have a large impact on his or her behavior. A spouse who considers the patient to be more dependent and disabled than he or she actually is can present a major barrier to rehabilitation by restricting the patient's activities or involvement. In addition, the appearance of anxiety or depression in the spouse can further stimulate these reactions in the patient.

Return to sexual functioning is another area of extreme importance that is often overlooked by the health-care team. Most patients with uncomplicated MIs are able to return to sexual activity approximately six to eight weeks after their attack. However, a large percentage of these patients evidence a greatly reduced frequency of or a total abstinence from sexual activity following the MI. In fact, Tuttle et al. (1964) report that 10 percent of their research sample developed impotence believed to be of psychological origin after their coronary attack. Hellerstein and Friedman (1970) report that, on the average, sexual activity is not resumed until approximately fourteen weeks postinfarction, and that two-thirds of the patients studied reported reductions in sexual frequency following their coronary episode. Interestingly, most of these patients related their decreased sexual activity to reductions in their sexual motivation or their wives' fears. However, these authors determined, in a controlled study, that sexual intercourse produces a strain on the heart that is approximately equivalent to climbing a flight of stairs or walking briskly. Extramarital sexual activity, on the other hand, is more stressful, and 80 percent of reported deaths during coitus are related to these circumstances.

Not only are the patient's perceptions of sexual capabilities related to oucome, but the reaction of the spouse is also a critically important determinant. The spouse must be included in any rehabilitation efforts and fears surrounding the impact of sexual activity on the partner must be addressed. If necessary, a set of structured and incremental tasks given to the couple can serve to desensitize them and reduce the anxiety that may impair their return to normal sexual activity.

Phase 3: Lifestyle Modification and Risk Factor Reduction

Having survived the MI and regained a state of cardiac stability, the patient returns to society and enters the third phase of recovery, which extends throughout the remainder of life. Since neither medication nor bypass surgery influence the process of atherosclerosis, the patient is usually required to make lifestyle changes in an attempt to retard the underlying disease process. These lifestyle changes are considered to be an essential part of the patient's medical care. As discussed earlier, it is the ability to influence the course of the disease by these lifestyle modifications that differentiates CHD from other terminal illnesses. However, changing lifelong behavior patterns is difficult and patients are often unable to effect such changes on advice alone.

Unfortunately, patients are often left to their own devices, or it is assumed that cardiac teaching, presented in the hospital, is sufficient to facilitate lifestyle change. While it is necessary for the patient to be aware of the deleterious consequences associated with risk-related behavior, this knowledge is not always sufficient to produce behavior change. Thus, it is important for the physician to monitor the patient's progress and, when necessary, to refer the patient to a structured cardiac rehabilitation program or a behavior modification clinic. Comprehensive cardiac rehabilitation programs (e.g., Carleton 1979; Granger 1974; and Rothman 1974) usually address the physical and psychological factors related to CHD in an attempt to return the patient to a productive and satisfying way of life. Physical reconditioning and lifestyle modification are essential components of these programs which typically employ a multidisciplinary approach to patient education and behavior change. The ultimate goal of cardiac rehabilitation is not only improvement in the quality of life, but also the extension of life by attempting to retard the underlying disease process through lifestyle modification and risk factor reduction. When attempting to reduce the risk of reinfarction and death, the CHD patient must identify risk-related behaviors and then modify these behavior patterns.

The remainder of this chapter is devoted to a discussion of self-control procedures and the major behavior change strategies that are employed in cardiovascular-risk factor reduction. Since space does not permit a step-by-step analysis of each procedure, the following discussion will only present the basic principles.

Behavior therapists are developing techniques that are effective in modifying an individual's risk-related behavior. Self-control procedures, derived from learning theory, are employed to produce and maintain these lifestyle changes. The self-control approach is based on the principle that an individual's behavior is a function of environmental events (Bandura 1969). Certain events in the environment serve as antecedents that prompt specific behaviors (e.g., finishing a meal may cue cigarette smoking). Positive and negative consequences are also associated with most behaviors and affect the probability that the behavior will occur again. For example, some obese individuals find that eating helps them relax, providing a positive consequence that makes it more likely that they will eat in response to subsequent tension. In a self-control behavior change program, the patient is taught the nature of the environmental consequence interaction and how it influences behavior. The patient can then modify environmental antecedents and consequences that in turn promote the desired behavior changes.

The basic procedures associated with the self-control approach include self-monitoring, functional analysis, stimulus control, behavioral contracting, relaxation training, and problem-solving. These components provide patients with the skills needed to understand the factors that influence their behavior and with the procedures to develop more adaptive behavior patterns. We believe that these procedures are indeed practical and cost-effective; moreover, they represent a highly humanistic program of clinical care for terminally ill patients.

SELF-CONTROL PROCEDURES

Self-Monitoring

Prior to any behavior change, information about the target behavior must be obtained. Self-monitoring is a procedure whereby an individual observes and records specific behavior. This consists of recording the occurrence of a specific behavior and keeping a frequency count. For example, a patient might monitor the number of cigarettes smoked, calories consumed, or the duration of time spent exercising. If the person records those events that precede the behavior (antecedents), as well as those that follow it (consequences), self-monitoring can also make the person more aware of those factors that influence the target behavior. Another benefit of self-monitoring a particular behavior is that it can often lead directly to therapeutic changes in that behavior (c.f. Kazdin 1974). Thus, self-monitoring cigarette consumption or caloric intake often results in a decrease in these behaviors. Finally, self-monitoring can be used to observe changes over time and determine if treatment is effective or if alternative treatment procedures are necessary.

Functional Analysis

Self-monitoring provides that data on antecedents and consequences, and functional analysis determines the specific relationship between the behavior and the environment. Functional analysis provides necessary information for the intervention program. With this information, an individual may learn to respond to situations with alternative (adaptive) behaviors. For example, a patient finds that smoking is relaxing and reduces tension. He or she can then employ alternative behaviors which promote relaxation or engage in relaxation exercises in response to tension. These new or alternative behaviors enable the individual to reduce smoking and still achieve tension reduction. Factors that contribute to the nonoccurrence of adaptive behaviors can also be determined through functional analysis. Desirable behaviors often do not occur because there are no existing cues that signal them or positive consequences that follow them.

Stimulus Control

Stimulus control procedures are structured techniques used to modify environmental cues which prompt behavior. Research demonstrates that when behavior has consistently occurred in the presence of a stimulus, future presentation of that stimulus increases the probability of that behavior occurring again (Garfield and Bergin 1971). Stimulus control can be used in two ways: (1) to eliminate, progressively, the cues associated with undesirable behaviors; and (2) to increase the cues associated with desirable behaviors. In stimulus narrowing, an individual restricts a behavior to a limited set of stimuli. For example, an obese individual who usually eats while watching TV, reading the paper, or listening to the radio, may limit eating to the dinner table at specified times while engaging in no other activity. In cue strengthening, an individual is encouraged to practice a target behavior in a specific situation. An obese individual may be encouraged to exercise every day at 8.00 a.m. so that the stimuli associated with that time cue exercise behavior.

Behavioral Contracting/Contingency Contracting

If a positive consequence (i.e., positive reinforcement) follows a certain behavior, the probability of that behavior being repeated will increase. Conversely, when negative consequences (i.e., punishment) follow a behavior, the probability of its recurring is decreased. These principles can be used in a systematic manner to increase the frequency of desired behaviors and decrease the frequency of problematic behaviors. Behavioral contracts can be established whereby an individual agrees that if a desired behavior (e.g., decreased caloric intake) is accomplished, then a positive reinforcer will follow (e.g., putting one dollar toward a gift). To further enhance the effectiveness of this contract, an aversive consequence (e.g., washing the floors) can be employed when the daily goal is not met (i.e., caloric intake exceeds the predetermined goal). It is best to put these contracts in writing, specifying the exact contingencies involved. It should be noted that in developing any behavior change program the initial goals should be relatively easy to attain. A graduated approach to goal attainment will help to maintain motivation, avoid frustration, and assure initial successes.

Relaxation Training

Self-control strategies often involve the use of alternative behaviors in situations that usually cue risk-related behaviors. As mentioned earlier, an individual can employ relaxation exercises to reduce tension instead of smoking. However, relaxation is a skill which must be learned. Training in progressive muscle relaxation requires a therapist to guide a patient in feeling the tension and relaxation associated with each of the major muscle groups in the body. Beginning with the muscles of the hand, the patient systematically tenses and releases the muscles in the forearm, biceps, head, neck, shoulders, chest, abdomen, upper legs, calves, and feet. Gradually, the alternating tension and release cycles are eliminated as the patient learns to release tension and produce a state of relaxation simply by recalling the feeling of relaxation for the muscle group involved. Eventually, the patient can evoke feelings of relaxation at will in any situation.

For a detailed description of the procedure, the reader is referred to Bernstein and Borkovec (1973). Imagery procedures, which consist of having the patient visualize the experience of peaceful, calming scenes, can also be incorporated. This can reduce thought patterns that engender tension and enhance the state of relaxation.

Problem-Solving

Once an individual identifies problematic behaviors, a specific plan for changing those behaviors is developed. If a program is not working effectively, an alternative approach is needed. Developing problem-solving skills can give individuals a greater sense of control and reduce anxiety in chronic worriers.

Accurate identification of the problem is the first of five steps involved in problem-solving. The problem should be specific and clearly indicate the behaviors involved (e.g., "I tend to snack during the day when I'm bored," rather than "I can't stay on my diet"). Second, a list of alternative ways to deal with the problem is constructed. When generating the list, the individual should develop as many plans as possible without evaluating them. Evaluating plans and deciding which to employe does not occur at this phase. Occasionally, difficulties arise in generating alternatives because the problem was not specified clearly enough. If this occurs, the individual can repeat step one. Third, positive and negative consequences associated with each alternative are listed. Fourth, the difficulty of implementing each plan is designated. This is done by assigning each plan a number from one (very easy to implement) to ten (very difficult to implement). Finally, the individual selects those strategies that are most easily employed and have the most favorable consequences associated with them. Once the plans are implemented, the person must determine if the problem has been satisfactorily solved. If not, the procedure can be repeated. For a more detailed description of problem-solving skills, see Goldfried and Davison (1976).

RISK FACTOR MODIFICATION

Smoking

Behavioral approaches to smoking cessation focus on either self-control, aversive conditioning, or gradual reduction of smoking. Self-control approaches to smoking cessation utilize self-monitoring, stimulus control, contingency contracting, and alternative behaviors, singly or in combination. With this approach, an individual is taught to observe smoking behavior, to manipulate the environment to extinguish cues for smoking, to set goals, to reinforce reductions in smoking, and to use alternative behaviors in problematic situations. Pomerleau and Pomerleau (1977) provide a detailed description of a multifaceted self-control procedure for smoking cessation. Research to date demonstates that this approach is effective in producing abstinence or reduced smoking during treatment (Lando 1977). However, dropout rates during treatment and lack of long-term maintenance are significant problems. For a recent review of this smoking cessation research, the reader is referred to Lando (in press) or Leventhal and Cleary (1980).

Aversive control procedures punish smoking behavior by pairing it with noxious stimuli such as shock, covert sensitization, or large doses of cigarette smoke. These procedures are based on the fact that aversive events contingent upon specific behaviors reduce the frequency of those behaviors. Shock and covert sensitization are relatively ineffective in reducing smoking behavior (Russell, Armstrong, and Patel 1976; Wagner and Bragg 1970). Rapid smoking is an example of an aversive control procedure that uses heavy cigarette consumption to produce noxious sensations. Thus, the act of smoking is associated with a highly aversive situation. In this procedure, an individual is required to puff a cigarette once every six seconds, until he or she feels unable to continue. Lichtenstein et al. (1973) report encouraging results using this procedure, with 60 percent abstinence at six-month follow-ups. Abstinence rates of 34 percent are reported at two-to-six-year follow-ups (Lichtenstein and Rodriguez 1977). Other studies (Lando 1976; Levenberg and Wagner 1976), however, have reported less successful results. Still, the data associated with this approach are the best in the area and indicate the need for further study and refinement. There is, however, considerable controversy surrounding the use of this procedure because of its physio-logical effects and related risks for the patient with heart disease. Rapid smoking increases heart rate, blood pressure, and carboxyhe-moglobin levels (Lichtenstein and Glasgow 1977). Concern has been expressed over the stressful effects of these procedures on the cardio-vascular system and its potential contraindication in patients with predetermined or undetected CHD.

Treatment approaches combining self-control and aversive proced-ures have been used. While the results of these approaches are mixed, the trend in their outcome is encouraging. For a review of these stud-ies, see Lando (in press). A recent innovative and nonaversive behav-ioral smoking treatment is nicotine fading (Foxx and Brown 1979). Nicotine fading consists of progressively reducing tar and nicotine content by changing brands of cigarettes. This procedure is based on the premise that cigarette smoking is a dependence disorder that is maintained by physiological and psychological factors. Nicotine has physiologicallly addicting properties and thus may cause with-drawal symptoms in patients attempting to quit smoking (Jarvik 1977). When the cigarettes they smoke contain only 0.1 mg. of nico-tine, their dependence is reduced and patients are encouraged to quit smoking altogether (Lichtenstein 1978). Initial results of this approach are promising. At 18-month follow-ups, Foxx and Brown (1979) report a 40 percent abstinence rate. Of those subjects who continued smoking, their nicotine and tar consumption was reduced 61 percent and 70 percent, respectively. The possibility that the topography of the person's smoking behavior changes as nicotine content is reduced has been raised (e.g., the individual will increase smoke inhalation and number of puffs). However, there is currently no controlled demonstration of this effect during nicotine fading.

For subjects who do not wish to be abstinent, a promising ap-proach is to combine nicotine fading with another innovative ap-proach known as controlled smoking (e.g., Frederiksen, Peterson, and Murphy 1976). Controlled smoking is based on the notion that rate and topography determine the amount of tar, nicotine, and noxious gases ingested by smokers. Fredriksen, Miller, and Peterson (1977) demonstrate that topographical variables can be reliably meas-ured, monitored, and modified. They identify five topographical variables: inter-puff intervals, cigarette duration, puff length, puff frequency, and percentage of tobacco burned. They found that with simple verbal instructions and practice, individuals can significantly change these topographical variables. Whether or not the patient chooses to pursue abstinence or controlled smoking, these procedures provide him or her with a way to potentially reduce the risk of CHD and improve pulmonary function by reducing nicotine and carbon monoxide consumption.

Obesity

Numerous studies employing self-control procedures have reported significant weight loss in obese individuals (Jeffery, Wing and Stunkard 1978; Stuart 1971; Wollersheim 1970). Successful programs tend to be multidimensional, modifying aspects of the individual's eating behavior and the environment. The energy balance model, which combines increased activity with decreased caloric intake, is an important component. Self-monitoring food intake is employed to make the individual aware of the amount eaten and the antecedents and consequences of eating. While self-monitoring alone can result in a loss of weight, it has not been found to produce a sustained weight change. Supplementary procedures are required to effect durable changes in eating habits. For example, the individual can reduce the number of antecedent situations by using stimulus control procedures (e.g., restricting eating situations, limiting the amount of food provided at each setting, and restricting the availability of food). Wollersheim (1970) reports an average weight loss of eleven pounds for women in a ten-session behavioral weight loss group, which was significantly greater than that obtained by women in a nonspecific therapy group, a social pressure group, or a no-treatment control group.

Behavioral contracts also increase the frequency of desired behaviors and decrease problematic ones. One innovative use of contracting involves the use of social support by significant others. Brownell et al. (1978) report significantly greater weight loss (thirty pounds) and better maintenance of weight loss in a group that included a family member in the treatment program. For a detailed description of behavioral weight loss programs, see Ferguson (1975) or Brownell (1979). While the data indicate that behavioral weight reduction programs can result in moderate amounts of weight loss (e.g., ten to twenty pounds), maintenance of weight loss remains a problem. For example, in the Wollersheim (1970) study, even women in the behavioral weight group had regained an average of two pounds at eight-week follow-ups. Behavior therapists are not yet sure how to maintain weight loss and are only now devoting their full attention to this area (Abrams, Follick and Thompson, in press). While techniques derived from behavioral principles have shown promise, their full potential has not yet been realized (Abrams 1979; Wilson 1978).

Hypertension

Research on behavioral approaches to the control of essential hypertension has emphasized relaxation techniques and biofeedback. Progressive muscle relaxation and meditation procedures, when practiced once or twice per day, can lead to a reduction in sympathetic activity and consequently to a lowering of blood pressure (Seer 1979). Shoemaker and Tasto (1975) report of a decrease of 6.8 mm. Hg. in systolic and 7.6 mm. Hg. in diastolic blood pressure in patients with essential hypertension following muscle relaxation training. While most individuals report pleasurable sensations during relaxation exercises, they often do not practice the procedure. Contingency contracting can be employed to provide reinforcements for daily practice of relaxation. For a detailed description of training in progressive muscle relaxation, the reader is referred to Bernstein and Borkovec (1973).

In blood pressure biofeedback training, information regarding the blood pressure is fed back to the subject in the form of a light or sound signal. This allows the subject to become aware of the fluctuations in blood pressure and to exercise voluntary control over these changes (Schwartz 1972; and Shapiro, Schwartz, and Tursky 1972). For example, Kristt and Engell (1975) report an average decline of 18.5 mm. Hg. in systolic and 7.5 mm. Hg. in diastolic blood pressure in patients with elevated blood pressure following feedback of systolic pressure. While progressive relaxation training and biofeedback procedures alone have been determined to produce statistically significant changes in blood pressure, the changes are small and of questionable clinical significance (Benson, Shapiro, Tursky, et al. 1971; Kristt and Engel 1975; Taylor et al. 1977). Furthermore, whether or not within-session blood pressure changes generalize to the natural environment has not yet been resolved. However, when one of these procedures is employed in conjunction with an antihypertensive regiment, they can provide the added increment necessary to promote a clinically significant change in blood pressure without the patient experiencing serious medication side effects (Jacob et al. 1977). For a detailed description of biofeedback procedures, the reader is referred to Gaarder and Montgomery (1977), and Basmajian (1979).

Stress and the Type A Coronary Prone Behavior Pattern

The rushed, competitive, achievement-oriented behavior of the Type A individual is not generally seen as psychopathological or physically harmful. On the contrary, these behaviors are often admired and reinforced in our society. However, the fact that this behavior pattern can increase the risk of a major coronary event suggests that its modification is important in the patient with CHD.

In order to effect a change in the Type A behavior pattern, it is necessary to challenge the individual's belief that these behaviors are necessary to achieve one's goals. Rosenman and Friedman (1977) have stated:

> We believe that Type A behavior cannot be changed unless patients are sufficiently motivated to do so, by being helped to achieve a certain level of philosophical awareness of their total life structure. This awareness should lead them to recognize, perhaps for the first time, that they have been falsely attributing many of their past successes to a behavior pattern which has not truly advanced their socioeconomic career. Indeed, such a pattern may have done just the opposite. They must be helped to recognize that, unless altered, this pattern will continue to impede their socioeconomic advance, and might also bring on cardiac catastophe (325).

Since Type A individuals are characterized by self-imposed stress (creation deadlines, competing regularly), and a tendency to respond maladaptively to uncontrollable stress, stress management procedures are employed with these individuals (Roskies 1979; Suinn et al. 1975). This approach consists of cognitive coping strategies and relaxation training to reduce autonomic arousal. These skills help the Type A individual modulate responses to stressful situations. As a result, maladaptive reactions can be ameliorated without changes in the individual's life aspirations. In addition, the person's perception of threatening situations can be changed (e.g., realizing that over-restrictive deadlines are not necessary for production). This is accomplished by helping the individual become more aware of irrational beliefs and employ more constructive self-statements in stressful situations (e.g., "If I take my time, I can still get everything accomplished") (c.f. Ellis 1962).

Roskies (1979) reports using stress management procedures, particularly relaxation training, with individuals who operate at a constantly high level of tension. Almost immediately, these individuals reported a sense of enhanced control and well-being. These techniques were judged to increase their efficiency and the ease with which they carried out their activity. In another study, 87 percent of the Type As treated believed that stress management training led to substantial improvement in their reaction to stress, and 83 percent believed that there were major changes in their lifestyle patterns (Suinn et al. 1975). While we do not know if the Type A behavior pattern can be permanently altered, it may be possible to help these individuals better manage stress and thereby reduce their risk of CHD.

Exercise

Since a sedentary lifestyle is believed to be related to the incidence of CHD, and since exercise is an important component of the recovery process, a primary focus of cardiac rehabilitation programs is physical reconditioning. Post–MI patients should be placed on individualized exercise programs. Exercises should be gradually increased in intensity and duration to the desired level, preceded by warm-up and followed by cool-down periods. It should initially be isotonic (aerobic), involving large muscle groups (e.g., walking, jogging, cycling, swimming), and patients should avoid competitive activity, sudden bursts of effort, and exercises that severely stress the lower back and knees (Hellerstein 1968; Leon 1976; Naughton and Hellerstein 1973; and Zohman and Tobis 1970). Usually, exercise is performed three to five times per week for thirty to sixty minutes.

A review of the literature by Leon (1976) found that the principal beneficial effects of long-term reconditioning programs are increased cardiac functioning and improved psychosocial adjustment. A major problem with structured exercise programs, however, is patient adherence. Bruce et al. (1975) report a 58 percent dropout rate among CHD patients in a structured physical activity program. While researchers now recognize adherence to exercise regimens as a problem, no investigation has been directed at improving motivation and participation in exercise programs.

REDUCTION OF RISK AND INCIDENCE OF CHD FOLLOWING LIFESTYLE MODIFICATION

In the previous section we reviewed the behavioral approaches to the modification of CHD risk factors. While it is necessary to demonstrate that these procedures result in the desired behavior changes, it is perhaps even more important to establish that these behavior changes alter those physical parameters known to reduce the risk of CHD and to ultimately reduce morbidity and mortality. Although definitive answers do not currently exist, data from epidemiologic studies and from primary and secondary prevention trials are quite encouraging. Although the focus of the chapter is secondary prevention (i.e., lifestyle modification in CHD patients), results of epidemiologic and primary prevention studies are included in the discussion because they are important, especially regarding changes in physiological mediating mechanisms.

A number of primary prevention studies document changes in the proposed mechanisms underlying the development of CHD. Follick, Henderson, Herbert, Abrams, and Thompson (1980) report reductions in serum cholesterol and increases in HDL cholesterol in obese women following a weight reduction program. Similarly, Brownell and Stunkard (in press) report a significant increase in HDL-cholesterol and a decrease in LDL-cholesterol in obese men immediately following behavioral weight loss. In addition, systematic exercise results in the elevation of HDL-cholesterol (Admer and Castelli 1980). Both the general level of carbon monoxide and its intake are reduced by cessation or changes in the topography of smoking behavior (Fredericksen and Martin 1979). Studies employing multiple risk factor reduction procedures (i.e., weight reduction, smoking cessation, dietary changes, and increased activity) also report decreases in plasma cholesterol, plasma triglycerides, and systolic and diastolic blood pressure (Meyer and Henderson 1974; and Meyer et al. 1980). Thus, it appears that changes in risk-related behaviors are associated with changes in physiological mediating mechanisms.

Changes in risk factors also appear to be related to a reduced incidence of CHD. Turpeinen (1979) reports that total replacement of dairy fats by vegetable oils in the diets of patients in two Finnish mental hospitals, between 1959 and 1971, substantially reduced CHD mortality in male patients. The Veterans Administration Cooperative Study (1967, 1972) demonstrates that the control of elevated blood pressure by antihypertensive medications significantly reduces the incidence of CHD. Epidemiological studies support the contention that smoking cessation reduces CHD mortality (Bain et al. 1978; Gordon et al. 1974; and Kleinman et al. 1979). In addition, current data suggest that even moderate activity levels can significantly reduce the incidence of MI (Morris et al. 1953; and Paffenberger and Hale 1975). Paffenberger et al. (1979), for example, report a decreased incidence of heart attack in individuals who have high energy expenditure occupations compared to those with low energy expenditure occupations. Stamler (1979) concludes that due to public education efforts, Americans have reduced the major risk factors of serum cholesterol, cigarette consumption, sedentary lifestyle, and essential hypertension; as a result, from 1968 to 1976, there were 100,000 fewer deaths from CHD each year in people aged 35 to 74.

Regarding secondary prevention, the report of the Task Force on Cardiovascular Rehabilitation (1974) indicates that compliance with risk factor modification regimes can influence the prognosis of CHD patients with uncomplicated first MIs. After approximately one year, the chance of reinfarction is no greater than the chance of an initial MI in individuals in the same age and risk factor index bracket. A number of studies utilizing structured exercise programs in CHD patients demonstrate improved cardiovascular functioning (Bergstrom et al. 1974; Bruce 1974; and Froelicker et al. 1980), and a reduced mortality rate (Brunner and Meshulam 1969; Hellerstein 1968; Rechnitzer et al. 1972). While promising and consistent with the hypothesis, these studies are inconclusive due to uncontrolled designs, insufficient sample size, and large numbers of drop-outs. However, the psychosocial benefits cited and the potential impact on the disease process strongly support the use of exercise in the rehabilitation process.

In a study of individuals who sustained an MI, those who stopped smoking or subsequently reduced their consumption had less than half the mortality rate of those who failed to do so over a five year period (Mulcahey et al. 1977). Suinn, Brock and Eddie (1975) report decreased serum cholesterol and triglyceride levels in Type A CHD patients receiving stress management training following their MIs. However, the effect of treating the Type A behavior pattern on subsequent morbidity and mortality is largely unknown.

While there are many comprehensive cardiac rehabilitation programs designed for post–MI patients, few have reported systematic analyses of their effectiveness. Rahe et al. (1979) report on the effectiveness of a group therapy program that was largely educational and supportive in nature. The treated group had significantly fewer reinfarctions and a reduced incidence of mortality compared to the controls. Perhaps the most promising data to date are reported by Kallio and his colleagues (1979). Following an MI, patients were assigned to a control group (routine follow-up by their private physicians) or a multifactorial risk factor reduction group (smoking and weight reduction, discussion of psychosocial problems, and structured physical exercise). At three year follow-ups, the cumulative coronary mortality rate in the intervention group was 18.6 percent compared to 29.4 percent in the control group. Thus, while definitive controlled studies are not currently available, there is substantial support for the hypothesis that risk factor modification can influence the pathogenesis of CHD and ultimately reduce morbidity and mortality.

ADHERENCE TO TREATMENT REGIMENS

We have discussed some of the behavioral approaches to lifestyle modification and how they may influence CHD morbidity and mortality. However, the most efficacious treatment is worthless if the patient does not comply with the treatment regimen. The adherence problem becomes even more pronounced when dealing with lifestyle changes. The more extreme the change required, the more unlikely it is that the individual will adhere to the regimen. Unfortunately, health providers do not usually consider the issue of compliance until it appears that the patient is not responding to treatment. While awareness of the adherence problem and its magnitude is the first step, there are a number of behavioral procedures that have been developed to manage this problem once it is detected (Dunbar and Stunkard 1979).

Unfortunately, there is no way to predict which patient will be compliant or which patient will have adherence difficulties. There are, however, a number of preventative interventions that the clinician can employ. Education of the patient is critical. The patient needs to understand the disease and its long-range implications. In addition, the patient must know the details of the treatment procedure and the goals of the regimen. A clear rationale that is both comprehensible and credible to the patient is necessary.

A major problem with treating an asymptomatic disorder, such as essential hypertension, is that the patient does not feel better after taking the medication and often feels worse. If the patient has a clear understanding of the goals of treatment, he or she will know that current efforts to control blood pressure are an attempt to reduce the probability of difficulties at some future time. The patient also needs to know what to expect as a result of treatment. This should include all side-effects and the likelihood of their occurrence. In addition, they should know what to do if side-effects occur. Accurate information about what to expect is important since adherence is known to decline when patients experience events that are incongruent with their expectations (Blackwell 1973). Information is best presented in categories so that each topic is presented separately (e.g., what is wrong; what symptoms are to be expected; what the treatment is; what the patient must do). It was found that this method increased patient recall by 25 percent to 50 percent and that visual aids further increased recall to 65 percent (Ley et al. 1973). Patient education, then, is the first step toward the development and maintenance of a therapeutic alliance between the patient and the clinician. Once the therapeutic alliance is established, the clinician can follow the patient's behavior as it regards the treatment regimen and not focus solely on the outcome of the intervention. Improvement in the patient's condition is not necessarily an indicator of patient adherence. Thus, adherence behavior and treatment effectiveness must be conceptualized and measured independently.

When the patient has difficulties following a specific treatment regimen, there are a number of behavioral techniques available to help the clinician assist the patient (Dunbar and Stunkard 1979). Tailoring the treatment regimen fits the regimen to the patient's daily routine and thereby minimizes the disruptive effects of the regimen and maximizes the likelihood of adherence. If enhanced exercise level is desired, the patient can be encouraged to park some distance from work and thereby increase the distance walked. Stimulus control procedures are also employed. For example, if the patient stores medication next to the toothbrush and takes it in the morning after brushing, brushing one's teeth can serve as a cue for medication-taking behavior. Self-monitoring is used to both assess and improve adherence. Patients can be instructed on how to self-monitor body weight or food intake. Graduated shaping procedures are particularly important in lifestyle modification. Shaping is a procedure whereby the patient is assisted in gradually building a set of skills until the criterion is achieved. For example, a patient on a low-cholesterol diet must first learn those foods that are low in cholesterol content. Skills in planning weekly dietary programs and new recipes for the preparation of foods low in cholesterol can then be acquired. The important component of this approach is that it is incremental and systematically develops the patient's behaviors, making it easier to master complex regimens. Contracting is another procedure which can improve adherence (Steckel and Swain 1977).

These behavioral procedures have been employed in a controlled clinical trial with hypertensive patients who were determined to be noncompliant. Haynes et al. (1976) found that self-monitoring, tailoring, and reinforcement procedures resulted in a significant improvement in compliance in the treated group as compared to the controls. The experimental group also evidenced a greater reduction in blood pressure. Thus, behavioral intervention procedures appear to hold much promise in the management of adherence and can ultimately increase the potential benefit of primary and secondary prevention efforts with patients suffering from coronary heart disease.

Two case examples illustrate a number of the problems and behavioral interventions that we have discussed in preceding sections.

CASE EXAMPLE 1

John G., aged 29, was a hyperlipidemic patient with a history of three MIs and a quadruple coronary bypass. Following each of his first two MIs, he evidenced a behavior pattern that suggested serious denial. Upon discharge, he would suddenly become very active in both social and athletic pursuits and ignored his gradual reconditioning program as well as other recommended lifestyle changes. In addition, he began to drink alcohol excessively. Following his third MI and coronary bypass surgery, he became depressed and recuperated alone at home. Apparently, he no longer denied the extent of his illness and conscientiously complied with recommended lifestyle changes and medical regimens. Eight weeks after his bypass operation, Mr. G. was readmitted to the hospital for left arm and chest pain. These symptoms, which had been associated with all of his prior MIs, were believed to represent unstable angina. A cardiac catheterization determined that this was the result of occlusions in the bypass graphs. There was no evidence of a recent MI, but significant obstruction was detected in still other coronary arteries.

Mr. G. had several episodes of angina while at rest and required increased dosages of medication to relieve his pain. His condition quickly deteriorated to where even the large doses of medication were providing little symptomatic relief. Knowing that he was seriously ill and had a guarded prognosis, Mr. G. consented to another bypass operation in an attempt to relieve his continuing pain. At the time of this decision, Mr. G. was becoming increasingly anxious and agitated, despite large doses of sedative medication. A psychiatric consultation was requested in order to assess the patient's concerns and assist in the management of his emotional distress. Mr. G. was evidencing marked anxiety that appeared to be related to his ruminations about postsurgical pain, the possibility of becoming totally disabled, and his fears of dying during the surgical procedure.

The psychological intervention with Mr. G. sought to help him express his concerns, cope with his fears, and reduce his emotional distress. Progressive relaxation that emphasized imaginal relaxation procedures was employed. He was asked to gently tense muscle groups. He was also to generate images of calming scenes and to imagine himself in those scenes. In addition, Mr. G. engaged in a problem-solving procedure and was asked to develop plans for psychological and vocational rehabilitation, postsurgery. He was also asked to rehearse, cognitively, his compliance with postoperative recovery regimens and distract himself with the procedure when he was in pain.

These procedures were designed to reduce his physiologic arousal, enhance his involvement in his treatment, and distract him from his discomfort and worry. During the first session, the patient was able to employ the relaxation procedure well and reported a significant reduction in his anxiety. He practiced the relaxation exercise twice daily and was ultimately able to produce a state of relaxation almost at will. Mr. G. reported a concomitant enhancement of his self-esteem. In addition, a decrease in rumination was also noted. There was also a marked reduction in the patient's complaints of pain during the time he was developing his coping skills. He found that planning how he would cope with postoperative pain and depression further served to reduce his ruminations about surgery.

Following his bypass surgery, the patient stated that he felt well and evidenced no signs of depression. It was noted that he was alert and cooperative, seemed in good spirits, and was willing to comply to the best of his ability. Unfortunately, this patient died two days after his surgery. However, this case does illustrate how behavioral interventions can be employed to reduce a patient's preoperative distress and help him or her cope with the fear of impending death.

CASE EXAMPLE 2

Mrs. C. was referred to the Risk Factors Clinic by her cardiologist following her first MI. At the time of her referral, she was 58-years-old, married, and working in a jewelry factory. Her MI had occurred eight months earlier.

At the beginning of treatment, her medical condition was very unstable. During a stress test, her EKG revealed dysrhythmias, couplets, and ventricular premature beats. The stress test was not completed because of her severely impaired cardiac functioning and the potentially dangerous results of continued activity. Similar results were found with an ambulatory cardiogram. She was Class D according to the New York Heart Association Functional and Therapeutic Standards (i.e., ordinary activity markedly reduced), and Functional Class IV (Hellerstein and Ford 1957) (i.e., worst class). In addition, her laboratory results indicated seriously elevated serum cholesterol and glucose levels. Her doctor prescribed a low cholesterol diet, restricted all physical activity except work (where she remained seated all day), and prescribed Mellaril, 50 mg. PRN, for anxiety.

Mrs. C. weighed 217 pounds and was 5 feet, 2 inches tall. According to the Metropolitan Life Insurance norms, she was 100 pounds over her ideal body weight. She reported being overweight since childhood, with her lowest adult weight being 187 pounds. She had tried unsuccessfully to lose weight during the past sixteen years through physician-prescribed diet pills, Weight Watchers, and fad diets. She was smoking approximately one pack of Newport 100s (19 mg. tar/1.4 mg. nicotine) per day. She had been smoking approximately thirty years, and had at one time smoked up to two packs per day. In addition, she was experiencing significant distress due to her CHD. She reported feeling anxious, despondent, helpless, and hopeless most of the time. She had lost initiative and interest in socializing, taking care of her house, and pursuing her hobbies and leisure activities. She stated that she had sleep disturbances, including difficulty falling asleep and early morning awakening, and frequent crying spells over the past few weeks.

Mrs. C. was placed on a weight control program that combined stimulus control procedures and modification of eating behaviors. Because of her restricted activity level, exercise was not possible. She also began a nicotine fading program as the first step toward smoking cessation. Finally, pleasant events scheduling and supportive psychotherapy were employed to help Mrs. C. cope with her depression. Weekly sessions were held during which the previous week's self-monitoring and pleasant events schedules were discussed, hand-outs of the new material for the weight loss program were presented and explained, and a change in cigarette brands was negotiated. Time was also spent discussing the course of her illness and its impact on her lifestyle.

At the end of five weeks of treatment, Mrs. C. had lost 12 pounds, had reduced her smoking to ten cigarettes per day, was smoking Merit 100s menthol (11 mg. tar/.7 mg. nicotine), was falling asleep within fifteen minutes of going to bed, was sleeping until her alarm went off the next morning, and had not needed the Mellaril in three weeks.

At that time, she returned to her cardiologist for a repeat stress test and follow-up appointment. She successfully completed her stress test with minimal cardiac dysfunction and was placed on a structured exercise program (primarily walking). She had improved to Class B (i.e., some reduction in ordinary activity) according to the New York Heart Association Functional and Therapeutic Standards, and Functional Class II (Hellerstein and Ford 1957). Her laboratory results also showed significant improvement, with her glucose levels within normal limits and with reduction in her total serum cholesterol.

Mrs. C. continued on her weight loss program with the addition of increasing her caloric expenditure through modified exercises. The nicotine fading procedure continued until she was smoking Carlton Menthols (1 mg. tar/.1 mg. nicotine). She then moved to stimulus control procedures and achieved total abstinence. At the end of a ten week treatment program, Mrs. C. had lost 25 pounds, had quit smoking, and continued to improve her cardiac functioning. Her laboratory results continued to be encouraging, with her glucose levels remaining within normal limits and her serum cholesterol approaching normal limits. These changes, with some additional weight loss, were maintained during an eight week maintenance program where sessions were scheduled every other week.

This case provides a good example of how self-control procedures can be employed to modify behavioral risk factors, leading to changes in physiological parameters associated with CHD. Not only was the patient able to improve the quality of her life through these modifications, but she was also able to influence the course of her illness and reduce her risk of reinfarction or death.

CONCLUSIONS AND SUMMARY

We have reviewed the behavioral and psychological factors related to the development of CHD and to the management of the patient following MI. The procedures and effects of lifestyle modification were reviewed in some detail in an attempt to give the traditional health caretaker an overview of this discipline. Lifestyle modification is an essential component in the care of the patient with CHD and represents the ideal of a humanistic behavioral medicine perspective. Our approach to the patient with CHD is obviously a divergence from traditional thanatology and is quite different from that taken by the other authors in this volume. Behavioral thanatologists, however, may not only be able to influence the quality of life through their interventions, but in some diseases, they may also begin to influence the course of the illness and the quantity of life. Lifestyle modification procedures are important tools for helping the terminally ill patient.

REFERENCES

Abrams, D.B. Clinical developments in the behavioral treatment of obesity. *Clinical Behavior Therapy Review*, 1979, *1*, 1-14.

Abrams, D.B., Follick, M.J., and Thompson, C.D. Worksite weight loss interventions: Procedures, problems and potentials. In T.J. Coates (Ed.), *Behavioral medicine: A practical handbook*. Champaign, Ill.: Research Press, (in press).

Adner, M.M. and Castelli, W.P. Elevated high-density lipoprotein levels in marathon runners. *Journal of the American Medical Association*, 1980, *243*, 534-536.

Bain, C., Hennekens, C.H., Rosner, B., Speizer, F.E., and Jesse, M.J. Cigarette consumption and deaths from coronary heart disease. *Lancet*, 1978, 1087-1088.

Bandura, A. *Principles of behavior modification*. New York: Holt, Rinehart and Winston, 1969.

Basmajian, J.V. (Ed.). *Biofeedback — Principles and practice for clinicians*. Baltimore: Williams and Wilkins, 1979.

Benson, H., Shapiro, D., Tursky, B., and Schwartz, G.E. Decreased systolic blood pressure through operant conditioning techniques in patients with essential hypertension. *Science*, 1971, *173*, 740-741.

Bergstrom, K., Bjemuff, A., and Erickson, U. Physical training after myocardial infarction. Metabolic effects during short and prolonged exercise before and after physical training in male patients after myocardial infarction. *Scandinavian Journal of Clinical Laboratory Investigations*, 1974, *33*, 1973.

Bernstein, D.A. and Borkovec, T.D. *Progressive relaxation training: A manual for the helping professions*. Champaign, Ill.: Research Press, 1973.

Blacher, R.S. On awakening paralyzed during surgery: A syndrome of traumatic neurosis. *Journal of the American Medical Association*, 1975, *234*, 67-68.

Blackwell, B. Patient compliance. *New England Journal of Medicine*, 1973, *289*, 249-252.

Brownell, K.D. Behavioral therapy for weight control: A treatment manual. Unpublished manuscript, University of Pennsylvania, 1979.

Brownell, K.D., Heckerman, C.L., Westlake, R.J., Hayes, S.C., and Monti, P.M. The effect of couples training and partner cooperativeness in the behavioral treatment of obesity. *Behavior Research and Therapy*, 1978, *16*, 323-333.

Brownell, K.D. and Strunkard, A.J. Differential changes in plasma high-density lipoprotein cholesterol in obese men and women during weight reduction. *Archives of Internal Medicine* (in press).

Bruce, R.A. The benefit of physical training for patients with CHD. In F. Ingelfinger (Ed.), *Controversies in Internal Medicine, II*. Philadelphia: W.B. Saunders Co., 1974.

Bruce, E.H., Fredrick, K., Bruce, R.A., and Fischer, L.D. Comparison of active participants and dropouts in Capri cardiovascular rehabilitation programs. *American Journal of Cardiology*, 1975, *37*, 53.

Brunner, D. and Meshulan, N. Prevention of recurrent myocardial infarction by physical exercise. *Israel Journal of the Medical Sciences*, 1969, *5*, 783.

Carleton, R.A. Cardiac rehabilitation: A biobehavioral approach. *Behavioral Medicine Update*, 1979, *1*, 9–11.

Cassem, N.H. and Hackett, T.P. Psychological rehabilitation of myocardial infarction patients in the acute phase. *Heart and Lung*, 1973, *2*, 382–388.

Castelli, W.P., Doyle, J.T., Gordon, T., Hames, C.G., Hjortland, M.C., Hulley, S.B., Kagan, A., and Zukel, W.J. HDL-cholesterol and other lipids in coronary heart disease: The cooperative lipoprotein phenotyping study. *Circulation*, 1977, *55*, 767–772.

Croog, S.H., Levine, S., Lurie, C. The heart patient and the recovery process. *Social Science Medicine*, 1968, *2*, 111–164.

Croog, S.H., Shapiro, D.S., and Levine, S. Denial among male heart patients: An empirical study. *Psychosomatic Medicine*, 1971, *33*, 385.

Daniel, A. Coronary heart disease: An overview. In M.L. Pollock and D.H. Schmidt (Eds.), *Heart disease and rehabilitation*. Boston: Houghton Mifflin, 1979.

Dunbar, J.M. and Strunkard, A.J. Adherence to diet and drug regimens. R. Levy, B. Rifkins, B. Dennis, and N. Ernst (Eds.), *Nutrition, lipids, and coronary heart disease*. New York: Raven Press, 1979.

Ellis, A. *Reason and emotion in psychotherapy*. New York: Lyle Stuart, 1962.

Ferguson, J.M. *Learning to eat: Behavior modification for weight control*. Palo Alto, Calif.: Bull Publishing, 1975.

Follick, M.J., Henderson, O., Herbert, P., Abrams, D., and Thompson, C. Plasma lipoprotein changes associated with behavioral weight loss intervention. Paper presented at the Second Annual Meeting of the Society of Behavioral Medicine, New York, 1980.

Foxx, R.M. and Brown, R.A. A nicotine fading and self-monitoring program to produce cigarette abstinence or controlled smoking. *Journal of Applied Behavior Analysis* (in press).

Fredericksen, L.W. and Martin, J.E. Carbon monoxide and smoking behavior. *Addictive Behaviors*, 1979, *4*, 21–29.

Fredericksen, L.W., Miller, P.M., and Peterson, G.L. Topographical components of smoking behavior. *Addictive Behaviors*, 1977, *2*, 55–61.

Fredericksen, L.W., Peterson, G.L., and Murphy, W.D. Controlled smoking: Development and maintenance. *Addictive Behaviors*, 1976, *1*, 193–196.

Friedberg, C.K. *Diseases of the heart*, 3rd Ed. Philadelphia: W.B. Saunders, 1966.

Froelicher, V., Jensen, D., Atwood, E. McKirnan, D., Gerber, K., Slutsky, R., Battler, A., Ashburn, W., and Ross, J. Cardiac rehabilitation: Evidence for improvement in myocardial perfusion and function. *Archives of Physical Medicine Rehabilitation*, 1980, *61*, 517–522.

Gaarder, K.R. and Montgomery, P.S. *Clinical biofeedback: A procedural manual*. Baltimore: Williams and Wilkins, 1977.

Garfield, S.L. and Bergin, A.E. (Eds.). *Handbook of psychotherapy and behavioral change*. New York: John Wiley and Sons, 1978.

Garrity, T.F. and Klein, R.F. Emotional response and clinical severity as early determinants of six month mortality after myocardial infarction. *Heart and Lung*, 1975, *4*, 73–1737.

Glass, D.C. *Behavior patterns and stress in coronary disease*. New York: John Wiley and Sons, 1977.

Goldfried, M.R. and Davison, G.C. *Clinical behavior therapy*. New York: Holt, Rinehart and Winston, 1976.

Gordon, T. and Kannel, W.B. Obesity and cardiovascular disease: The Framingham study. *Clinics in Endocrinology and Metabolism*, 1976, *5*, 367–375.

Gordon, T., Kannel, W.B., McGee, D., and Dawber, T.K. Death and coronary attacks in men after giving up cigarette smoking. *Lancet*, 1974, *2*, 1345.

Granger, J.W. Full recovery from myocardial infarction: Psychosocial factors. *Heart and Lung*, 1974, *3*, 600–610.

Hackett, T.P., Cassem, N.H., and Wishnie, H.A. The coronary care unit: An appraisal of its psychologic hazards. *New England Journal of Medicine*, 1968, *274*, 1365–1370.

Haynes, R.B., Sackett, D.L., Gibson, E.S., Taylor, D.W., Hackett, B.C., Roberts, R.S., and Johnson, A.L. Improvement of medication compliance in uncontrolled hypertension. *Lancet*, 1976, *1*, 1265–1268.

Hellerstein, H.K. Exercise therapy in coronary disease. *Bulletin of the New York Academy of Medicine*, 1968, *44*, 1028.

Hellerstein, H.K. and Friedman, E.H. Sexual activity in the post-coronary patient. *Archives of Internal Medicine*, 1970, *125*, 987–999.

Horan, J.J. "In vivo" emotive imagery: A technique for reducing childbirth anxiety and discomfort. *Psychological Reports*, 1973, *32*, 1328.

Jacob, R;G., Kraemer, H.C., and Agras, W.S. Relaxation training in the treatment of hypertension. *Archives of General Psychiatry*, 1977, *34*, 1417–1427.

Janis, I.L. Psychological stress among surgical patients. In I. Janis (Ed.), *Psychological stress*. New York: John Wiley and Sons, 1958.

Jarvik, M.E. Biological factors underlying the smoking habit. In M.E. Jarvik (Ed.), *Research on smoking behavior*. Washington, D.C.: National Institute on Drug Abuse, 1977.

Jarvinen, K.A. Can ward rounds be a danger to patients with myocardial infarction? *British Medical Journal*, 1955, *1*, 318–320.

Jeffery, R.W., Wing, R.R., and Strunkard, A.J. Behavior treatment of obesity: The state of the art in 1976. *Behavior Therapy*, 1978, *9*, 189–199.

Jenkins, C.D. Recent evidence supporting psychologic and social risk factors for coronary disease. *New England Journal of Medicine*, 1976, *294*, 987–994.

Johnson, J.E. Effects of structuring patients' expectations on their reactions to threatening events. *Nursing Research*, 1972, *21*, 499.

Jones, P.M. *The heart health guide.* Unpublished manuscript, Pawtucket Heart Health Program, 1979.

Kallio, V., Hamalainen, H., Hakkila, J., and Luurila, O.J. Reduction in sudden death by a multifactorial intervention programme after acute myocardial infarction. *Lancet*, 1979, 1091–1094.

Kannel, W.B. Recent findings of the Framingham study. *Resident and Staff Physician*, 1978, 56–71.

Kannel, W.B. and Gordon, T. Physiological and medical concomitants of obesity: The Framingham study. In G.A. Bray (Ed.), *Obesity in America.* Washington, D.C.: U.S. Department of Health, Education and Welfare, NIH Publication No. 79–359, 1979.

Kaplan, N.M. The control of hypertension: A therapeutic breakthrough. *American Scientist*, 1980, *68*, 537–545.

Kazdin, A.E. Self-monitoring as a behavior change. In M. Mahoney and C. Thoresen (Eds.), *Self-control: Power to the person.* Monterey, Calif.: Brooks/Cole, 1974.

Kendal, P.C., Williams, L., Pechacek, T.F., Graham, L.E., Shisslak, C., and Herzoff, N. Cognitive-behavioral and patient eduction interventions in cardiac catheterization procedures: The Palo Alto Medical Psychology Project. *Journal of Consulting and Clinical Psychology*, 1979, *47*, 49–58.

Kleinman, J.C., Feldman, J.J., and Monk, M.A. The effect of changes in smoking habits on coronary disease mortality. *American Journal of Public Health*, 1979, *69*, 795–602.

Kristt, D.A. and Engel, B.T. Learned control of blood pressure in patients with high blood pressure. *Circulation*, 1975, *51*, 370–378.

Lando, H.A. Self-pacing in eliminating chronic smoking: Serendipity revisited. *Behavior Therapy*, 1976, *7*, 634–640.

Lando, H.A. Successful treatment of smokers with a broad spectrum behavioral approach. *Journal of Consulting and Clinical Psychology*, 1977, *45*, 361–367.

Lando, H.A. Behavioral treatments in the modification of smoking. In J. Reed (Ed.), *Clinical behavior therapy and behavior modification*, Vol. 2. New York: Garland, (in press).

Leon, A.S. Review of literature on cardiac rehabilitation for stratified coronary care workshop. Working Committee on Cardiac Rehabilitation, 1976.

Levenberg, S.B. and Wagner, M.K. Smoking cessation: Long term irrelevance of mode of treatment. *Journal of Behavior Therapy and Experimental Psychiatry*, 1976, *7*, 93–95.

Leventhal, H. and Cleary, P.D. The smoking problem: A review of the research and theory in behavioral risk modification. *Psychological Bulletin*, 1980, *88*, 370–405.

Lewinsohn, R.M. A behavioral approach to depression. In R.J. Friedman and M.M. Katz (Eds.), *The psychology of depression: Contemporary theory and research*. New York: John Wiley and Sons, 1974.

Ley, P., Bradshaw, P.W., Eaves, D., and Walker, C.M. A method for increasing patients' recall of information presented by doctors. *Psychological Medicine*, 1973, *3*, 217–220.

Lichtenstein, E. Future needs and directions in smoking cessation. In *Progress of smoking direction*. New York: Publication of the American Cancer Society, 1978.

Lichtenstein, E. and Glasgow, R.E. Rapid smoking: Side effects and safeguards. *Journal of Consulting and Clinical Psychology*, 1977, *45*, 815–821.

Lichtenstein, E., Harris, D.E., Brichler, G.R., Wahl, J.M., and Schmahl, O.P. Comparison of rapid smoking, warm smoky air, and attention placebo in the modification of smoking behavior. *Journal of Consulting and Clinical Psychology*, 1973, *40*, 92–98.

Lichtenstein, E. and Rodrigues, M.P. Long term effects of rapid smoking treatment for dependent cigarette smokers. *Addictive Behaviors*, 1977, *2*, 109–112.

McIntosh, H.D., Eknoyan, G., and Jackson, D. Hypertension—A potent risk factor. *Heart and Lung*, 1978, *7*, 137–140.

McIntosh, H.D., Entman, M.L., Evans, R.I., Martin, R., and Jackson, D. Smoking as a risk factor. *Heart and Lung*, 1978, *7*, 145–149.

McIntosh, H.D., Stamler, J., and Jackson, D. Introduction to risk factors in coronary heart disease. *Heart and Lung*, 1978, *7*, 126–131.

McNeer, J.F., Wagner, G.S., Ginsburg, P.S., Wallace, A.G., McCanto, C.B., Conley, M.J., and Rosati, R.A. Hospital discharge one week after acute myocardial infarction. *New England Journal of Medicine*, 1978, *298*, 229–232.

Meyer, A.J. and Henderson, J.B. Multiple risk factor reduction in the prevention of cardiovascular disease. *Preventive Medicine*, 1974, *3*, 225–236.

Meyer, A.J., Nash, J.D., McAlister, A.L., Maccoby, N., and Farquhur, J.W. Skills training in a cardiovascular health education campaign. *Journal of Consulting and Clinical Psychology*, 1980, *48*, 129–142.

Morris, J., Heady, J., Raffle, P., Roberts, C., and Parks, J. Coronary heart disease and physical activity of work. Part I. *Lancet*, 1953, *2*, 1053.

Mulcahey, R., Hickey, M., Graham, I.M., and McAirt, J. Factors affecting the five year survival rate of men following acute coronary heart disease. *American Heart Journal*, 1977, *93*, 556–559.

Nagle, R., Gangola, R., and Picton-Robinson, F. Factors influencing return to work after myocardial infarction. *Lancet*, 1971, *2*, 454–456.

Naughton, J.P. and Hellerstein, H.K. (Eds.). *Exercise testing and exercise training in coronary heart disease*. New York: Academic Press, 1973.

Paffenberger, R.S., Jr. and Hale, W.E. Work activity and coronary heart mortality. *New England Journal of Medicine*, 1975, *292*, 545.

Paffenberger, R.S., Jr., Wing, A.L., and Hyde, R.T. Current exercise and heart attack risk. *Cardiac Rehabilitation*, 1979, *10*, 1-4.

Pomerleau, D.F. and Pomerleau, C.S. *Break the smoking habit: A behavioral program for giving up cigarettes.* Champaign, Ill.: Research Press, 1977.

Rahe, R.H. and Lind, E. Psychosocial factors and sudden cardiac death: A pilot study. *Journal of Psychosomatic Research*, 1971, *15*, 19-24.

Rahe, R.H., Ward, H.W., and Hayes, V. Brief group therapy in myocardial infarction rehabilitation: Three to four year follow-up of a controlled trial. *Psychosomatic Medicine*, 1979, *41*, 229-242.

Rakoczy, M. The thoughts and feelings of patients in the waiting period prior to cardiac surgery: A descriptive study. *Heart and Lung*, 1977, *6*, 280-287.

Rechnitzer, P.A., Pickard, H.A., Paivio, A.U., Yuhasz, M.S., and Cunningham, D. Long-term follow-up study of survival and recurrence rates following myocardial infarction in exercising and control subjects. *Circulation*, 1972, *45*, 853-857.

Rosenman, R.H. and Friedman, N. Modifying Type A behavior pattern. *Journal of Psychosomatic Research*, 1977, *21*, 323-333.

Rosenman, R.H., Friedman, M., Straus, R., Jenkins, C.D., Zyzanski, S.J., and Wurm, M. Coronary heart disease in the Western collaborative group study: A follow-up experience of four and a half years. *Journal of Chronic Diseases*, 1970, *23*, 173-190.

Roskies, E. Considerations in developing a treatment program for the coronary prone (Type A) behavior pattern. In P.D. Davidson and S.M. Davidson (Eds.), *Behavioral medicine: Changing health lifestyles.* New York: Brunner/Mazel, 1980.

Rothman, R.M. A comprehensive cardiac rehabilitation program. *Heart and Lung*, 1974, *3*, 578-580.

Russell, M.A.H., Armstrong, E., and Patel, U.A. Temporal contiguity in electric aversion therapy for cigarette smoking. *Behavioral Research and Therapy*, 1976, *14*, 103-123.

Sanne, H. Exercise tolerance and physical training of non-selected patients after myocardial infarction. *Acta Medica Scandinavica*, 1973, *551*, 1-124.

Scalzi, C.C. Nursing management of behavioral responses following an acute myocardial infarction. *Heart and Lung*, 1973, *2*, 62-69.

Schwabb, J. A summary of a symposium on counseling the cardiac patient on work and sex. *Ohio State Medical Journal*, 1970, *66*, 1003.

Schwartz, G.E. Voluntary control of human cardiovascular integration and differentiation through feedback and reward. *Science*, 1972, *175*, 90-93.

Seer, P. Psychological control of essential hypertension: Review of the literature and methodological critique. *Psychological Bulletin*, 1979, *86*, 1015-1043.

Seligman, M.E. *Helplessness.* San Francisco, Calif.: W.H. Freeman and Company, 1975.

Shapiro, D., Schwartz, G.E., and Tursky, B. Control of diastolic blood pressure in man by feedback and reinforcement. *Psychophysiology*, 1972, *9*, 296–304.

Shoemaker, J.E. and Tasto, D.L. The effects of muscle relaxation on blood pressure of essential hypertensives. *Behavior Research and Therapy*, 1975, *13*, 29–41.

Stamler, J. Research related to risk factors. *Circulation*, 1979, *60*, 1575–1587.

Steckel, S.B. and Swain, M.A. Contracting with patients to improve compliance. *Hospitals—Journal of the American Hospital Association*, 1977, *51*, 81–84.

Stuart, R.B. A three-dimensional program for the treatment of obesity. *Behavior Research and Therapy*, 1971, *9*, 177–186.

Suinn, R.M., Brock, L., and Eddie, C. Behavior therapy for Type A patients. *American Journal of Cardiology*, 1975, *36*, 267–270.

Task Force on Cardiovascular Rehabilitation, National Heart and Lung Institute. Needs and opportunities for rehabilitating the coronary heart disease patient. Bethesda, Maryland: DHEW Publication No. (NIH) 75–750 National Heart and Lung Institute, 1974.

Taylor, C.B., Farquhur, J.W., Nelson, E., and Agras, S.W. The effects of relaxation therapy upon high blood pressure. *Archives of General Psychiatry*, 1977, *34*, 339–342.

Theorell, T. and Rahe, R.H. Psychosocial factors and myocardial infarction, 1. An inpatient study in Sweden. *Journal of Psychosomatic Research*, 1971, *15*, 25–31.

Turpeinen, O. Effect of cholesterol-lowering diet on mortality from coronary heart disease and other causes. *Circulation*, 1979, *59*, 1–7.

Tuttle, W.B., Cook, W.L., and Fitch, E. Sexual behavior in post-myocardiac infarction patients. *American Journal of Cardiology*, 1964, *13*, 140.

Veterans Administration Cooperative Study Group on Antihypertensive Agents. Effects of treatment on morbidity in hypertension—Results in patients with diastolic blood pressures averaging 115 through 129 mm. Hg. *Journal of the American Medical Association*, 1976, *202*, 1028.

Veterans Administration Cooperative Study Group on Antihypertensive Agents. Effects of treatment on morbidity in hypertension III. Influence of age, diastolic pressure and prior cardiovascular disease. Further analysis of side effects. *Circulation*, 1972, *42*, 991.

Wagner, M.K. and Bragg, R.A. Comparing behavior modification approaches to habit decrement-smoking. *Journal of Consulting and Clinical Psychology*, 1970, *34*, 258–263.

Weisman, A.D. *On dying and denying: A psychiatric study of terminality.* New York: Behavioral Publications, 1972.

Wilson, G.T. Methodological considerations in treatment outcome research on obesity. *Journal of Consulting and Clinical Psychology*, 1978, *46*, 687–702.

Wollersheim, J.P. Effectiveness of group therapy based upon learning principles in the treatment of overweight women. *Journal of Abnormal Psychology*, 1970, *76*, 462–474.

Zohman, L.R. and Tobis, J.S. *Cardiac rehabilitation*. New York: Grune and Stratton, 1970.

AUTHOR INDEX

SUBJECT INDEX

Adaptive behavior, 182, 186–87, 190, 192, 274
Advocate-shaman-therapist, 209–210
Affective reactions
  as component of pain, 98, 101, 111
  and stress in terminal care, 229–30, 234–35
Age. *See also* Elderly
  -appropriate peer relationships, 182
  and depression reaction, 76
American Heart Association, 253
Anger, 190
Anticipatory coping, 105–107
Anticipatory grief, 55, 125, 138–41
Anxiety, 220
  and assertive training, 241–43, 246–47
  in cancer patients, 15–16
  and dying, 45, 53, 55–57
  and information, 104
  in MI, 260–62, 267–69, 271
  myths, 31
  and relaxation method, 89
Appropriate death, 92
  definition of, 43–44
Assertion
  and behavioral skills, 241–42, 246
  and cognitions, 240–41, 246
  and coping, 239–40
  definition of, 238–39

obstacles to in terminal care, 242–44
Assertive training, 230–31, 245–47, 247–48
  components of, 245–47
  obstacles to, 242–44
  for stress, 238–42
  techniques, 82–83
Assessments
  behavioral, 13–14, 16
  family, 180–85
  of grief, 141, 142–44
Attention deversion, 113–15
Attribution, 78
Avoidance, 237–38

Behavioral contracting/contingency contracting, 275, 287. *See also* Positive reinforcement
Behavior modification, 78
Behavior patterns, and CHD, 254–57, 269–70, 281–82, 283–85, 285–87
Behavior skills, and assertion, 241–42, 246
Behavioral techniques
  cognitive method as, 70, 78–86
  in cognitive therapy, 80–83, 92
  for depression in terminal illness, 90–92

ABOUT THE EDITOR

Harry J. Sobel received his M.S. degree from Purdue University in 1973 and his Ph.D. from Boston College in 1977. Following his clinical internship at Massachusetts General Hospital (MGH), he was a Postdoctoral Fellow at Harvard Medical School and MGH where he began his work on the coping process, cancer, stress, and behavioral medicine. Dr. Sobel has spent four years with Avery D. Weisman and the Omega Project investigating the uses of problem-solving therapy with newly diagnosed cancer patients. He is currently an assistant professor of Psychiatry at Harvard Medical School, a staff clinical psychologist at Massachusetts General Hospital, and an adjunct assistant professor at Boston College. Since 1978, Dr. Sobel has served as a supervisor for the MGH Clinical Psychology Internship Program, a consultant to numerous organizations and centers, and is a frequent contributor to professional journals. Most recently, he and J. William Worden designed and co-authored a program on *Helping Cancer Patients Cope*, which is currently used by health care practitioners around the country. Dr. Sobel conducts workshops on this topic for professionals from many health care disciplines. His present interests also include long distance running, Chinese cooking, teaching, and solitude in New Hampshire.

ABOUT THE CONTRIBUTORS

Jeanne Achterberg received a Ph.D. in 1973 from Texas Christian University, with a major course of study in physiological psychology. She developed the initial research program for the Cancer Counseling and Research Center in Fort Worth, and has consulted with numerous private clinics and state agencies. She was co-director of an evaluation team for a Cancer Demonstration Project at the University of Texas Health Science Center, Dallas, where she currently holds the academic rank of assistant professor of Physical Medicine. Her primary areas of interest are behavioral medicine and the clinical uses of imagery. Dr. Achterberg co-authored a book entitled *Imagery of Cancer.*

James R. Averill received his B.A. in philosophy and psychology from San Jose State College and his Ph.D. in physiological psychology from the University of California, Los Angeles. He also studied at the Dusseldorf Medical Academy and the University of Bonn, Germany, while on a Fulbright Fellowship. After obtaining his doctorate, Dr. Averill spent five years at the University of California, Berkeley as an assistant research psychologist and lecturer. Since 1971, he has been at the University of Massachusetts, Amherst, where he is currently professor of Psychology.

Elizabeth Keating Cohen received her Ph.D. from Boston College in 1981. She was a clinical fellow in the Department of Psychiatry, Harvard Medical School, from 1977 to 1978 and is currently a staff psychologist at the Douglas A. Thom Clinic for Children in Boston. Her major interests are family therapy, child psychotherapy, and brief problem-solving treatment approaches.

Martin S. Cohen was awarded his Ph.D. from the George Washington University in 1980. He is presently employed as a staff psychologist at the Chelsea Unit of the Massachusetts General Hospital and at Psychological Associates of Framingham, Massachusetts. Dr. Cohen holds an appointment in the Department of Psychiatry, Harvard Medical School. His primary areas of interest include family therapy, individual psychotherapy, and organizational consultation.

Albert Ellis is executive director of the Institute for the Advanced Study of Rational Psychotherapy in New York City. He has published more than 400 articles in psychiatric, psychological, sociological, and popular periodicals. His many well-known books include such titles as *Sex Without Guilt, Humanistic Psychotherapy, Reason and Emotion in Psychotherapy* and *A Guide to Rational Living.*

Michael J. Follick received his Ph.D. in clinical psychology from the University of Iowa in 1977. He is currently an assistant professor of Psychiatry in the Brown University Program in Medicine, and is director of the Miriam Hospital Risk Factors Clinic, in Providence, Rhode Island. Dr. Follick is a consultant to the Pawtucket Heart Health Program and is on the consultant roster of the National Heart, Lung, and Blood Institute. In addition, he is the associate editor of *Behavioral Medicine Update*, a publication of the Society of Behavioral Medicine. His major interests include cardiovascular risk factor modification, stress and illness, and worksite health promotion.

Joanne L. Fowler received her Ph.D. in clinical psychology from the University of Georgia in 1980. She is presently a postdoctoral fellow in behavioral medicine at Miriam Hospital, a Brown University affiliated hospital in Providence, Rhode Island. Her major interests are weight reduction, smoking cessation, and stress management among medical patients.

Bruce S. Gottlieb received his Master of Arts degree from Ohio University. He is presently a clinical psychology intern in the Brown University Psychology Internship Consortium and is completing the requirements for his Ph.D. degree. His major interests include behavior therapy and self-control procedures.

Richard A. Kolotkin received his Ph.D. from the University of Minnesota in 1978 following a one-year appointment at Harvard Medical School and the Massachusetts General Hospital. He is currently an assistant professor at Moorhead State University and a Clinical Instructor at the University of North Dakota School of Medicine. Dr. Kolotkin also serves as a consultant for Lakeland Mental Health Center and is in private practice. His primary interests include assertion training, behavior therapy, and stress management.

G. Frank Lawlis received his Ph.D. in psychology in 1968 from Texas Tech University with a specialization in rehabilitation. He completed his internship at the New York University Medical Center. After serving as director of research at University of Arkansas Rehabilitation Research Center, he returned to Texas Tech and became director of Rehabilitation Psychology from 1970 to 1975. Dr. Lawlis is currently professor of Psychology at North Texas State University and clinical professor of Physical Medicine and Orthopaedics at the University of Texas Health Science Center at Dallas. He holds a Diplomate degree in counseling psychology and has authored or coauthored a number of books.

Jerrold M. Pollak received his Ph.D. from Boston College in 1977. He is a clinical fellow in Psychology in the Department of Psychiatry, Massachusetts General Hospital, and an adjunct assistant professor at Boston College. Dr. Pollak is presently pursuing postdoctoral training in psychoanalytic psychotherapy at the Boston Institute for Psychotherapies and in pediatric neuropsychological assessment at Children's Hospital Medical Center, Boston. His interests are in thanatology, psychodynamic psychotherapy, and psychological testing.

Karen S. Rennert is a doctoral candidate in the clinical psychology program at Yale University. She served as a clinical intern in the counseling and health psychology section of the West Haven Veterans Administration Medical Center in 1980. Ms. Rennert's major areas of interest are stress, coping, and chronic illness.

Wendy K. Sobel received her Master's degree from Purdue University in 1973 and her Ph.D. from Boston College in 1977. She was a predoctoral intern at Worcester State Hospital from 1976 to 1977. Since completing her graduate studies, she has been a clinical psychologist within the University Counseling Services at Boston College. Her major interests include psychotherapy with women, assertiveness training, behavioral treatment of depression, and grief counseling.

Dennis C. Turk received his Ph.D. in clinical psychology from the University of Waterloo in 1978. He was a clinical intern in the Division of Health Care Psychology at the University of Minnesota Hospital from 1976 to 1977. Dr. Turk is presently an assistant professor in the Department of Psychology at Yale University. He has been the director of the Psychological Services Research and Training Clinic at Yale since 1979. Dr. Turk serves as a consultant to the Counseling and Health Psychology Section at the West Haven Veterans Administration Medical Center and was acting director of the Yale Center for Health Psychology during the year 1980-81. His major interests are in the areas of stress, coping, and behavioral medicine.

Patricia A. Wisocki received her Ph.D. from Boston College in 1971. She is currently an associate professor of Psychology at the University of Massachusetts in Amherst. Dr. Wisocki has specialized in the area of clinical behavior therapy and has contributed numerous publications to the field. Her recent interests are in designing treatment programs for the elderly, and training staff within geriatric settings.